The Great Cooks
COOKBOOK

The Great Cooks COOKBOOK
A Good Cooking School Cookbook

JAMES BEARD
ALEXIS BESPALOFF
PHILIP BROWN
JOHN CLANCY
EDWARD GIOBBI
GEORGE LANG
LEON LIANIDES
HELEN McCULLY
MAURICE MOORE-BETTY
JACQUES PÉPIN
FELIPE ROJAS-LOMBARDI

FERGUSON/DOUBLEDAY
THE GOOD COOKING SCHOOL

Acknowledgments

The Good Cooking School
and the members of its faculty
who contributed to this book
would like to thank
the following people for their
encouragement and assistance
in developing it.

Susan Bromer
Louella Culligan
Frank Fenno
Frances Field
Helen Finegold
Louise Gault
Marta Hallett
Becky Jones
Barbara Kafka
Barbara Kiernan
Catherine Oleson
Donald Roughan
Eugene Stuttman
Robert Thorborg
Xandy Wilson

JACKET AND BOOK DESIGN
Milton Glaser, Vincent Ceci
COLOR PHOTOGRAPHY
Walter Storck
ILLUSTRATIONS
Mel Furukawa

List of Color Plates

Table of Contents

Introduction

This book is about a number of people who love good food and good wine, who have learned a great deal about them and devoted their lives to them. These people have joined to enrich their own knowledge and share it. That is what the Good Cooking School is about and that is what this book is about.

The authors are chefs and painters, writers and restaurant creators, cooks, teachers, magazine editors and restaurant owners from places as distant as Peru and Greece, the State of Washington and Hungary, France, Italy, the Midwest and New York.

Each has chosen to write about a group of foods for which he or she has a particular feeling. Each has written a chapter filled with his own personal recipes and, even more, particular style. This book, then, is a collection of eleven different points of view and working styles, as well as of fine and tested recipes.

However, all of these people have worked closely together to make a comprehensive book. Wines, for example, have been written about not only in a general way but have been chosen for different menus, different kinds of foods in each section of the book. The whole has been unified under the guidance of James Beard. Thus, Mr. Beard, who by any measure is America's preeminent authority on food and wine, reflects a particularly American experience in his blending of elements from all the world's cuisines to make memorable meals. His discussion in this volume is on the planning and coordination of menus,

and while he offers some individual recipes of his own, his main thrust is on the architecture of a great experience in entertaining.

Alexis Bespaloff, a well-known writer and lecturer on wines, believing that wines should be enjoyed, has tried to make them more available in his contribution to this book. He has written a general introduction for the use of wines in the meal and then has generously contributed a section to each chapter about the wines that go with that particular kind of food.

Helen McCully is well known throughout America as a food editor, columnist and educator. Here, she delves into her own special love, the hors d'oeuvre that set the tone and tenor of the meal to follow.

George Lang brings to his discussion of soups a gusto and verve that derive from his Hungarian background and his years of experience as a restaurateur. In his treatment, soups become not merely traditional courses within a menu, but achievements in and of themselves, even the main substance and center of memorable meals.

Edward Giobbi is a painter of international reputation whose works are in the world's leading galleries and museums. He is passionately devoted to fine foods and wines, raises his own fruits and vegetables and is known throughout the food world as a master Italian cook. In this chapter, the author of *Italian Family Cooking* delves into the techniques, the family secrets and the delights of infinite forms of pasta.

Leon Lianides, owner of the famed Coach House Restaurant in New York's

Greenwich Village, reflects his Greek origins in the sureness, simplicity and integrity with which he treats the fruits of the seas.

Felipe Rojas-Lombardi, a young, intense, talented Peruvian, has worked closely with James Beard. He brings to poultry and game a highly individual standard of excellence based on the views of a man who has hunted and fished—and cooked— in many parts of the world.

Meat has traditionally formed the core of the American diet, and its preparation has become almost institutionalized. Philip Brown goes back to basics, offering a thorough understanding of the special qualities and properties of each different cut of meat, as the underpinning for free, inventive, creative expression.

Jacques Pépin grew up in Lyon, France, and knew his way around a restaurant kitchen by the time he was eleven. He went on to a distinguished career as Chef to General Charles de Gaulle and some of the great restaurants of Europe and America. In Lyon, vegetables occupy a special place; often, instead of accompaniments to other courses, they are served as courses in themselves. Their treatment in his chapter reflects the special regard of this Lyonnais.

Americans have recently begun to explore anew the infinite world of breads, cakes, rolls and pastries available beyond the ordinary commercial product. John Clancy is perhaps as responsible as anyone for this rediscovered delight. The baker's craft becomes in his hands not only a high art, but a cause to which he daily converts new *aficionados,* through his classes and demonstrations.

Maurice Moore-Betty brings to desserts not only a global range of experience, but a distinctly British sense of balance and proportion. His focus, in this volume, is on selecting and designing that finale which not only completes but properly complements all that has gone before.

A note of caution: This book, as mentioned earlier, is not intended as a road map, by which one starts from Beard's menus and drives relentlessly to Moore-Betty's desserts, compiling a meal by selecting one item from each section along the way. Each chapter has a unity and a completeness of its own. Many, in fact, can easily suggest complete meals. Each offers an insight into tastes, attitudes, profound knowledge and infinite sensitivity in the uniquely human achievements of fine eating, drinking and entertaining.

James Beard
Milton Glaser
Burton Richard Wolf

The Good Cooking School

The Great Cooks
COOKBOOK

Menus

What's the secret of a good menu? It must tempt, entertain, satisfy, spur conversation, and leave pleasant taste memories.

There must be balance of flavor and texture. Never a meal which is all soft—monotone to the tooth—never. A crisp salad contrasts with a serving of perfectly sautéed sweetbreads. Crusty bread is always a vis-à-vis for most any textured offering.

Never follow cream with cream. If you serve a cream soup resist the temptation to offer cream in other sauces and to have an elaborately creamy dessert.

Today's dinners are not the marathon meals of the Edwardians and Victorians—not at all. Two or three courses—and these of the highest quality—can suffice in our modern world. They must be of the best and accompanied by good wine.

There must be good conversation, soft lights, lovely china and napery. It is a sensual delight for all the senses. This is good menu-making and successful dining. Also good entertaining!

The first three menus that follow I have used both in my own house and in the advanced classes of my school. They include some of my most favorite dishes and they offer, I think, an interesting variety of foods.

Menu-planning I find to be an intriguing project, but I must admit that I sometimes change my mind at the last minute and substitute another dish. I think this is quite within the realm of good living because all of us cannot be expected to plan weeks ahead for any type of menu. Whenever something new comes into the market, or when the particular thing we have chosen for a menu is not the quality we want, we have to be elastic.

These menus and recipes have all been tested and tried, most of them dozens of times, and I trust you find them as interesting and as pleasant as I have.

The rest of the menus have been chosen from the many excellent recipes of my colleagues in this book. All menus will comfortably serve eight. My colleague Alexis Bespaloff has suggested wines for each menu.†

Bon Appétit
James A. Beard

---

† Indicated by a † in the text.

An Informal Winter Dinner

Cauliflower and Seafood Salad
Veal Cutlets Siciliana
Poppy-Seed Noodles
Savarin with Apricot Glaze

The cauliflower-seafood mixture is extremely interesting. It is a blending of flavors and textures. The veal is a Sicilian dish.

The noodles are a pleasant accompaniment because they will absorb the sauce from the veal very nicely, and the dessert is a classic which can be made early in the day.

It would be nice to have some crisp Italian bread and serve a bowl of watercress with it.

†A robust red wine with some acidity is needed to stand up to this flavorful veal dish—an inexpensive Chianti, say, or a Barbera from Northern Italy or California. If you want to start with a white wine, try a Verdicchio or Frascati.

Cauliflower and Seafood Salad

1 head cauliflower divided into flowerets
4 cups mixed seafood (may be cooked shrimp, crabmeat, lobster or raw bay scallops, or a combination of two)
4 tablespoons finely chopped onion
2 tablespoons chopped parsley
1 teaspoon fresh tarragon, if available
1 cup MAYONNAISE *
1 cup sour cream
Additional chopped parsley
Cherry tomatoes

Blanch the cauliflower flowerets in boiling, salted water for 2 minutes. Drain and cool. Toss with the mixed seafoods, onion, parsley and tarragon. Blend with the MAYONNAISE and sour cream. Serve on individual plates on a bed of greens and garnish with chopped parsley and the cherry tomatoes.

* See page 36.

AN INFORMAL WINTER DINNER

Veal Cutlets Siciliana

3 large, very thin veal cutlets, from the leg, about 12 by 6 inches
¼ pound salami
¼ pound mortadella or bologna
¼ pound prosciutto or cooked ham
¼ cup bread crumbs
2 cloves garlic, peeled and chopped
Chopped parsley
½ teaspoon fresh sweet basil, chopped
5 or 6 hard-cooked eggs
Olive oil
Salt
Freshly ground black pepper
5 or 6 bacon slices
2 cups tomato sauce
2 whole cloves garlic

Leave veal slices in whole pieces, but remove bones. Pound veal very thin. Arrange slices side-by-side (the long sides adjoining) so they overlap slightly. Pound overlapping areas thoroughly to press them together. On veal, arrange rows of overlapping slices of salami. Top with rows of sliced mortadella or bologna and finally with sliced prosciutto or cooked ham.

Heat oven to 350 F. Sprinkle surface of meat with fine bread crumbs, garlic, parsley, and basil. Down the center place a row of shelled, hard-cooked eggs. Sprinkle with olive oil, salt and freshly ground black pepper. Roll up very carefully as for jelly roll, making certain that eggs stay in place in center. Place roll in lightly greased oven-proof glass baking dish and top with bacon. Pour tomato sauce, with whole garlic cloves, over veal. Bake for 1 hour. Remove to a hot platter and slice, or serve from baking dish.

NOTE: This is also exceptionally good sliced cold.

Poppy-Seed Noodles

In a large kettle, place 3 quarts water and 1 teaspoon salt; bring to a boil. Add 1 stick of butter, melted, 12–16 ounces of green or egg noodles. Cook at high heat until tender to your taste. Drain thoroughly, and toss with 1 stick butter, melted; salt and freshly ground pepper, to taste; and 2–3 tablespoons poppy seeds.

Savarin with Apricot Glaze

½ cup warm water (105 F.—115 F. for dry
    yeast; 95 F. for compressed)
3 tablespoons sugar
2 packages or cakes of yeast, active dry or
    compressed
2½ cups unsifted, all-purpose flour
4 eggs, slightly beaten
½ teaspoon salt
⅔ cup soft corn-oil margarine

APRICOT GLAZE
Fresh fruits and whipped cream or rum
    syrup

Measure warm water into small, warm bowl. Add 2 tablespoons sugar. Sprinkle or crumble in yeast; stir until dissolved. As soon as the mixture bubbles, add it to the flour in a large bowl; then add eggs. Beat with spoon for 2 minutes. Cover; let rise in warm place, free from drafts, about ½ hour, or until bubbly and doubled in bulk. Stir down; add remaining sugar, salt and soft margarine. Beat again until dough is elastic when dropped from spoon (about 4 minutes).

Turn into well-greased 3-quart mold (ring). Heat oven to 450 F. Again, let dough rise in warm place until doubled in bulk, about 30 minutes. Bake in a very hot oven 10 minutes; reduce heat to 350 F. and bake 20 minutes longer, or until done. Unmold. Brush with APRICOT GLAZE.

When ready to serve, fill center with fresh fruits and whipped cream or pour rum syrup * over the cake, which may be served warm or cool.

APRICOT GLAZE
Melt a 1-pound jar of apricot jam in a heavy saucepan over high heat. When it is melted and bubbling, remove from heat and strain through cheesecloth. Keep warm until ready to use.

• See page 213.

A Fall Dinner for Close Friends

Cold Spinach Soup with Seafood
Beef Stroganoff
Onions Braised with Madeira
Tomato Compote

It is still warm enough in autumn to offer a cold soup. Because of its quick cooking and rather spectacular seasoning, the BEEF STROGANOFF may be prepared at the table in an electric skillet.

The tomatoes, a novelty in many ways, make a thoroughly delicious dessert.

†BEEF STROGANOFF is a difficult dish with which to match a wine. Uncomplicated wines with some flavor of their own are best—Moulin-à-Vent or Morgon from the Beaujolais region, Rioja from Spain, or Zinfandel from California.

Cold Spinach Soup with Seafood

3 pounds spinach
2 quarts strong chicken stock
Juice of 1 lemon
1 teaspoon dried tarragon or 1 tablespoon chopped fresh tarragon
1 clove garlic, chopped
Pepper, salt
Mashed potato (about ¾ cup)
Finely chopped shrimp, crabmeat or lobster—about 1 tablespoon per serving
Sour cream, chopped parsley

Wash the spinach well, blanch it and drain thoroughly. Press to remove excess liquid. Chop as finely as possible. Put spinach in a saucepan with chicken stock, lemon juice, tarragon, garlic, freshly ground pepper and salt to taste; cook over low heat for 10 minutes. Beat in mashed potato—enough to give it the consistency of thick soup. Chill well and correct seasoning.

Garnish each serving with chopped seafood; top with a large dollop of sour cream and sprinkle with parsley.

Beef Stroganoff

There are many different versions of this dish. Beware of those that specify long cooking. BEEF STROGANOFF is much better when prepared quickly, a few minutes before it is to be eaten. It is one of the specialities that is fun to do at the table if you have an electric chafing dish or skillet.

1½ pounds fillet of beef
6 tablespoons butter
Olive oil
2 tablespoons chopped green onions (white part only)
¼ cup white wine or vermouth
A-1 sauce or Worcestershire sauce
1½ cups of sour cream
Salt
Pepper
Chopped parsley

Ask the butcher to cut the meat into very thin slices. You can try it yourself, but it is difficult to do a neat job.

Melt 4 tablespoons of butter in the chafing dish or skillet; get it as hot as you can without burning. Adding just a bit of olive oil to the butter helps prevent it from turning brown. Sauté the beef slices in the hot fat very quickly, stirring. When they are delicately browned on both sides and done (this takes only 1 or 2 minutes), remove them to a hot platter. Add the remaining butter and chopped onions and cook for 1 minute. Then add wine or vermouth, a dash or two of A-1 sauce or Worcestershire sauce and the sour cream. Stir well and heat through, but do not boil or the sour cream will curdle. Salt to taste and pour the sauce over the beef. Top with a sprinkling of freshly ground black pepper and chopped parsley. Serve with rice.

Onions Braised with Madeira

2 tablespoons olive oil
2 tablespoons butter
4 large onions, peeled and sliced 1 inch thick
1 teaspoon salt
½ teaspoon freshly ground pepper
¼ cup beef broth
¼ cup Madeira

Melt oil and butter in a heavy pan. Add onions and sear over high heat 2 minutes. Season with salt and pepper; add broth; cover and simmer for 10 minutes, or just until tender. Add Madeira and let the sauce cook down slightly.

Tomato Compote

2 pint baskets cherry tomatoes
Their weight in sugar
Approximately ½ cup water
Juice of ½ lemon
Heavy cream, whipped cream or sour cream

Scald the tomatoes for 1 minute and peel carefully, being certain you do not break the flesh. Combine the weighed sugar with the water; bring to a boil; reduce heat to medium and cook for 10 minutes. Add the tomatoes and cook very slowly, skimming off any scum that rises to the top, until the tomatoes are thoroughly tender but not mushy. Stir in lemon juice; remove to a serving dish and cool. Serve with heavy cream, whipped cream or sour cream.

An Excellent Sunday Lunch or Dinner

Shrimp Kiev
Gigot à la Ficelle, Anchovy Sauce
Carrot Quiche
Omelette Soufflé Flambé

The shrimp may be prepared and served at once. The lamb, which has a most intriguing sauce, is such a surprise that it is worth springing on your best friends, and the CARROT QUICHE is a pleasant addition. It is most tasty this way because of the crust, which takes the place of a starch, in addition to presenting the vegetable.

The soufflé may be prepared in advance, to a great extent; but it is better to have the guests wait for the soufflé than to have the soufflé wait for the guests.

You might add a simple green salad to this meal if you wish.

†Start with a Pouilly-Fuissé or California Pinot Chardonnay; continue with a young red Bordeaux, and—for a change—finish with a glass of Sauternes.

Shrimp Kiev

Shell jumbo shrimp, leaving tails on. Allow 4–6 shrimp per person. Split shrimp on *inside,* flatten and pound slightly between wax paper. Put tiny pieces of frozen butter on inside of shrimp and roll them around butter. Dip first in flour, then in beaten egg—allow about 1 egg per person—and finally in very fine bread crumbs. Chill very well or freeze. Fry in 375 F. fat. These may be served with MUSTARD MAYONNAISE (see page 45) or with lemon.

Gigot à la Ficelle

Bone and tie a 5-pound leg of lamb and stud it with 1 clove garlic, cut in slivers. Roll in a linen towel or cloth and tie securely. In a deep pan combine enough water to cover the lamb, the lamb bones, 4 cloves crushed garlic, 1 bay leaf, 1 tablespoon dried tarragon, 4 tablespoons freshly ground black pepper, 3 dried red peppers and 2 tablespoons salt. Bring to a boil and cook for 1 hour over medium heat. Tie the cloth in which the lamb is rolled to the handles of the pan so that the lamb hangs clear of the bottom, or place it on a rack. Bring broth to a boil once more; then reduce to a simmer and cook the lamb, allowing approximately 14–15 minutes per pound boned weight for rare lamb. Remove lamb; keep warm. Strain broth; use ½ cup for ANCHOVY SAUCE.

ANCHOVY SAUCE
1 clove garlic, finely chopped
12 anchovy fillets, finely chopped
12 black olives, Italian or Greek, pitted and chopped
1 or 2 hot peppers, seeded and chopped
2 tablespoons olive oil
1 teaspoon lemon juice
1 teaspoon grated lemon rind
½ cup lamb broth

Combine all the ingredients and cook, stirring, over medium heat until smooth and heated through. Correct the seasoning. The sauce should be very hot, with a pronounced anchovy flavor. You may wish to add a dash of Tabasco.

Carrot Quiche

1 recipe sour-cream pastry
1½ pounds carrots
6 tablespoons melted butter
5 eggs
1½ cups light cream
Salt to taste
Nutmeg to taste
Chopped parsley

SOUR CREAM PASTRY
2¼ cups flour
½ teaspoon salt
¾ cup (6 ounces) butter
1 egg
Sour cream

Sift flour and salt onto a board or into a bowl and make a well in the center. Add the butter, broken into small pieces, the egg and a very little sour cream—just enough to make the pastry hold together. Work with the fingers, blending the ingredients into the flour until it forms a soft ball. Add a little more sour cream, if necessary, but not enough to make the pastry floppy. Roll into a ball, wrap in waxed paper or foil and chill for ½ hour before rolling out.

Meanwhile, peel and grate the carrots. Blanch them for 2 minutes in boiling water and drain well.

Heat oven to 400 F. Roll out pastry and line an 8- or 9-inch glass pie shell. Cover the inside of the shell with foil and weight down with rice or beans. Bake for 12 minutes; remove beans and foil and bake a few minutes longer, or until center is baked.

Reduce oven heat to 375 F. Toss carrots in melted butter and arrange in pie shell. Beat eggs and cream together lightly; season to taste with salt and nutmeg and pour over carrots. Sprinkle top with parsley. Bake until custard is set—about 40 minutes. Serve warm.

Omelette Soufflé Flambé

8 eggs
½ cup sugar
⅓ cup Cognac or rum
Butter
Granulated sugar
¼ cup Cognac, warmed

Separate the eggs and beat the yolks until light and lemon-colored. Gradually beat in the sugar. Add ⅓ cup cognac or rum. Heat oven to 375 F. Separately, beat the egg whites until they stand in firm peaks, and fold ⅓ of them into the egg-yolk mixture; then fold in the rest of the whites.

Heat a 10-inch skillet on top of the stove and butter it well. Sprinkle with granulated sugar. Pour the soufflé mixture into the skillet and bake for about 15 minutes. Remove from the oven, sprinkle with granulated sugar, pour the warmed cognac over it and ignite. Serve at once from the skillet.

A Gutsy Dinner for Hearty Appetites

Egg and Lemon Soup with Tripe
Baked Tongue in Mustard Crumbs
New Potatoes
Petits Choux Braisés
Deep Dish Apple Pie
Cream

Have your coziest friends who love eating in for this dinner. It's hearty and delicious. Sit back and enjoy—have full wines. A dinner for good appetites and good talk!

This is not the moment for delicate red wines; try a Chateauneuf-du-Pape, Rioja Reserva, or a Cabernet from Argentina, Hungary or Yugoslavia.

Black Tie Formal Dinner

Caviar
Striped Bass à la Grecque
Concombres Persillés
Felipe Rojas-Lombardi's Saddle of Venison
Purée de Marrons
Laitues Braisées
Fromages
Iced Coffee Mousse

A most elegant sitdown dinner with caviar served in the drawing room. Have plenty—with crisp toast and accessory foods: lemon, onion and egg. Be careful that neither the fish nor the venison is overcooked! The marrons should be creamy and rich, and the braised lettuce crisply soft. Continue with wine, along with cheese and dessert. Have a fun dessert wine.

†If you enjoy serving a series of wines, this is your chance. Begin with Champagne before dinner, then a fine dry white wine with the bass—a Meursault, Chassagne-Montrachet, or California Pinot Chardonnay. With the venison, look for a fine Bur-

BLACK TIE FORMAL DINNER

gundy such as Chambertin, Clos Vougeot, or Corton, or a mature château-bottled Bordeaux from the Médoc or St. Emilion. If you want to go all out, serve the Bordeaux with the venison, and then a Burgundy with the cheese. A glass of Sauternes or Barsac, or an Auslese from the Rhine, will complete this meal with a flourish.

Luncheon in the Garden

Eggs in Aspic
Pasta con Vongole al Brandy
Crisp French Bread
Tossed Salad
Cheese
Fresh Berries with Cream

The delicious eggs, the hot pasta, crisp bread, and salad are pleasant fare for a garden luncheon. Choose the season's bounty in berries. Sugar and cream with the fruit.

†Soave, Orvieto, Alsatian Riesling, California Dry Sauvignon Blanc—choose a dry white wine with a distinct taste.

A Dinner Where There is a Gathering of Children as Well as Adults

Predinner Cocktails
Cokes for the Junior Set
Tuna Pâté   Nuts   Les Crudités
Ed Giobbi's Lasagne (Double or triple
recipe)
Continue with Les Crudités
Crisp hot bread
Cheese
Bread Pudding, French Style,
with Sabayon Sauce

This could be a family reunion or minor celebration where everyone is together, including the children. The predinner snacks are slanted toward the junior palates, as is the entire meal.

†Don't fuss over the red wine on this informal occasion—a dependable red wine from California or New York State, or Chianti or Valpolicella will do nicely.

THE GREAT COOKS COOKBOOK

Sunday Supper

Fish Soup of the Islands
Garlic Bread
Tossed Salad
Dolce Maddalena

A simple supper to have around the fire on small tables. A great tureen of the soup is the mainstay, and the salad and dessert only additives. It's a pleasant dinner experience.

A dry white wine with enough flavor to balance the fish soup is called for, such as Mâcon Blanc or Muscadet, Soave or Verdicchio, or a California Riesling or Dry Semillon.

An Informal Dinner Before the Theater

Aji de Gallina
Boiled New Potatoes in Their Jackets
Spinach and Endive Salad, Vinaigrette
Sauce
Cheese
Crisp Bread Throughout; Butter
with Cheese

Start with wine or an apéritif and have the food ready. It's hot and spicy, so choose a simple wine for the dinner. Serve the salad and cheese together, and tear to the opera or theater. This could serve as well for after the theater or concert or the fights.

† This dish will overwhelm delicate white wines, so try a white Rioja, Graves, or well-chilled California Chablis in carafes.

Formal Luncheon

Avocado Soufflé with Lemon Sauce
Ham Chablisienne
Pommes Persillées
Timbales d'Épinards
Uncooked Almond Pudding

The elegant sit-down luncheon, catering to both sexes, is becoming more and more accepted. It is a pleasant time to entertain. A glass of wine or a light apéritif is preferred at this hour, and one usually serves lighter wines than at dinner.

†A dry rosé with some flavor would accompany the ham nicely—Tavel, Provence rosé, California Gamay Rosé—or else a full-bodied white such as Puligny-Montrachet, Sancerre or an Alsatian Riesling.

A Company Dinner

Fresh Oysters Ambassadeur
Pepper Duck
Courgettes Farcies
Endive and Beet Salad
Pear and Strawberry Compote

The peppered duck is crisp and pungent. A proper entrée after the oysters. The addition of beets to greens is classic and is a real contrast of tastes and textures. The dessert may be the combination of the two fruits or one or the other alone.

†Start with Chablis, Muscadet or California Pinot Chardonnay; then go on to a distinct red wine that will stand up to the duck—an inexpensive young Bordeaux, or a Cabernet wine from Hungary, Yugoslavia, Chile or California.

A Pleasant Dinner

Risotto con Frutta di Mare alla Genovese
Chicken Provençale
Salad—thinly sliced raw mushrooms
with Bibb lettuce
Lemon Ice Cream

One could serve this delicious meal on the terrace or around the pool, as well as in the drawing room. Chicken Provençale is deliciously seasoned. Make ice cream in the afternoon so that it will mellow properly.

†Start this meal off with a carafe of white wine, or a bottle of Soave or Muscadet. With the chicken, continue with the white wine, or change to a Côtes-du-Rhône, Barbera, or California Petite Sirah.

A Late Breakfast or Buffet

Pizza Siciliana
Gnocchi Parisienne with Sauce Mornay
Broiled Quail
Crisp Bacon
Les Crudités
Hot Biscuits   Butter and Jam
Very Sticky Buns
Pear and Strawberry Compote
Coffee   Tea

Serve pizza with drinks. Have buffet arranged so guests can navigate easily. Put the quail on a hot tray with crisp bacon and plenty of hot biscuits and sticky buns. Serve gnocchi in a chafing dish. Champagne is delightful, or serve some country wine. Have plenty; be leisurely.

†Serve Champagne or sparkling wine throughout, just for the fun of it; or else put out generous amounts of such red wines as California Mountain Red, a young Beaujolais or a Chianti.

A Perfect Holiday Dinner

IN THE DRAWING ROOM
Pâté de Foie   Onion Cocktail Sandwiches
DINNER
Roast Wild Turkey
Baked Oysters
Whipped Potatoes
Gratin de Poireaux Savoyarde
Cranberries
Braised Parsnips
Cheese
Simple Syllabub
Mince Pies

Such a meal could be served perfectly for Thanksgiving or Christmas. If you want the elegance, and can afford it, add caviar to the beginning. If wild turkeys are not available in your markets, find good fresh-killed ones. Buy mince pies for an added dessert or make your own mincemeat.

†Get things off to a lively start with Champagne; then go on to mouth-filling wine: a Vosne-Romanée, Chambolle-Musigny or Pommard from Burgundy; a Côtes-du-Rhône or Châteauneuf-du-Pape; or a Barolo from Italy.

A Homely Dinner for Winter

American Corn Chowder
Roast Lamb with Garlic and Olives
Hot Ratatouille
German Apple Pie
Cream

Corn chowder is so thoroughly American —heartwarming—delicious. The lamb has a taste of Provence. Hearty apple pie is the perfect ending for a particularly good meal.
†A good, château-bottled red Bordeaux is always a good bet with lamb, although the distinct taste of this particular dish would also be nicely set off by a California Zinfandel, Chianti Classico Riserva or Rioja Reserva.

An Hors d'Oeuvre Buffet—Beach or Country

Ed Giobbi's Insalata di Riso
Stuffed Ham Rolls
Shrimp with Mustard Mayonnaise
Cold Roasted Pork Loin with Green
Pepper Butter
Cold Ratatouille
Sliced Tomatoes with Basil
Hot French Bread
Rhubarb or Raspberry Fool
Fresh Fruit

Perfect for a luncheon or supper after swimming! This might even be an elaborate picnic. No last-minute cooking— merely assemblage. Served with hot breads or rolls or small French loaves.

† Let your guests choose for themselves between red and white wines. Set out open carafes of California or New York State burgundy or chablis, or of jug wines from Spain, Portugal or Italy. Chill the whites; cool the reds.

A Game Dinner

Mousse de Saumon Fumé
Roast Pheasants in Madeira Sauce
Crêpes de Maïs
Endives Meunière
Cheese
Strawberry Sorbet, Sauce Dijonnaise

Pheasants, well hung before roasting, are far more to be desired than those which are spanking fresh. Cook them carefully, for it is easy to dry out the breasts. This could easily be a black-tie dinner if you have enough pheasants. Bring out your best wines.

Start with a good white Burgundy—Puligny-Montrachet, Chassagne-Montrachet or Meursault. With the pheasant, choose a good red Burgundy or a château-bottled Bordeaux from St. Emilion, Pomerol or the Médoc. If you can find an older California Cabernet Sauvignon, this is a good time to open it. Be sure to have enough wine on hand to complement the cheese also.

A Good Autumn Dinner for Friends

Fresh Mushrooms Rémoulade
Roast Liver with Bacon
Gratin Dauphinois
Chopped Spinach, Tarragon Butter
Cheese
Orange Moss

Be sure you know your guests' tastes when you invite them for roast liver. It is very special. It's such a simple dinner that it encourages you to more entertaining. The dessert will hold, I'm sure.

A good wine with plenty of character is needed here—a Médoc or St. Emilion from Bordeaux, or a California Cabernet Sauvignon. You might also want to bring out a bottle of fine Burgundy, such as Nuits-Saint-Georges or Gevrey-Chambertin, with the cheese.

After Theater Supper

Lobster Bisque
Crisp Rolls
Classic Green Salad
Cold Apricot Soufflé

On a winter night, after the opera, concert or the theater, this rib-sticking, luscious soup will revive and restore you. One can leave the soup on a warming tray. The salad greens are ready. The dressing made.

† Make the evening especially gay with Champagne or sparkling wine. As an alternative, choose a rich Rhine wine from Johannisberg or Nierstein, or a white Burgundy from Chablis, Meursault or Mâcon.

Autumn Sunday Lunch

Liver Pâté   Salami
Celeriac in Mustard Sauce
Irish Stew
Crisp Hot Bread
Stalks of Endive, Celery and Fennel
German Crumb Cake
Coffee

A pleasant meal to serve outdoors. Linger over drinks and snacks. Serve a great tureen of stew with hot bread. Arrange endive, fennel and celery in deep pots with ice. Relax. Take your time.

† A fresh, light wine, such as a Fleurie or Brouilly from Beaujolais, a Gamay or Zinfandel from California, or a Rioja from Spain will suit the menu and the mood.

Summer Garden Lunch

Balkan Yogurt and Cucumber Soup
Ed Giobbi's Insalata di Rigatoni
Melba Toast
Meringue aux Pommes

A pleasant menu for the late spring or early fall when the days call for meals outside. Everything is ready. This luncheon serves itself.

† Serve a carafe of California Burgundy or Mountain Red, or a bottle of Valpolicella or Beaujolais—casual and copious.

Spring Luncheon

Eggs in Aspic
Chicken Panné
Rice
Asparagus Maltaise
Baba au Rhum with Whipped Cream
and Strawberries

The menu is gay and light—a sheer delight for the palate. It can be prepared pretty well in advance. It's a colorful menu as well.

† A flowery white wine, not completely dry, would suit the chicken and the time of year: a Moselle such as Bernkasteler or Piesporter, a Vouvray, California Chenin Blanc, or New York State white wine. If your natural preference is for reds, choose a light one such as Beaujolais Brouilly or Bardolino.

Soup and Salad Luncheon

Kettle Gulyás
Rye Breads and Sweet Butter
Salad of Endive, Rugala
and Cherry Tomatoes
Cheese
Fresh Fruit

A remarkably heavy soup and a most appealing, crisp salad balance wonderfully. This luncheon may also be served as a Sunday Supper or as a supper before the theater or a concert.

† You'll want a full-flavored wine here —Côtes-du-Rhône from France, Egri Bikavér from Hungary or a California Zinfandel.

Wine is one of life's most accessible pleasures, and its tremendous variety is a source of continuing fascination and enjoyment to the serious enthusiast. Not everyone shares this fascination, of course, but even those with only a casual interest in wine will want to serve wines that reflect to some extent the style and variety of the dishes described in this book.

Fortunately, choosing a wine to accompany a specific dish does not require precise calculation. There are times, for example, when the choice depends more on the occasion, the guests, or the time of year than on the menu. A celebration dinner may call for champagne. A grilled steak with casual friends may be accompanied perfectly by a bottle of Beaujolais, Chianti, or California Zinfandel, or—when knowledgeable and appreciative wine buffs come for dinner—a fine bottle of château-bottled Bordeaux. A chicken dish with which you usually serve a red wine may be even more enjoyable with a light white wine if it is served outdoors on a summer day.

As a matter of fact, the people who make wine are themselves casual about its presentation. Their choice of wine is based as much on what they produce as on any formal rules. A *coq au vin* in Beaune or Nuits-Saint-Georges would be cooked and served with red Burgundy; an Alsatian would use white wine. Most people prefer sweet white wines with dessert; but vineyard owners in Sauternes enjoy their wines with fish and cheese as well. Sausages would be accompanied by Beaujolais in Lyon, and by a white wine along the Moselle. It's helpful to remember that the wines and cuisine of a country, or of a particular region, generally complement each other. Some natural combinations include pasta and Chianti, *boeuf bourguignon* and red Burgundy, *paella* and Rioja, QUICHE LORRAINE and an Alsatian Riesling, steak *bordelaise* and red Bordeaux. Regional pairings of this kind are not only simple and appropriate, but also provide the opportunity to drink a variety of wines.

As you experiment with various combinations of wine and food, you will discover that certain foods spoil the taste of wine. Vinegar, whether it appears in a salad or an appetizer, emphasizes the natural acidity of wine and makes it taste sour. Overly spicy foods, peppery dishes, and curries overwhelm wine and destroy its taste. The yolk of egg gives wine an odd taste, so it's best not to serve wine with such dishes as *oeuf en gelée* or Eggs Benedict. A light red wine would go very well with a cheese or mushroom omelet, however. Red wine is rarely served with fish because the oiliness of the fish seems to bring out a metallic taste in red wine.

These few warnings apart, there is ample scope for imagination and personal preference in the choice of wines to accompany the recipes in this book. For example, many people serve white wine with veal or chicken; others will choose a light red. The choice depends partly on the preparation of the dish, partly on whether you and your guests prefer white or red wine. Perhaps the most useful principle to keep in mind is to match the weight of the wine with that of the dish. Rich foods overwhelm light wines; rich wines overwhelm delicate dishes. In the

THE GREAT COOKS COOKBOOK

wine sections that follow, red and white wines are grouped by style, from light and delicate to rich and full-flavored. As a matter of fact, anyone who wants to enjoy wine without making a study of it can limit his or her cellar to a light red and white, and a bigger-bodied red and white, each to be used with the appropriate dishes. It would also be useful and generous to have a few bottles of really fine wine in this simple cellar, to be brought out when an elaborate party dish has been prepared.

Although pink wines are a simple and popular way around the question of which wine to serve with which food, rosé is more often a compromise than a solution. For all its appeal, rosé lacks the interest and complexity of many red and white wines that cost the same or even less, and consequently does not always go as far in enhancing the food you have prepared. There are many occasions when rosé is the perfect wine— informal luncheons, picnics, with a *salade niçoise,* and so on—and at such times, the choice of rosé depends on whether you prefer dry wines or those that are slightly sweet. Semisweet rosés are produced in Portugal, in the Anjou district of France, in California and New York State. Provence rosé and Tavel are two well-known dry rosés from southern France, and there are good examples to be found in Italy, Switzerland, Spain, and, of course, California.

Another factor that enters into the choice of a wine is its place in the meal. When you are planning a menu that includes two or more interesting dishes, you may want to serve different wines to set off each dish. There's nothing complicated or unusual about this, and it's a gesture that will please your guests while also offering you a chance to use your imagination in deciding on the sequence of wines.

The simplest progression would be a dry white wine with the first course, then a red wine with the main dish. If you were planning to continue with a fine dessert, you might also add a sweet dessert wine such as Sauternes. This sequence suggests some general guidelines that are useful to remember. White wines are served before red wines, not only because this conforms to the order of dishes in most menus—fish before meat—but also because a white wine will taste particularly weak and washed out if served after a fuller-flavored and more complex red wine. The exception to this rule is, dry before sweet, since a sweet wine will make any dry wine that comes after it taste bitter by comparison.

You may occasionally want to serve two red wines at one meal, one with the roast, another with the cheese. Two sound precepts to remember are young before old, light before full. This is based on the concept that a progression of wines should lead up to the best, to avoid the anticlimax that would result if a lighter, younger, less interesting wine were served after a bigger-bodied, mature, and complex wine.

Just how much wine is needed for a dinner party depends on whether your guests enjoy wine, of course, and also on whether you plan to serve a progression of wines with several courses, or just one wine with, say, beef stew and salad. Remember also that the more people there are, the more wine each person will drink. Two people may be satisfied to share a half-bottle at an informal lunch, four people will certainly consume two bottles, and a convivial dinner party of eight may drink five or six bottles of wine. It's best always to have an extra bottle or two on hand, to avoid the awkwardness and disappointment of running out of wine in the middle of dinner.

Once you have decided on the style of wine that you would like to serve with a particular dish, you must also decide how much you want to spend. At one end of the scale are the many inexpensive jug wines that sell for $4 to $8 a gallon—the equivalent of 80¢ to $1.60 a bottle. These wines, from California, New York State, France, Spain, Portugal, and Italy certainly represent good value, and are the simplest solution to serving wine regularly and generously. As you experiment, you will find red and white jug wines that are more or less dry, and lighter or fuller in style. If you buy gallon jugs regularly, remember that air is the enemy of wine. If you open a jug and don't plan to use the wine all at once, decant it into five wine bottles or four 1-quart soda bottles. If the bottles are clean, filled right to the top, and sealed tight, the wine should last for a week or more, and can be used as needed.

Apart from jug wines, the range of wines available in America from $2 to $5 a bottle is enormous. Americans may not take wine with meals for granted, as is done in Europe and South America, but we do have a much greater choice of wines than do the citizens of any other country —much of it inexpensive. Try different and unusual wines, at least from time to time. Buy a mixed case of wines from a store with a large selection, and see for yourself how varied the taste of wine can be and how much imagination you can use in matching up specific dishes with specific wines. Occasionally, you may want to serve one of the world's finest wines—just as you will sometimes want to spend several hours in the preparation of a single dish—to find out for yourself what it tastes like, and to add another dimension to your enjoyment of wine and food.

In the wine sections that follow some of the recipe chapters, I have suggested a number of choices—varying in style and in price—that would be appropriate with the dishes mentioned. HORS D'OEUVRE and DESSERTS permit the widest and most original choices, since one can serve sparkling wines, such as champagne; fortified wines, such as sherry and port; and any number of table wines, which include all still wines with no more than 14 per cent of alcohol, whatever their price. The other wine sections are concerned solely with the wide range of red and white table wines that are readily available in most cities, and these wines are most fully described after the chapters on MEAT and FISH AND SEAFOOD. Fine red wines are discussed in conjunction with POULTRY AND GAME. A number of wines are also suggested after the chapters on SOUPS and PASTA, with particular attention to the wines of Hungary and Italy respectively. Although a special vegetable dish, such as a soufflé, might call for wine, it is not usually thought of as an accompaniment to vegetables. On the contrary, vegetables are served as a separate course in certain countries precisely so that their taste does not conflict with that of the wine

THE GREAT COOKS COOKBOOK

served with the principal dish. Since the BAKING chapter includes recipes for appetizers, main dishes, and desserts, the appropriate wine suggestions can be found elsewhere, and are not repeated.

We are not limited in our choice of wines to those of a particular region or even of just our own country—as is so often the case in Europe and South America. In America, we have the opportunity to use as much imagination as we want in choosing wines to accompany our meals. The suggestions that follow are meant to take advantage of the great variety of wines available to us.

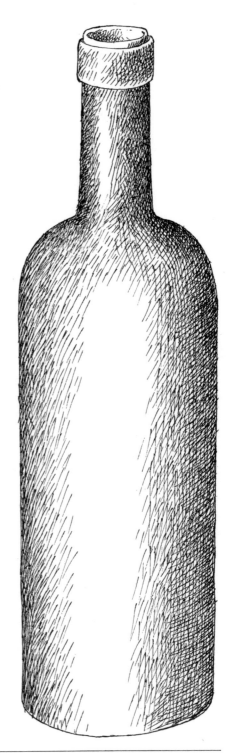

Hors d'Oeuvre and Canapés

In André Simon's FRENCH COOKBOOK,* he writes, *"Hors d'oeuvre* means 'outside the meal' and regardless of how many different sorts may be provided 'outside' or before any one meal, there is but one meal or *oeuvre* [work], so that, in French, *oeuvre* remains in the singular and *hors d'oeuvre* never is written *hors d'oeuvres."* Despite M. Simon's pronouncement, all too frequently *hors d'oeuvre is* pluralized in the press and in cookbooks and, unfortunately, even in WEBSTER'S NEW INTERNATIONAL DICTIONARY, second edition.

In modern restaurants, the *hors d'oeuvre* is presented on the menu as the first course, preceding the soup and the *entrée.* This is interesting primarily because correctly *entrée* means *"le premier plat du 'corps de repas,' c'est-à-dire du rot."* ** (the first plate of the meal, which is to say, the roast). Classically, fish is the first dish after the soup. Thus, the *entrée* is actually the third course. With a few exceptions the *hors d'oeuvre* I present here are not, as you can clearly see, *entrées* or first courses but rather small bites to forestall instant malnutrition while enjoying a drink or two.

In her fascinating book, FOODS IN HISTORY,*** Reay Tannahill suggests that it may have been the Athenians who, in the third century B.C., developed the original *hors d'oeuvre* trolley **** serving such things as garlic, sea urchins, a "sweet wine sop," cockles and sturgeon, each on a small plate, the whole presented on a large tray. I was amused on pursuing the subject a bit

* English Edition.
** DICTIONNAIRE DE L'ACADÉMIE DES GASTRONOMES.
*** Stein and Day, New York, 1973.
**** Trolley, for your enlightenment, is English for a low cart.

further to learn that caudel (also spelled caudle), first served in England in the 12th century, "warmed you, fed you, and kept you going till you could obtain a solid meal." * A mixture of eggs, cereals, malt, etc., caudel might well be considered the forerunner of the *hors d'oeuvre.*

Wherever the idea of the *hors d'oeuvre* originated, it has its counterpart in many other countries. In Italy, it is the *antipasto* (before the meal); in Germany, *vorspeisen* (before the meal); in Russia, *zakouski* (small bites); and in Sweden, the *smörgasbørd* (untranslateable), which traces its origin to *Brannvinsbørd* (aquavit buffet), which in the 18th century was an appetizing introduction to a festive meal. To some extent the foods offered sometimes parallel each other. In Italy, for example, you could be served cooked or raw vegetables, fish, bread, olives, ham, perhaps sausage; in Germany, salads of lobster or crabmeat, broiled mushrooms in a rich sauce, puff pastry shells with fish or meat fillings. In many instances, the *vorspeisen* is formidable enough to be served as a main course. In Russia, the *zakouski,* originally an array of "small bites" accompanied by vodka, was probably spawned in country houses on vast estates to which guests came over long distances on bad roads, often in sub-zero weather, arriving in desperate need of sustenance. As a consequence the *zakouski* became a permanent fixture on a table in the hall, parlor or an alcove in the reception room. Foods included a variety of fishes, cheeses, meats, bread and smoked eel. But the most important item on the table was caviar, the

* Dorothy Hartley, FOOD IN ENGLAND, MacDonald, London, 1954.

THE GREAT COOKS COOKBOOK

quality of which depended on the host's solvency. Like the *zakouski*, the *smörgasbørd* was set on a separate table in a corner of the dining room or in an adjoining room and was enjoyed while standing, before guests were seated at the meal proper. Along with several kinds of aquavit, the buffet included herring, home-cured sprats, breads, salt pretzels, and sharp cheeses. More and more dishes were added to this herring buffet and gradually it developed into the giant *smörgasbørd* which today, both in restaurants and homes, makes up the whole meal.

"The first sign of the *hors d'oeuvre* in this country," James Beard writes in his book, *Hors d'Oeuvre and Canapés*, "probably appeared in some roughly-hewn, pioneer bar on the California coast. Perhaps some homesick Frenchman, longing for the customs of his faraway homeland, set up a simple *hors d'oeuvre* tray on the bar of his ramshackle saloon. News spread around town that there was a free lunch at Frenchie's bar. Thus came the day of the five-cent beer and free lunch throughout America."

Although I was unable to track down any reference to free lunches in the English "pub," I discovered in THE AMERICAN HERITAGE COOKBOOK * that our nineteenth-century saloons, all strictly male institutions, featured free-lunch counters which offered salty hams and pretzels obviously designed to whet the customers' thirsts.

Hors d'oeuvre, in the French sense—and here we quote Elizabeth David, the great English food authority writing in FRENCH PROVINCIAL FOOD **—should consist of "something raw, something salt,

something dry or meaty, something gentle and smooth and possibly something in the way of fresh fish." Known as *hors d'oeuvre varié* they are always eaten with knife and fork. There are, of course, certain *hors d'oeuvre* that are always served on their own. For example, QUICHE LORRAINE, AVOCADO SOUFFLÉ, and EGGS IN ASPIC. All of which I have included, among others, in this chapter. It is worth pointing out here, I think, that *hors d'oeuvre* can make a light, but satisfying, main course.

Hors d'oeuvre, as the Europeans understand the meaning, are not widely used in the United States. We have adopted the term and use it interchangeably with appetizers and canapés and even snacks. The cocktail *hors d'oeuvre,* essentially finger food, is really an American innovation as is also the cocktail hour—now almost universal. *Canapé,* from the French, originally meant, according to Mr. Webster, "A couch with mosquito curtains," later a "piece of fried bread." Today it means toasted or fried bread spread with various mixtures.

When I give a big "cocktail" myself, I serve rather sturdy fare for two reasons: one, I don't want my guests, on leaving my house, to rush to the nearest restaurant to sustain themselves; two, I prefer to see all my guests perpendicular rather than horizontal. Here is a menu I serve often with great success.

Apricot Glazed Ham
Dijon Mustard
Fresh Mushrooms Rémoulade
Mousse de Saumon Fumé Toast Triangles
Brie
French Bread

* American Heritage Pub. Co., Inc., New York, 1964.
** Harper & Row, New York, 1962.

Although on the surface this may not appear to be finger food, it turns out that way. The ham, carved in the kitchen, then reshaped makes a handsome presentation but, further, makes it easy for guests to make their own delicious *hors d'oeuvre*—with ham, bread and a dash of mustard. As for the MOUSSE, it is soft enough to spread on a piece of toast, so each one helps himself. The fresh mushrooms are eaten by dipping into the RÉMOULADE. So that the "cocktail" will run smoothly, I have a man and his wife, a splendid team, to make the drinks, serve and tidy up. This expense provides a hostess who is having a good time.

Avocado Soufflé with Lemon Sauce *

Serves 6

BÉCHAMEL

4 tablespoons butter, approximately
4 tablespoons flour, approximately
1 cup milk
1 teaspoon salt
Freshly ground white pepper
Good pinch freshly grated nutmeg

SOUFFLÉ

4 whole eggs, separated
2 very ripe medium avocados or 1 large
    (1½ cups, puréed)
2 extra egg whites
Pinch of salt
Pinch cream of tartar

*B*utter heavily a 2-quart glass soufflé dish, then coat with flour, dumping out any excess. Refrigerate. Place a baking sheet in the oven and turn oven heat to 375 F.

Melt 4 tablespoons butter in a heavy saucepan (not aluminum). Stir in the

* Rather than the LEMON SAUCE you may like to serve SAUCE RÉMOULADE (page 37).

flour until smooth to make a *roux*. Cook slowly, stirring constantly with a wooden spatula, until the mixture froths—about 3 minutes. Take care not to allow it to brown. Beat in milk. Continue cooking slowly, beating constantly with a wire whip, until the BÉCHAMEL comes to a boil and thickens noticeably. Remove from the heat and beat in the seasonings. Cool slightly. Add the 4 yolks, one at a time, to the cooled BÉCHAMEL, beating hard after each addition. Set aside. *The soufflé can be made in advance to this point*—in which case, seal with plastic wrap to prevent a skin forming.

Peel the avocados; discard the pits and scoop the flesh out with a spoon. Push through a fine sieve, or purée in a food mill. *Measure exactly 1½ cups.* Combine with the BÉCHAMEL and egg-yolk base.

Add to the 6 egg whites a pinch of salt and the cream of tartar. Beat in an electric mixer or with an electric beater until the whites hold firm shiny peaks when the beater is held straight up. Using a wire whip, beat about a third of the whites into the avocado mixture. Pour the whole mixture over the remaining whites, and fold in with a rubber spatula.

Taste for seasonings. It may need both salt and pepper. Pour into the prepared soufflé mold, place on the baking sheet and bake for 35 minutes, or longer if you like a dry soufflé. Serve immediately on a tray with a folded napkin under it.

LEMON SAUCE

1 package (8-ounce size) cream cheese, softened
3–4 tablespoons finely chopped parsley
3–4 tablespoons finely chopped chives
Juice 2 lemons (about), strained
Salt
Freshly ground white pepper

Place the cheese, herbs and half the lemon juice in the container of the electric blender and blend at high speed to a smooth purée. Add salt and pepper to taste. Taste here, too, for lemon and add more if you like. Serve in a suitable sauceboat at room temperature. Makes about 1½ cups.

Asparagus Maltaise

Serves 6

Look for firm, crisp stalks with compact, tightly closed tips. If the tips are open, the asparagus is well past its prime.

I buy asparagus loose, rather than by the bunch, because I can choose each stalk and stalks all of a size.

36 medium-size stalks fresh asparagus (about 6 per person)

SAUCE MALTAISE

To prepare the asparagus, peel it. This gets rid of the tough outer flesh and makes the whole stalk edible. Cut off the root ends; then, with a vegetable peeler, peel from the tip down, rolling the stalks around as you work.

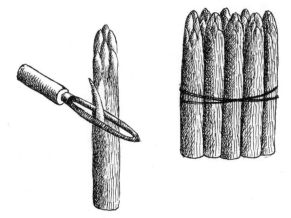

Wash the asparagus thoroughly in cold water and drain.

To cook, take stalks, a few at a time, and tie into small bundles with soft white string. Lay the bundles in rapidly boiling salted water in a heavy sauce-pan. Cook, uncovered (this keeps them green), until tender when the stem end is tested with the point of a sharp paring knife.

Young, fresh asparagus will cook in a matter of minutes (I allow 3–5) after the water comes back to a boil. Lift from the saucepan and place in a napkin-lined veg-etable dish. Cut off and discard the string. Wrap the napkin around the asparagus to keep it warm.

If the asparagus is to be served cold, run under cold water the minute you take it from the stove to stop the cooking. Then drain, wrap in a fresh dish towel and refrigerate until cold.

With hot asparagus, serve SAUCE MAL-TAISE made with a HOLLANDAISE base; with cold, serve SAUCE MALTAISE made with a MAYONNAISE base.

SAUCE MALTAISE (WITH HOLLANDAISE)
2 cups HOLLANDAISE (page 34)
Grated rind of 1 navel orange
Juice 1 navel orange, strained

Stir the rind and juice of the orange into the HOLLANDAISE. Pour into a warm (not hot) sauceboat. Serve with hot aspar-agus.

SAUCE MALTAISE (MAYONNAISE)
2 cups MAYONNAISE (page 36)
Grated rind 1 large navel orange
Juice of ½ a navel orange, strained

Stir the rind and juice into the MAY-ONNAISE. Serve with freshly cooked, cold asparagus or lukewarm cauliflower.

Classic Hollandaise

Makes 2 cups

4 egg yolks
2 tablespoons water
3 sticks (1½ cups) sweet butter, melted
    and hot

Salt
Freshly ground white pepper
Cayenne
1 tablespoon lemon juice, strained

ombine the yolks and water in the top of a double boiler (not aluminum). Beat for 1 minute with a whip; place over simmering water, or on a "flame tamer" over medium heat. Using a wire whip, beat vigorously for 8 to 10 minutes or until the mixture is thick and creamy. Take care not to curdle the eggs, but, if that happens, see below. When perfectly combined, you can see the bottom of the pan between strokes and the mixture will never be so hot you can't dip your finger into it.

Remove from the heat, place the pan on a damp cloth to keep it from turning as you beat. Add the hot butter in dribbles—beating constantly. When all the butter has been added, season with salt, pepper and cayenne to taste. Finally, stir in the lemon juice. Keep warm in a pan of tepid water, not hot or your sauce will separate. Hollandaise is always served lukewarm or tepid.

Blender Hollandaise

Makes about 1¾ cups sauce

1½ cups (3 sticks) unsalted butter
4 egg yolks
2 tablespoons water
Dash salt
Dash freshly ground white pepper
Dash cayenne
1½ teaspoons lemon juice, strained

elt the butter in a small saucepan over low heat until bubbling but *not brown.*

Place all the remaining ingredients in the container of the electric blender. Cover; turn motor to high; at once remove cover and add the hot butter in a slow, steady stream. When all the butter has been added, turn off the motor. Good as this recipe is, I do not think it matches the classic recipe.

TO SALVAGE HOLLANDAISE (either blender or classic), that has not thickened properly or has curdled: Place 1 teaspoon of lemon juice and 1 tablespoon of the sauce in a bowl that has been rinsed out in hot water and dried. Beat with a wire whip until the sauce becomes creamy and thickens. Then, beat in the remainder of the sauce, about 1 tablespoon at a time, whipping vigorously until creamy before adding next tablespoonful.

LEFTOVER HOLLANDAISE, tightly sealed in plastic wrap, can be refrigerated successfully for a few days, or it can be frozen. *To heat:* place in a pan of tepid (not hot) water until the *right temperature* has been reached. *To thaw:* take from the freezer a couple of hours before you plan to use it, then heat as directed. It is important to remember that Hollandaise is always served *warm,* never hot.

Classic Mayonnaise

Makes about 2 cups sauce

2 egg yolks
1 teaspoon Dijon mustard
1 tablespoon tarragon or wine vinegar
Salt
Freshly ground white pepper
1½ cups peanut oil, vegetable oil or olive oil *

* Or half olive oil and half peanut or vegetable.

*P*lace the yolks and mustard, *half the vinegar* and salt and pepper to taste in a generous bowl. Beat for 1 minute with a wire whip. Then begin to add the oil, almost drop by drop, whipping vigorously and constantly until all the oil is incorporated. If the mayonnaise seems too thick, beat in the remainder of the vinegar.

Blender Mayonnaise

Makes about 1¼ cups

2 egg yolks
½ teaspoon dry mustard
½ teaspoon salt
2 tablespoons vinegar or lemon juice
1 cup vegetable oil or half vegetable and half olive oil

*P*lace the yolks, mustard, salt, vinegar and ¼ *cup of the oil* in the container of the electric blender. Cover and turn the motor to high. Remove cover at once, and add remaining oil in a slow, steady stream. When all the oil has been added, turn off the motor.

TO SALVAGE CURDLED MAYONNAISE (either type): Place 1 tablespoon of the curdled mayonnaise in a warm, dry bowl with 1 teaspoon prepared French or domestic mustard. Beat with a wire whip until creamy. Add remaining mayonnaise, tablespoon by tablespoon, beating vigorously after each addition until creamy.

Fresh Mushrooms Rémoulade

*T*his is a splendid idea for a cocktail party. Buy a 3-pound basket of whole fresh mushrooms. To make sure they are absolutely fresh and clean, order them to be delivered to your market the day of the party. Do not wash or wipe them because any dampness darkens the caps; but do snip off the ends of the stems. Line a large bowl with either pale blue tissue paper (comparable to the paper they are packed in), which shows them off beautifully, or use a linen napkin.

The Rémoulade is served in a separate crystal or silver bowl, guests dipping the caps of the mushrooms into the sauce. If other foods are served, this will be sufficient for 15 to 20 people.

SAUCE RÉMOULADE
3 cups MAYONNAISE (page 36)
2 generous teaspoons Dijon mustard

4 tablespoons each of chopped gherkins, capers (well drained), fresh tarragon or chervil (if available),* parsley and a "whisper" of anchovy paste

Mix all ingredients together well; then, allow the sauce to stand, sealed with plastic wrap for a couple of hours to mellow. Not only delicious with mushrooms but with sliced hard-cooked eggs, shellfish and cold meats.

* If not, increase the parsley.

Celeriac in Mustard Sauce

Serves 6

*I*n buying celeriac, look for roots that are on the small side, 2–2½ inches in diameter, firm and clean. Scrub thoroughly; cut off tops; peel with a sharp knife, and cut into slices about 1/16-inch thick. Cut the slices into strips (in short, *julienne*) as thin or thinner than a toothpick. Mix with MUSTARD SAUCE.

1 pound of celeriac (celery roots) makes 3–3½ cups when cut. 3 medium celeriac plus MUSTARD SAUCE will serve 6 as an *hors d'oeuvre*.

MUSTARD SAUCE
1 egg yolk
2 teaspoons white wine vinegar
1 tablespoon Dijon mustard

Salt
Freshly ground pepper
¾ cup oil (half olive and half peanut)
Lemon juice to taste
Water
Minced parsley

Place the yolks in a mixing bowl with the vinegar, mustard and salt and pepper to taste. Start beating with a wire whip (you can use an electric beater, if you like), adding the oil very gradually. Continue beating until all the oil is used up and the mayonnaise is thick. Stir in lemon juice to taste. If the sauce seems too thick to mix comfortably with the celeriac, add a little water by the drop, beating steadily. Use parsley as a garnish.

Gnocchi Parisienne with Sauce Mornay

Serves 6–8

GNOCCHI

6 tablespoons sweet butter
2 cups water
8 tablespoons (½ cup) freshly grated Parmesan cheese (about 2 ounces)
Salt
Dash of cayenne
1 teaspoon Dijon mustard
2 cups flour
6 eggs

*C*ombine butter, water, cheese, salt, cayenne and mustard in a heavy saucepan. Bring to a boil. Add the flour all at once. Take off the heat and beat hard with a wooden spatula until the dough leaves the sides of the pan. Place in the bowl of the electric mixer until cool.

When cool, add the eggs, one at a time. Beat at medium speed until each egg has been completely absorbed before adding another. Have ready a large saucepan with simmering, salted water.

With two tablespoons, dipped into hot water, mold the dough into egg shapes and drop into the simmering water. Poach only a few gnocchi at a time (they should not touch) and turn over occasionally with a spoon. Cook, all told, about eight minutes. Lift to paper toweling with a slotted spoon.

Refrigerate, covered, or freeze. If frozen, defrost before finishing.

SAUCE MORNAY

6 tablespoons unsalted butter
6 tablespoons flour
2 cups milk
½ cup heavy cream, heated
4 to 6 tablespoons (about 1 ounce) freshly grated Gruyère
Salt
Freshly ground white pepper
Parmesan cheese, freshly grated, about ½ cup
4 tablespoons unsalted butter, melted

*M*elt the 6 tablespoons of butter in a heavy saucepan. Stir in the flour until smooth and cook over moderate heat, stirring occasionally, for 3–4 minutes to cook the flour. Do not brown. Add the milk and cook, whipping constantly with a wire whip, until smooth. Stir in the grated Gruyère, salt and pepper to taste; add heavy cream; bring to boil. Take off the heat and set aside for the moment.

TO FINISH: Heat oven to 350 F. Butter an 8″ x 12″ baking dish that can go to the table. Cover the bottom with a thin layer of the SAUCE MORNAY. Add a layer of the gnocchi; cover with sauce and sprinkle with grated Parmesan; add another layer of gnocchi, sauce and Parmesan. Coat with the melted butter and bake for 15 minutes. Place under the broiler to melt the cheese.

Classic Quiche Lorraine

Serves 6

PASTRY

Recipe for PASTRY (page 225)—omit sugar
1 egg yolk, lightly beaten

FILLING

6 to 8 slices bacon
3 eggs
2 cups heavy cream
Salt
Freshly ground pepper
Freshly ground nutmeg

*R*oll the PASTRY out on a lightly floured board or pastry cloth into a circle about 1/8-inch thick, and 2 inches larger, all around, than a 9-inch pie plate—about 13″ diameter. Roll up on the rolling pin, center over the pan and unroll. Fit the pastry loosely into the pan, taking care not to stretch it, and press it lightly into the bottom of the pan. With a sharp paring knife, cut off the surplus overhanging dough, leaving an inch extending all around. Fold the extra pastry under, and press together to form a high, standing rim, then flute. Chill for 30 minutes.

Pre-heat oven to 425 F. Place a piece of aluminum foil in the pastry shell to form a lining; then fill with dry beans or rice, making certain the beans are well distributed and push against the sides of the pastry shell. This trick keeps the shell from puffing during baking.

Bake in oven for 15 to 20 minutes or until the bottom is set and the edges are lightly brown. Remove from the oven and lift out the foil and beans. (Save the beans for the next time you bake a shell.)

Using a pastry brush, coat the shell all over with the beaten yolk. This seals the crust and prevents its soaking up the custard mixture. Return to the oven for 2 minutes to set the yolk. Cool. Reduce oven heat to 375 F.

Fry the bacon until crisp; drain; then crumble. Scatter over the bottom of the pastry shell.

Beat the eggs and cream together *with a wire whip* (do not use a beater). Then stir in salt, pepper and nutmeg to taste. Pour over the bacon.

Place on a baking sheet in oven and bake for 25–30 minutes, or until a paring knife inserted *one inch from the center* come out dry—that is, without any custard clinging to it. Serve piping hot as an *hors d'oeuvre* to 6.

Eggs in Aspic

Serves 6

---

6 tender eggs *(oeufs mollets)*
3 egg whites
3 cans (10½-ounce size) condensed chicken
    broth
3 envelopes unflavored gelatine
A few grains of cayenne pepper
1 tablespoon tomato paste
¼ cup dry sherry
Fresh tarragon leaves
Thin slices of ham
Fresh watercress

---

*O*EUFS MOLLETS, one of the most delicious ways to eat eggs, has been described as "betwixt and between" because they are simmered longer than soft-cooked eggs but not as long as hard-cooked ones. They can be served hot (on a bed of puréed spinach, for example) or cold in aspic with RICH SAUCE VINAIGRETTE (page 41).

To cook the tender eggs (they must be at room temperature), place in boiling water that covers them by at least an inch. Cook, just below simmering, for 5½ to 6 minutes. Remove immediately and place in cold water to stop the cooking; shell as soon as they are cool enough to handle.

TO MAKE THE ASPIC: Combine the egg whites, broth, gelatine, cayenne pepper, tomato paste and sherry in a heavy enamel or glass saucepan. Mix well. Over moderate heat, bring to a rolling boil, whipping constantly with a wire whip. Take off the heat and let it stand for 15 minutes. Line a colander with a dish towel wrung out in cold water and strain the liquid aspic through it into a bowl.

TO FINISH THE DISH: Pour a thin layer of the liquid aspic into the bottom of 6 oval ½-cup metal molds or custard cups. Refrigerate until set. Chill the remaining aspic until syrupy.

Dip the tarragon leaves in the syrupy aspic and arrange in a design on top of the set aspic in the molds. Chill briefly to set the tarragon leaves.

Place 1 tender egg in each mold. Cut the slices of ham in the shape of the mold, then place on top of each egg. Gently pour in enough of the almost-set jelly to fill the mold.

Refrigerate until firm. Pour the remaining aspic into a shallow pan and let it set to use for garnish.

TO SERVE: Dip the bottom of each mold into hot water for 3 or 4 seconds. Run a knife around the edge of the jelly and turn upside down on a cold platter. If the egg doesn't drop out easily, give the mold a sharp tap. Garnish the platter with clusters of watercress and a garland of chopped aspic. Serve with RICH SAUCE VINAIGRETTE.

Combine the yolk, vinegar, mustard, shallots, salt and pepper to taste. With a wire whip, beat together for about 1 minute. Then begin to add the oil very slowly, almost drop by drop, beating constantly with the whip. Makes 1 cup. Serve with EGGS IN ASPIC or green salads.

Hors d'Oeuvre Varié

*A*rrange on a large serving platter some of each of the following: salami or pepperoni, sliced very thin; shiny black olives or stuffed olives; stuffed, hard-cooked eggs; raw celery and carrot sticks; pimiento cut in julienne; sliced tomatoes with a sprinkling of oil and, if available, a tiny sprig of fresh basil. Serve with sturdy bread.

Jean=Claude Szurdak's Smoked Salmon Mousse

Serves 12 or more

---

1 pound Nova Scotia smoked salmon
2 cups heavy cream
Juice 1 lemon, strained
3 tablespoons sweet butter, melted
Freshly ground white pepper
Salt
Capers, well drained

---

*C*ut up the salmon into relatively small pieces, cutting out any discolored bits and eliminating any bones. Combine about half the salmon and half the cream at one time in the container of the electric blender and purée until smooth. Empty into bowl. Then purée the remaining salmon and cream. Add to bowl with lemon juice and butter; mix. Finally, stir in a few twists of pepper from the peppermill. It should be quite spicy with pepper. Taste for salt.

To serve, spoon into a crystal bowl and garnish with capers. Serve with small toast points.

Stuffed Ham Rolls

Serves 6

1 medium carrot, peeled
⅓ cup peeled and diced white turnip,
　　¼-inch cubes
⅓ cup fresh or frozen peas, defrosted
12 green beans, ends cut off
1 medium potato, scrubbed
⅓ cup peeled and chopped onion
1 tablespoon finely chopped parsley
½ cup MAYONNAISE (see page 36)
Salt, pepper and cayenne to taste
6 large slices boiled ham, ⅛-inch thick

Boil all the vegetables separately until done. Allow 20 minutes for the carrot, 15 for the turnip, 5–6 for the peas, 8–10 for the string beans and 25–30 for the potato. Immediately cool the peas and string beans under cold running water. Peel the potato and cut it and the carrot into ¼-inch dice. Cut the string-beans into ¼-inch lengths. Combine the cooked vegetables with all the other ingredients except the ham. Put this mixture in the refrigerator, covered, for 20 minutes. Spread an equal amount of the vegetable mixture on each slice of ham and roll up as you would a jelly roll. Arrange on a platter, seam-side-down, with a garnish of Bibb lettuce.

Les Crudités

[RAW VEGETABLES]

A delicious crisp addition to the *hors d'oeuvre* table—vegetables that taste good raw. Sliced cucumbers or tomatoes, dressed with oil, lemon juice and seasonings, garnished with minced parsley; radishes, washed, then trimmed of all but a tuft of their green leaves; fennel, cut in julienne and dressed with oil, lemon and salt; sweet red or green peppers, seeds and core removed, cut into thin slivers; celeraic, peeled, cut in julienne and dressed with MUSTARD MAYONNAISE (page 45); scallions, roots removed and leaves cut fairly short. A bowl of kosher salt should accompany the platter.

Onion and Cheese Tart

Serves 6

---

1 recipe PASTRY (page 225)—omit sugar
4 large onions, peeled and sliced thin
3 tablespoons butter
1 cup water
2 cups half-and-half cream
4 eggs
1 cup grated swiss cheese (about ¼ pound)
Salt
Freshly ground white pepper
8 to 10 parsley sprigs, minced
¼ cup bread crumbs (1 slice firm bread) *

---

*M*ake PASTRY as directed (page 225) and bake as directed for QUICHE LORRAINE (page 39). Do not use any sugar.

* Can be done in the electric blender.

Place the onions with the butter and a cup of water in a skillet. Bring to a boil and cook until the onions are soft and all the water has boiled away. Set aside. Combine the half-and-half with the four eggs and beat *with a wire whip* or fork only until well mixed. Stir in the cheese, salt, pepper and parsley.

Spread the onions in the partially cooked pastry shell. Add the egg mixture and sprinkle with the bread crumbs. Bake in a preheated 350 F oven for 25 to 30 minutes or until a paring knife inserted *one inch from the center* comes out dry— that is without any custard clinging to it. Serve piping hot as a first course.

Oysters à la Jacques

Serves 6

---

3 dozen oysters with their liquor
1 cup dry white wine
4 shallots, peeled and minced very fine
2 eggs plus 2 tablespoons water
1 teaspoon salt
2¼ cups fresh bread crumbs *
Oil for deep-fat frying

---

*P*our the oysters and their liquor into a deep saucepan. Stir in the wine and the shallots. Marinate for at least 1 hour. When marinated, place over moderate heat and bring to a boil.

* Use fresh, firm-textured bread and grate in the container of the electric blender.

Reduce heat and simmer from 2 to 4 minutes or until the edges of the oysters begin to curl. Do not overcook. Drain, reserve the liquor. Freeze, and if not used immediately, use next time you are making a fish soup.

Beat the eggs with the water and salt thoroughly. Dip each oyster first in the egg mixture then roll in bread crumbs. Place on a wire rack and dry for ½ hour.

Heat the oil in a deep-fat fryer to 350 F. Fry the oysters, a few at a time (don't crowd the fryer), until golden— about 2 minutes. Drain on paper towels.

Keep warm in a low (200 F.) oven. Serve with TARTAR SAUCE as an *hors d'oeuvre* or with cocktails.

TARTAR SAUCE
Makes about 2½ cups sauce

2 cups MAYONNAISE (page 36)
5 to 6 shallots, peeled and minced very fine

4 tablespoons chopped dill pickle
8 to 10 parsley sprigs, minced
Lemon juice to taste

*M*ix all ingredients together thoroughly, adding just enough lemon juice to give the sauce a nice zing.

Pâté de Foie

[LIVER PÂTÉ]
Serves 8–10

A good country pâté that you would find in any French *charcuterie*. Refrigerated, it will keep about two weeks. In France, it is usually served as a first course for lunch accompanied by Dijon mustard, small *cornichons* (gherkins in vinegar) and dry white wine, although a red Burgundy or rosé is perfectly acceptable.

2–4 (depending on size) strips of fat back *
1 pound pork jowls, cut up
½ pound pork liver, cut up
⅓ cup dry white wine
¼ cup Calvados or applejack
1½ tablespoons salt
Dash freshly ground white pepper
1 bay leaf

*L*ine 1½-quart earthenware or other ovenproof terrine or baking dish with some of the strips of fat back. Refrigerate.

Using the finest blade, put the jowls and liver through the meat grinder twice.

* If not available, buy salt pork or fat bacon, then blanch in simmering water for 10 minutes or so to remove the salt.

It is of the utmost importance to have the mixture very fine, almost pastelike.** Mix the wine, Calvados, salt and pepper into the mixture thoroughly. Wrap in foil and refrigerate overnight to give the pâté more flavor and aroma.

To cook the pâté, fill the lined terrine and cover the top with the rest of the strips of fat back. Place the bay leaf on top. Place the terrine in a deep pan and fill the pan with cold water to *almost* reach the top of the dish. Bake in a preheated 325 F oven for approximately 2 hours, or until the pâté registers 150 F to 155 F when tested with a meat thermometer. Cool. When cold, place a piece of foil on top of the pâté, then a weight on top of that (any 10- to 15-ounce can of food will do). This helps the pâté to release fat, which rises to the surface. Refrigerate for at least 24 hours. This gives the pâté a chance to rest.

To serve, unmold the pâté and discard all the soft fat around it. Slice into 8 to 10 slices. Place on a platter, surround with lettuce leaves and mounds of *cornichons*.

** The meats can be puréed, a small amount at a time, with the wine and applejack in the blender.

Shrimp with Mustard Mayonnaise

To serve as an hors d'oeuvre, allow about 2 pounds for six

To cook, wash thawed or fresh shrimp under cold water. Place in a large heavy skillet with all the water that clings to them. Place over moderate heat, covered, until the shrimp turn pink. About 3 minutes. Cool immediately under cold water to stop the cooking. Shell and devein. Arrange on individual plates with a little bouquet of watercress.

MUSTARD MAYONNAISE: To 1½ cups MAYONNAISE (page 36) add 3 to 4 tablespoons of Dijon mustard or to taste. It should be quite vivid. Then add enough heavy cream to bring the mayonnaise to a light consistency. Spoon into a serving bowl.

Tuna and Pistachio Terrine

Serves 6–8

1 can (7-ounce) tuna in oil
2 to 3 tablespoons Cognac
2 hard-cooked eggs
2 three-ounce packages cream cheese, at room temperature
Good dash freshly ground white pepper
3 tablespoons pistachio nuts out of the shell, coarsely chopped
Consommé (refrigerated until almost jellied)

Break the tuna up into small pieces. In the container of the electric blender, purée a small amount at a time, with the tuna oil and Cognac. Then add the eggs. Add the softened cream cheese and the pepper. Blend again at high speed until you have a very smooth, suave mixture. Place in a bowl. Taste for seasoning. It may (doubtful) need salt. Stir in the pistachio nuts. Spoon into a 1½- to 2-cup mold that can go to the table. Smooth the surface with a metal spatula. Cover with consommé that is just beginning to jell, and refrigerate until firm.

Serve straight from the terrine with plain, unflavored crackers, heated, or French bread. A delicious addition to the cocktail table.

Roquefort Cheese Spread

Makes about ¾ Cup

Cream 4 ounces of Roquefort, or other blue cheese, with ½ stick sweet butter, softened. Add Cognac and freshly ground pepper to taste. To serve, spread on buttered rounds of French bread and sprinkle with paprika.

Anchovy Canapés

Take an eight-ounce package of cream cheese, softened, and mix with anchovy paste to taste. Spread on rounds of French bread and sprinkle with caraway seeds.

Anchoyade

[ANCHOVY SPREAD]

1 can (2 ounces) fillets of anchovies
1½ tablespoons olive oil
Juice 1 lemon, strained
2 garlic cloves, peeled and minced
Handful parsley sprigs, minced
Salt
Freshly ground pepper

Soak the anchovies in cold water for half an hour to remove the salt; then, dry on paper towels. Place all ingredients, *except the salt and pepper,* in the container of the electric blender. Blend to a smooth purée. Taste for seasoning. Serve with hot, fresh toast.

James Beard's Potato-Skin Canapés

Take Idaho potatoes, wash and dry well. Place in a preheated 450 F. oven and bake until soft when pierced with a sharp paring knife. This will take about 30 minutes or a bit longer, depending on the size. Slit, then scoop out all the potato. (Use as a vegetable with your next dinner.)

Cut the skin in strips, butter well, sprinkle with salt and pepper. Brown under the broiler. An unusual bite with cocktails. They can be frozen successfully.

Chicken Liver Pâté

1 pound chicken livers
1 can (10½-ounce size) condensed chicken broth
1 cup (2 sticks) sweet butter, melted
4 to 5 shallots or green onion bulbs, peeled and chopped fine

Salt
Freshly ground pepper
Cognac
1 envelope unflavored gelatin

Cut the livers in half and cut away fibers and any bits of fat. Place in a saucepan with cold water. Bring to boil to get rid of any scum. Drain, and rinse under cold water. Rinse out the saucepan and return the livers. Add the chicken broth and bring to a boil slowly. Reduce heat and simmer for about 10 minutes or until the livers are extremely soft when pierced with the point of a paring knife. Drain through a sieve lined with several layers of cheesecloth wrung out in cold water. Reserve the broth.

While still warm, cut the livers up coarsely and purée, about half at a time with half the melted butter and half the shallots in the container of the electric blender. When you have a smooth purée, turn into a bowl and season with salt, pepper and Cognac to taste.

Cut a piece of kitchen parchment to fit the bottom of a 2-cup mold. Spoon in the pâté and smooth the surface. Seal with plastic wrap and refrigerate.

Pour the reserved broth into a *small* saucepan. Sprinkle with the gelatine. Place over low heat and stir until the gelatine has dissolved. Pour into a shallow pan and refrigerate until the jelly is firm.

To serve, turn the pâté out on a platter. Garnish the platter with the jelly chopped fairly fine. Serve with unseasoned crackers, French bread or toast points.

Crabmeat Spread

Take a can of regular or "flake" crabmeat (8-, 10- or 12-ounce); drain and pick it over. Combine crabmeat with enough well-seasoned MAYONNAISE (page 36) to hold it together; add some finely chopped green onion bulbs (scallions) with a bit of the green top, minced parsley, and salt and freshly ground pepper to taste. To serve, spread on rounds of toast or French bread.

Cream Cheese and Caviar Canapés

Mix together an 8-ounce package of cream cheese, softened, with about one cup of commercial sour cream. Spread on rounds of toast and top with a little dollop of red caviar.

Liederkranz Spread

Combine in these proportions: 1 (4-ounce) package Liederkranz cheese with 2 tablespoons softened butter and a few drops of Tabasco. Work together with an electric beater until you have a smooth paste. Stir in some finely chopped chives and freshly ground pepper to taste. Spread on cocktail pumpernickel or rye bread. Delicious!

Liverwurst Spread

Cream 4 ounces of liver sausage with ½ stick (¼ cup) sweet butter, softened. Add Cognac and freshly ground black pepper to taste. Spread on rounds of French bread and sprinkle with finely-chopped ripe olives.

James Beard's Onion Cocktail Sandwiches

Using a biscuit cutter, cut very thin slices of firm white bread into circles about two inches in diameter. Spread each circle with a thin coating of MAYONNAISE (page 36). Peel sweet mild onions. Slice very, very thin. Arrange a slice on one of the circles of bread, then top with another circle, mayonnaise side down. Brush the edge of each little sandwich with MAYONNAISE, then roll the edge in minced parsley.

I warn you: you can't make enough of these. Even non-onion types love them.

Wines for Appetizers

ALEXIS BESPALOFF

Although many Americans still drink Scotch, gin, vodka, bourbon or mixed drinks before dinner, an increasing number of people prefer a glass of wine instead. The choice of apéritif wine traditionally served in different parts of the world varies from bone dry to very sweet, so you need not hesitate to choose any wine that pleases you and your guests. A fairly dry white wine is one drink that most people will enjoy, however. It can range from a gallon jug of Mountain White to a fine German Moselle or white Burgundy of a good vintage. If you do choose a jug wine, you may find it easier and more attractive to serve your guests from a carafe instead of the original gallon bottle. The container need not be elaborate. There are now a number of inexpensive clear glass carafes available in a variety of sizes and shapes in most housewares stores.

As an alternative to the many red, white and rosé wines that would make an excellent beginning to the evening, you can occasionally serve one of three popular wine-based drinks—a spritzer, kir or sangria. A spritzer is nothing more than a mixture of white wine and soda—with or without ice—and is a refreshing long drink that is also low in alcohol. Kir, which originated in the Burgundy district of France, is a glass of white wine to which you add a spoonful of crème de cassis, a black currant syrup. It is a mild, semisweet alternative to cocktails. Sangria can be bought already bottled or made at home with red wine, a few slices of orange and lemon, sugar to taste, and lots of ice.

Wine is the simplest and least alcoholic apéritif you can enjoy, but there are other choices that are increasingly found in many homes. Among these is sherry, a popular and traditional apéritif that ranges in taste from very dry to very sweet. The driest of all Spanish sherries is labeled *manzanilla,* not often seen here. More easily found are those labeled *fino* and— not quite as dry—*amontillado.* Interestingly enough, more sherry is now produced in this country than in Spain, and American examples from California and New York State offer good value. Most American wineries market a medium-dry wine labeled "sherry," as well as a drier "cocktail sherry" and a sweet "cream sherry." Although it is traditional to drink dry sherry before a meal and sweet sherry afterwards (just as we serve the sweetest dish at the end of the meal), there's no reason not to drink a cream sherry from Spain or the United States before dinner, if you prefer.

Vermouth is a wine-based mixture flavored with various combinations of herbs. Both dry white and sweet red vermouth have long been popular as an alternative to spirits. Vermouth is usually served on the rocks, sometimes with a splash of soda. There are also a number of proprietary apéritif wines, such as Dubonnet, Raphael and Lillet, which are also flavored wines, though with a more distinct and individual taste than vermouth.

The most glamorous way to greet your guests is with Champagne. The classic Champagnes of France are readily available from a number of different firms, and the driest examples, labeled Brut, are available both with a vintage date and as a nonvintage blend. Nonvintage Champagne usually costs about $2 less per bottle, and is a better buy, although it will still cost $10 or more. There are less expensive sparkling wines from France, known as *mousseux,* including those from Vouvray, Saumur, and Seyssel. There are also dry sparkling wines from other countries. Those from Germany are labeled *sekt,* those from Italy, *spumante* (excluding Asti Spumanti—perhaps the best known—which is sweet). Most of the sparkling wines consumed here, however, come from California and New York State, and most American brands cost about half the price of French Champagne. Whether you choose one of the least expensive California sparkling wines for as little as $2.50 or a celebrated example from France for as much as $25, you are sure to get the evening off to a lively start.

Whether you and your guests begin the evening with one or another red, white, or rosé table wine, with sherry or vermouth, or with a sparkling wine depends not only on personal preference, budget, and the choice of food, but also on whether you are serving *hors d'oeuvre* informally before dinner, or a more elaborate appetizer as a first course. Once you sit down to dinner, table wine is the most appropriate choice, and the kind of wine you serve with the first course will also be determined by the food and wines to follow.

Soups

It was just over two centuries ago that M. Boulanger opened his small soup shop on the Rue Bailleul in Paris, taking advantage of a loophole which enabled him to sell food to the public without belonging to a guild. When all those with cooking skills—rotisseurs, ragout-makers, pastry-vendors, bread-bakers, and the like—organized themselves into guilds, there was no such thing as a soup-makers' guild. By serving sheep's feet cooked in white broth, M. Boulanger was able to start a new kind of establishment: the public restaurant.

For years, some of us have been saying that a good soup is the only possible substitute for mother love: it gives the child the emotional strength to grow up. This brings us to the revelation that the very word "restaurant" derives from the sign on M. Boulanger's shop, which indicated that these magical soups would *restore* you, if you happened to need any restoration.

Before I started writing this little essay, I promised myself that I would not mention the heritage of Esau, the stone broth or pebble-soup tale, or any of the other old chestnuts which come instantly to mind when the subject is soup. It is difficult to resist, because there are endless vignettes. To give you some vintage trivia: the good Joan of Arc never ate anything but a concoction of wine and five different soups, poured over toast. This sort of morsel is suitable only for bedside reading for would-be gourmets or saints in training.

And I shall barely touch upon the history of soups, fascinating as it is, because even a superficial treatise on the subject would take a good-sized book without giving a single recipe.

But perhaps you knew that, from findings in prehistoric caves, we learn that our ancestors apparently made a vessel out of sheepskin, filled it with water and the cracked bones of captured and killed animals. They then heated large pebbles and dropped *them* into the water, thus making the first meat stock, or, rather, a bone soup.

In the Middle Ages, if a meat was not roasted it was cooked in "long broth." In other words, it was a cross between a stew and a soup. Since the eighteenth century, the honey sweetening of soups has been gradually eliminated. This is perhaps the major change that occurred in soup flavoring. There are nations where a touch of sugar is put into salt-based soups, but in Western cuisines, it is only the tomato soup, some of the cabbage soups, and the fruit soups which are on the sweet side.

Rice soup, which was made with fruit and honey and milk, gradually became thicker and thicker. Sometime in the last century it became rice pudding.

The first person to approach soup-making in a fairly scientific way was probably the great nineteenth-century French-English chef, Alexis Soyer. Soyer created some of the most elaborate soups for his famous Reform Club kitchen in London. It is even more significant that, when the great Irish potato famine starved more than a million people to death, he invented a special steam boiler with a three hundred-gallon tank, the soup from which fed eight thousand people a day. The marvelous thing about this blessed invention was that the soup, apparently, was excellent. Even

THE GREAT COOKS COOKBOOK

people who didn't need it stood in line so they could enjoy the flavor.

He was sent, in 1855, to the Crimean War front, where he met Florence Nightingale in her hospital in Scutari. She led him to the smoky, messy hospital kitchen. There, he took a tasteless liquid being served to wounded soldiers, flavored it, and instantly transformed it into a delicious soup. Immediately, the mood of the soldiers changed for the better.

My wife and I love soup so much we decided to make an entire soup dinner for the birthday of a friend of ours who loves soup as much as we do. We tried to create a menu that would be completely balanced despite the obvious problems. The balancing act involved countless considerations: basic ingredients, texture, color, and so on —even the pronunciation of the name of each dish. Finally, we came up with the following menu: *

White Tomato Soup with Whole Vegetables
Beef broth simmered with vegetables and tomatoes, and strained so that the broth is flavored by the tomatoes while remaining clear. Served with freshly made Melba toast.
Hungarian Fisherman's Broth
Made with carp and other sweetwater fish. Served with potato bread.
Lentil Soup with Partridge
Served with buttered black bread spread with a purée of the partridge's liver.
Peach in Champagne Soup (in individual crystal soup dishes)
Served with sugared wafers.

* Based on recipes in *The Cuisine of Hungary*, George Lang (Atheneum, 1971).

Some of my friends and all of my enemies are tired of my statement: The only person who considers himself or herself "original" is the person who didn't study the past masters long enough. I must admit that we felt rather proud of that menu until one day, during my research in connection with a Renaissance dinner, I found that on October 30, 1563, in the house of one J. Malavergne, a midday repast was served entirely made up of soups—the first made of capons, the second of partridge and cabbage, the third of kidneys and cockscomb, the fourth of minced capon, and the fifth of partridge with lentils. While I must say the composition leaves something to be desired, nonetheless the idea was already there. I immediately put on my tailor-made shirt of humility.

When I was asked to contribute the soup chapter to this book and was limited to twenty recipes—a limit I have not been able to observe—I felt like President Lincoln, who could give a speech instantly as long as it could last for several hours, but who had difficulty with specified time limitations. After going over the great variety of possibilities—and they included my favorite soups, some rather unusual potages that probably cannot be found in cookbooks, and those recipes I've made up myself—I suddenly recalled the often quoted lines of the Mock Turtle in Lewis Carroll's *Alice's Adventures in Wonderland:* " 'Beautiful soup, so rich and green . . . / Soup of the evening, beautiful Soup!' " It occurred to me that there are soups which would be perfect for breakfast, others for a midday meal and, of course, soups for the evening, as Mr. Carroll prescribed.

Up to the mid- or late-eighteenth century, only two meals were served: early morning and late afternoon. *Nuncheons* (as the luncheons were called then) were introduced as an in-between snack and, with it, the dinner hour was postponed to the evening. But soup-stews were served in the morning for many centuries before this time-change occurred, so our suggestion of soup for breakfast is not a revolutionary idea.

For instance, there is an entire category of soups thickened at the last minute with egg yolk; many of these would be great to start the day. The robust soup-stews, accompanied by a crusty bread and sweet butter, and perhaps a salad and cheese, will make perfect luncheon meals. For the evening, you can serve almost anything, as long as it fits into the orchestration of the menu itself.

The soups in each of these categories have certain affinities to one another. All of them are hardy soups cooked in peasant kitchens or, in some instances, by housewives in the provinces. Most of them are spoon-knife-fork soups.

Another common denominator is that most of them use a single pot—none of this complex cooking of various ingredients separately and then putting them together.

These magical restoratives rarely use flour, and they are not fancied-up (to use a polite verb) with a variety of alcohols. For certain broths or soups I can imagine a touch of port or sherry, but never that gross practice of second-rate French chefs who pour cupfuls of Cognac into their *bisques* or *consommés*, ruining even the

little taste put into them originally. This I consider more criminal than many acts found in the criminal code.

One final point: Grimod de la Reynière wrote somewhere that soup is to dinner what an overture is to an opera. Perhaps you should be warned that the following soups are often entire operas in themselves.

In the court of Louis XI, the ladies apparently lived on broths because they thought that chewing food would distort the face by developing ugly facial muscles. If you still believe this theory, you had better not cook or eat the following soups, because they all have substance and richness. They are not the overrefined Victorian variety either—they will definitely restore you.

Kettner, who wrote the invaluable *Book of the Table* in 1877, compares, in his chapter on soups, some of the great masters' soup recipes, and finds "a remarkable difference of opinion on virtually every part of the recipes." He continues, saying, "It is because cookery, though a science, is not and cannot be an *exact* science, while at the same time the professors of cookery propound their recipes as if they were exact. A good deal must be left to the judgment of the cook who has to take into account the result which he or she desires to obtain."

My fellow author, John Clancy, who wrote the excellent chapter on BAKING, must ignore the above observation, but when you are cooking soups, Mr. Kettner's point should be remembered.

THE GREAT COOKS COOKBOOK

Soup of the Morning

Purée of Potato and Watercress

Serves 6

6–8 medium-size raw potatoes, peeled and
    grated
½ teaspoon dried rosemary
7 cups beef stock
1 bunch watercress (leaves only), finely
    chopped
2 egg yolks
1 tablespoon heavy cream
Salt to taste
Pinch crushed chili pods (or powder)

Cook grated potatoes and rosemary in the beef stock for about 15 minutes, or until they soften and dissolve. In the container of an electric blender, purée all the potato stock. Return to the pot and, over moderate heat, bring to a simmer. Add finely chopped watercress and simmer a few minutes. Meanwhile, mix egg yolks and cream in a soup tureen. Pour soup into the tureen, stirring gently to properly combine egg yolks and cream. Season with salt. Sprinkle with powdered chili.

NOTES:

1. Although I received this recipe from the **S**ociety **O**f **U**nderstanding **P**leasure, it is actually Central American in origin. There, a similar version is served under the name of *Sopa de Patatas Com Agrio*.

2. If you can't take the heat, don't leave the kitchen; just eliminate the chili pods.

Dill Soup, Polish Style

Serves 6

Big bunch of fresh dill
1 tablespoon butter
8 cups (1½ quarts) strong chicken broth
Salt to taste
Pinch sugar
½ cup sour cream
2–3 egg yolks

*P*are dill from stems, and use only leaves. Wash well and chop very fine. It is difficult to say how big a bunch is, but, fortunately, it doesn't make much difference if you end up with ½ cup or 1 cup of chopped dill. (It shouldn't be more than 1 cup, loosely filled; but, if you use only ¼ cup, you will still have a good soup.) Sauté the chopped dill in the butter very slowly, stirring constantly (about 2–3 minutes). Add broth, salt, and sugar and bring to a gentle simmer. Mix sour cream and egg yolks together; then, whip it into the soup. Remove from heat immediately and serve it forth.

NOTES:

1. You may serve this soup with freshly made chunky croutons, or with rice.

2. In several countries, the people have a strong predilection for dill, but none more than in Poland. In Hungary, dill is relegated to four or five specific dishes. One is a dill soup similar to this one, but made with potatoes. Another, which is quite interesting, is a salty (not sweet) cheese strudel, made with a generous amount of chopped dill mixed into the cheese and sour cream filling.

3. In one of my seventeenth-century herbariums, dill is prescribed: "Eat and it will improve your dreams." I'd like to think it was not a prescription analagous to our sleeping pills but a magic ingredient that made everything and anything possible in one's dreams.

Le Mourtaidol

Serves 6

2 quarts (approximately) of chicken stock
Pinch saffron
Freshly ground black pepper to taste
1 pound sliced French bread

*M*ake a strong chicken stock. Season with saffron and black pepper.

Heat oven to 375 F. Line a large ovenproof serving casserole with the slices of French bread. Depending on how you slice it and the size of the casserole, you may have more than 1 layer. Pour chicken stock over bread slowly; make sure it is being absorbed and not accumulating in the bottom of the casserole. When the bread cannot absorb more broth, stop; reserve any remaining broth, and place the casserole, uncovered, in oven.

In about 10 minutes, add a few tablespoons of the reserved broth to the bread. You will probably have to keep adding broth to the bread during the next 30 minutes—which is about the length of time necessary to use up what's left of the chicken stock.

NOTES:

1. You may also use the large round French-type white bread, but the texture will be different.

2. This is a curious preparation, and its only equivalent, perhaps, is French toast. Actually, it is an ingenious French peasant device to serve bread which contains soup. It originated in the Aveyron region. In an increasingly meatless society, this might be an interesting dish to serve 6 as a meal at a reasonable cost.

Aquacotta

[COOKED WATER]
Serves 6

¼ cup olive oil
2–3 medium-size onions, sliced
3–4 medium-size ripe tomatoes; peeled, seeded and chopped
3–4 medium-size ripe (red) bell peppers; deveined, cored and thinly sliced
2 stalks celery, peeled and chopped
1 tablespoon salt
Pepper
3 whole eggs
½ cup grated romano cheese

Use a dutch-oven-type pot for this. Heat oil in it and, over low heat, sauté onions until transparent and completely cooked (about 15–20 minutes). Add tomatoes, peppers, celery and salt. Stir well and cook, covered, for about ½ hour, or until peppers are done. Add 2 quarts of water; bring to a boil; then, lower heat, and simmer for 6–7 minutes. Check salt, and add pepper if you wish. Beat eggs and cheese in a soup tureen and pour soup over this mixture. Stir well, and serve immediately.

NOTES:

1. Again, this is a soup that can be eaten with toast, or toast can be placed in individual soup plates and the soup ladled over it. You may also serve it with fried bread rubbed with garlic and sprinkled with a mixture of anchovies and minced parsley.

2. This, too, belongs to the simple village soups made in every part of the world, and which are based on available products. In this one, the basic ingredient is the fruitlike fleshy red ripe green pepper. If it is not in the market, I don't think you should make this soup—even if in Italy they occasionally use green peppers; the soup has a completely different taste from one made with the red bell pepper.

3. The name of this soup means "cooked water." Among peasant soups one often comes upon amusing or poetic titles.

Potage Tourin
Serves 6

1 tablespoon lard
3 small or 2 large Bermuda onions
4 egg yolks, lightly beaten
Bread for toast
Clove of garlic
1 tablespoon salt

Heat lard in a soup pot to just below smoking point. Slice Bermuda onions very thinly; toss them in the lard, and cook over low heat until they color and are wilted. Stir every now and then. It will take about 20 minutes for the onions to have just the right texture. Add 1 quart of boiling water, and simmer mixture for about 10 minutes. Meanwhile, put the egg yolks into a soup tureen. Toast a thick slice of bread and rub it with garlic. Correct salt in soup and, stirring rapidly, pour it over the egg yolks. Serve immediately.

NOTES:

1. Toast can be placed either in individual soup plates and soup ladled over it, or it can be passed separately.

2. Butter may be substituted for lard, but do not substitute oil for lard.

3. You must use Bermuda or Spanish onions for this soup because they have the highest sugar content, and the slow cooking carmelizes it—a factor which contributes significantly to the soup's final texture, flavor and color.

4. Of course, you cannot reheat this soup unless you want to have little pieces of scrambled egg swimming unhappily amidst the onion.

5. If you say flour, everyone automatically thinks "wheat flour"; eggs are associated instantly with chicken eggs, snail preparation with garlic butter, and onion soup with cheese in some form or other. There are many dishes in our Western cuisines that are eaten in only one or two ways. This onion soup, however, is different from the traditional French variety and, I think, is a most rewarding approach to this most satisfying dish.

Midday Soup

Oyster and Pasta Soup

Serves 6 to 8

¼ pound salt pork, finely chopped
1 large onion, peeled and very finely chopped
1 quart shucked oysters in their liquor
1 tablespoon tomato paste
1 teaspoon salt
4 cups milk
½ cup parsley, very finely chopped
1 cup thick spaghetti, broken into 2-inch lengths
1 cup light cream
Parmesan cheese, freshly grated (optional)

Cook salt pork for a few minutes until it gives off enough fat in which to fry the onions. Add onions; stir for a few moments; then cook over low heat—covered, for about 10 minutes, or until onion is fairly soft but not brown.

Meanwhile, strain the shucked oysters; reserve the liquor.

Over very low heat, add tomato paste and salt to the onion, and stir well. Stirring constantly to prevent burning, add oyster liquor and cook, uncovered, for about 2 minutes. Add milk and parsley, and bring to a simmer. Pour in spaghetti and cook until tender.

Add oysters and cream, bring to a simmer and continue to cook 3–4 minutes or until edges of oysters ruffle. Take care not to overcook or the oysters will become rubbery. Adjust salt to taste, and serve with oyster crackers on the side and cheese if desired.

NOTES:

1. As I have pointed out in another recipe, you have to be careful when you cook with milk. Unless you keep it only slightly above the simmering point, it will separate; it will also boil out of the pot.

2. Only Heaven knows why certain foods are always married to certain ingredients. I have rarely seen an oyster soup which is not made with celery in one form or another and sprinkled with cayenne pepper. But I think you'll find the combination of milk, cream, and oyster with a touch of tomato paste very pleasing. And the addition of spaghetti makes this soup very much like the kind you taste in Louisiana, if you happen to be invited to a fisherman's table.

3. A foreign correspondent once told me about a recipe created in Italy for a legendary dish combining oysters with champagne which resulted in the most luxurious oyster soup in the world. I've experimented with it, and concluded that it spoils two good things: oysters and champagne.

4. Opening oysters is not easy unless you have trained sea gulls that will drop them from great heights to rocks below and crack the shells. (According to some historians, man learned to eat oysters by observing birds.) However, most good fish stores provide shucked oysters by the half pint—which generally contains 12 to 18 oysters, depending on their size. To make a generous oyster soup, you need 1½ pints for 6 to 8 people. If you want to use it as an aphrodisiac, as Casanova supposedly did, according to his formula you must have at least "fifty each evening with your punch."

A Pot of Mackerel

Serves 6

FISH STOCK:
Fish heads, bone and skin
Bouquet garni in cheesecloth bag
2 leeks, well cleaned
2 carrots, peeled and sliced
4 cups dry white wine
4 cups water
Juice of 1 lemon

INGREDIENTS TO COMBINE WITH STOCK:
3 tablespoons butter
1 large onion, peeled and cut into chunks
2–3 large potatoes, peeled; cut into chunks (about 1½ pounds)

About 2 pounds whole fillet of mackerel
¼ cup chopped parsley

Combine all ingredients for fish stock and cook ½ hour. Strain, and add water, if necessary, to have 6 cups of stock. Set aside.

Meanwhile, melt the butter in a soup pot; for 5 minutes, sauté the chopped onions and potatoes, stirring now and then. Add the fish stock, and cook vigorously until potatoes are almost tender—perhaps, another 10 minutes. Add fish and parsley;

cook over high heat for another 5 minutes. Most mackerel cooks in that length of time. Serve it from the pot.

NOTES:

1. For a variation of the dish, you may remove fish and serve it separately with a thick vinaigrette made with chopped onions, chopped chives, chopped hard-boiled eggs, mustard, oil and vinegar. If you plan to do it this way, use more fish, and serve it as a separate course. Very good with it, too, is a traditional *Salsa Verde.*

2. Originally, I planned to write an "authentic" *Cotriade,* the fish soup of Brittany. I recalled many a fine *Cotriade* I've eaten; but, to make sure I had covered the field, I read another dozen or more recipes. That was the end of my *Cotriade* venture, because one of them used peanut oil and saffron; Raymond Oliver added curry; the third made it more complicated than any of the recipes of Jules Gouffé. What clinched my decision to stop seeking the "real *Cotriade"* was a recent book by Courtine, the high priest and taste-maker of French gastronomy. He not only added a glass of hard cider to 4 cups of fumet (fish stock), which would cancel out any taste the fish might have, but asserted that in this simple fisherman's stew he can perceive the Breton reefs, spray, the massive silhouettes of the fishermen in yellow oilskins, gorse of the dunes, the crushing weight of the menhirs, the disturbing beauty of the spirits that haunt them, the secrets of the Druids, the eternal Celtic hope and a sigh from Melusine—the fairy from the legends of Poitu. Not wanting to subject my reader-cooks to such an extraordinary jambalaya of mixed metaphors, I abandoned the search.

3. And by the way, that dear old standby, the *Larousse Gastronomique,* very sensibly suggests a very simple fish-tomato-onion-herbs recipe using plain water—as the Breton fishermen probably do.

Halászlé

[[HUNGARIAN FISHERMAN'S BROTH]]
Serves 6

Carp should be alive when you buy it. Ask your fishman to bone it, remove the skin and cut the meat into 4–5-inch chunks. Be sure he gives you the skin and bones. Also, be sure you purchase female carp with a good amount of roe; purchase extra milt. If you buy a male carp with milt, buy extra roe. Do not wash the inside of the fish; the blood makes the dish tasty.

1 whole live carp, 5–6 pounds, or a piece weighing the same amount
Salt
3–4 medium-size onions (about 1 pound), peeled and chopped fine
2 tablespoons paprika, sweet such as "Noble Rose"
1 green pepper, seeded and cut across in very thin slices

*B*oil skin, bones and head of carp in 2 quarts of water with 1 teaspoon salt for 20 minutes. Strain the broth. Set fish pieces aside.

Cook the onions in the fish broth for about 30 minutes over medium heat; strain and reserve broth; force cooked onions through a sieve or purée them in a blender; put back into the broth.

In a 4-quart soup or stew pot, place pieces of fish next to each other. Pour onion broth over fish, and add as much water as necessary to cover it. Bring liquid to a boil; add 1 tablespoon salt, the paprika and the green pepper. Do not stir, but shake the pot.

Add the whole roe and milt and cook for an additional 4–5 minutes. Let the soup stand for 5 minutes before serving.

NOTES:

1. In the city of Szeged, four or five different types of fish are used in addition to the carp. None of these fish is available in Western Europe or North America. Use catfish, pike, brill, etc. You may add some small fish to the chopped onion and cook them together. Then purée onions and fish through a sieve and use this broth as a base for the soup.

2. There are many variations on this theme in different parts of Hungary. One of the most interesting excludes the paprika, thickens the broth with a mixture of walnut paste and flour, and flavors it with lemon juice and a touch of sugar. Another variation cooks the broth with lots of diced vegetables, such as parsnips, carrots, kohlrabi, knob celery and potatoes, and flavors the soup with dill.

I have always felt that an essential element in dealing with gastronomy is an over-all view of culinary history in terms of different cultures, giving a keen sense of precedent and fostering a continuing search for parallels. I have found an amazing number of seafood soup-stews—all the way from southern Italy to Java—to be almost identical. The fisherman uses available fish and cooks it in the simplest way, adding only one or two ingredients to achieve a particular flavor and texture. In Hungary, these two would be onion and paprika.

Perhaps a description of how a Hungarian Danube fisherman makes his HALÁSZLÉ would be not only of intellectual interest but may inspire you to make one for a big party—especially in the country, where your barbecue setup accommodates a large kettle; HALÁSZLÉ would be a suitable big-party dish.

Use a very large cast-iron kettle. If you are going to cook 10 pounds of fish, the proper proportion of onion to add would be $3\frac{1}{4}$ pounds (proportion of onion to fish, then, is one-third more onion, because it is not puréed).

Line the bottom of the kettle with paper-thin onion slices, and on top of them add split heads of fish with the boney part pointing toward the bottom—to be sure the flames do not scorch them right from the start. Place the remaining pieces of fish on top of the heads, and add water to cover.

Salt it at the very beginning. Salt has a chemical property that keeps the flesh of the fish intact; it will ensure your not ending up with hundreds of little pieces.

THE GREAT COOKS COOKBOOK

At any rate, undersalt it; you can always adjust the seasoning when the soup is done. Start it on fire which is at its hottest; this, too, will help to keep the fish from falling apart. Just before it begins to boil, add paprika—as much as your lips and stomach can take—but for the amount suggested above, at least 3 tablespoons—or possibly a mixture of half sweet and half hot paprika. Lower heat to simmer. You cannot stir, of course. With potholders grab either side of the top, and make a very fast semicircular motion, which has the same effect as stirring, but does not break up the fish.

How do you know when it's ready? Well, first of all, you will see three rings around the inside of the kettle; these appear after a certain length of cooking time. Put your palm over the simmering kettle for a while, and then make a fist; if your hand is sticky, you will know the fisherman's broth is done. Of course, for the uninitiated, the easiest way is to take a piece of the fish out and taste it. Make sure—and this is vital!—that the fish is cooked to the texture of Chinese "doneness." In other words, underdone, and almost like meat in texture.

The real thing will have three flavors, possibly four; fish, onion, paprika and maybe just a touch of singed twigs, if you are really authentic and do this over an open wood fire.

When you taste it, you will realize that this simple combination is a perfect example of the adage: art is the demonstration that the ordinary is extraordinary.

American Corn Chowder

Serves 6

2 slices bacon, diced
2 tablespoons chopped onion (1 small chopped onion)
1 small, seeded and coarsely chopped green pepper (optional)
5 cups milk
About ¾ pound potatoes, peeled and cut in small dice (2 cups)
Kernels of 6 ears of fresh corn (discard cobs)
1½ teaspoons salt
Pinch white pepper

Render bacon in a pot for 2–3 minutes, or until there is enough fat to start frying the onion. Let onion cook over low heat for about 10 minutes, adding peppers during the last few minutes. Stir, and cook a little longer. Add milk and potatoes; simmer for about 10 minutes, but watch milk, its boiling point comes without warning! Add corn kernels, and cook another 10 minutes or until corn is just tender. Add salt, pinch of pepper and serve.

NOTES:

1. Green pepper is optional. If you don't use it, add a little finely chopped parsley when the corn is done.

2. When cooking a milk-based soup, especially one involving the subtle, elusive

taste of corn, be very careful not to use any method or any ingredient that might overpower its flavor. Therefore, it is absurd to use lots of onion, heavily smoked bacon, all kinds of spices and other ingredients I so often see called for in some cookbooks.

3. There are enough apocrypha about the origin of the word chowder to fill a huge *marmite.* Actually, it is an archaic French word referring to a fish soup-stew called, logically enough, *chaudmer,* via *chaudière.*

Three-Helping Bean Soup
Serves 6

2 smoked pigs' feet
½ pound smoked pork ribs
1 knob celery, peeled and diced
¼ pound fresh shell beans *
1 medium-size onion, peeled and chopped
1 tablespoon lard
1 tablespoon chopped flat (Italian) parsley
1 tablespoon flour
½ tablespoon paprika
1 garlic clove, mashed
½ pound smoked pork sausage, cut into
    1-inch pieces
Salt
2 tablespoons sour cream

Cook pigs' feet and pork ribs in 2 quarts of barely boiling water until the meat comes off the bones—about 2 hours. Remove meat and bones from broth. Reserve meat pieces; discard bones.

Add diced celery and beans to the broth and, over medium heat, cook until beans are tender (about 20 minutes).

Meanwhile, fry onion in lard over low heat. When onion is soft, add chopped parsley and flour and, over the lowest heat

possible, make a brown *roux,* stirring often to prevent burning. When the *roux* is light brown, mix in paprika and garlic and, immediately, add 1 cup of cold water. Whip until smooth, then pour into the cooked beans. Add smoked sausage and ½ tablespoon salt; stir and simmer for 10 minutes more.

Cut reserved, cooked smoked meats into small pieces and add to the bean soup. Adjust salt. Add the sour cream, and serve with LITTLE DUMPLINGS (page 79).

NOTES:

1. *The best time to make this soup is when fresh shell beans are available. However, the soup can be made with dried beans too. Almost any type fresh shell bean can be used—cranberry or pinto beans, for example. If you use dried beans, soak them overnight.

2. In the United States, smoked pork rib and smoked pig's feet are generally sold in Southern-style butcher shops. Any part of pork can be used.

3. If you use dried beans, add the salt at the very end of the cooking, otherwise the skin of the bean will remain hard.

THE GREAT COOKS COOKBOOK

Veal Potage

Serves 6

---

1 good tablespoon butter, plus 1 teaspoon
    for croutons
1 pound very lean veal, cut fine
4–6 ounces very lean raw ham, or
    tenderloin of pork (all fat
    removed), cut into shreds
½ pound potatoes, peeled and thinly
    sliced
2 medium onions, peeled and thinly sliced
2 leeks, whites only, sliced thinly across
2 quarts veal stock
1 glass fruity, but not sweet, wine (a
    Riesling-type, perhaps)
Pinch powdered coriander
Bunch of chervil (or parsley)
1½ cups light cream
Salt
Pepper, freshly ground
2 slices rye bread

Melt 1 tablespoon butter in a soup pot and, over very low heat, sautée the veal, ham or pork, potatoes, onions and leeks for about 10 minutes. Add stock, wine, spice and herbs. Cook, covered, until meat is soft; about 1½ hours.

In the container of an electric blender, blend stock and all until it is completely puréed. Return to the pot and add 1½ cups light cream, or enough to give it a heavy soup texture. Adjust salt, and add a bit of crushed pepper.

Meanwhile, cut the bread into ¼-inch cubes. Melt the teaspoon of butter in a small frying pan and toss the cubes until they are nicely coated and crisp and become croutons. Serve them on the side with the soup, or if you have a little extra time make THIMBLE DOUGHNUTS (page 80) and serve them instead.

NOTES:

1. In my seventeenth- eighteenth-century books, I read so often of great *potages* which were basically puréed lean meats. I decided to re-create one while keeping in mind twentieth-century ingredients as well as twentieth-century stomachs.

2. I'm sure you realize that the potato acts only as a thickening agent.

3. As a slight variation, you may add 1 bay leaf to the soup, but be careful not to leave it in for more than 10 minutes. It is a common oversight among cookbook authors not to specify the length of time bay leaves should go on cooking. This factor is neglected, despite the fact that in this soup, for example, if the bay leaf were to cook for the duration of the 1½ hours, you would taste nothing but bay leaf.

4. This is a truly fine soup, and a very expensive one to make, I hasten to add. Yet it is not very glamorous-looking. You might enhance its appearance by rolling the croutons in very finely chopped parsley.

5. As a novel idea for a garnish, use individual onion-soup crocks and cover tops with a standard baking biscuit dough in the manner of a pot pie. Place in 350 F. oven for 10–12 minutes.

Chopped Beefsteak Soup

Serves 6

1 medium-size onion, peeled and finely
    chopped
1 tablespoon olive oil
½ cup raw rice
5 cups cold water
¾ pound sirloin or round steak, fat
    removed, ground twice
½ green pepper, seeded and chopped fine
A good pinch dried orégano
Salt to taste
1 tablespoon finely chopped chives

Sauté onion in the oil over very low heat for about 10 minutes, or until it is completely soft. Meanwhile, boil the rice in 1¼ cups of the water for about 15 minutes, or until cooked. Set aside.

Mix ground beef, remaining cold water, green pepper, the cooked rice and orégano. Add mixture to the cooked onion, and bring to a boil. Adjust salt to taste. Sprinkle with chives when ready to serve.

NOTES:

1. The origin of this soup is South American—most probably Paraguay—where they make a similar mixture but one which is much thicker. I have always been fascinated with it because it is not a "short-cut" soup, yet if you co-ordinate your cooking procedures, you have good, freshly made soup in about 20 minutes.

2. The ideal recipe is *any* recipe in the hands of a sensible cook. By adding eggs or different vegetables, herbs or spices, for example, you can create your own variation, using this recipe as a base.

Zuppa di Cavolata

[CAULIFLOWER COOKED WITH PIGS' FEET]
Serves 6

2 pigs' feet, cut lengthwise, then across
½ pound pork rind (see note 2)
1 large onion, peeled
4 peeled carrots, whole
Bunch parsley, flat (Italian) if possible
4 ripe tomatoes
½ large or 1 small head cauliflower, cut
    into flowerets
1 teaspoon salt
Freshly grated pecorino sardo cheese

Scald pigs' feet and pork rind, then discard water. Rinse with cold water. Put pigs' feet, pork rind, onion, carrots, parsley, tomatoes and 1 teaspoon salt into large pot with 4 quarts of water. Cook for about 2 hours, or until meat of pig's feet comes easily off bone. Strain broth; set pork aside to cool.

Pigs' feet absorb a great deal of water while cooking; fortunately, therefore, the broth will be very concentrated. Add enough water to it to have 2 quarts liquid in which to cook cauliflower. Cook the flowerets in the adjusted broth for about 15 minutes over medium heat, or until it's done but still has "bite" (or "al dente," as is said of properly cooked pasta).

Meanwhile, bone pigs' feet, and dice meat, as well as the pig rind. Put diced meat and rind into finished cauliflower soup; adjust salt. Serve with freshly grated pecorino sardo.

NOTES:

1. This is a soup from the island of Sardinia, but you don't have to be Sardinian to love it. It reminds me of the menu of a midtown New York restaurant, where George Lois wrote a throwaway line which reads: "My chef decided to have all sea-food appetizers. I told him, 'Marvelous, as long as one of them is pigs' knuckles.'" Personally, I feel the same way about pigs' feet.

2. Make sure the pork rind is completely scraped and clean before scalding it. It's not difficult to get it from a co-operative butcher. Ours, the Nevada on Broadway, for example, does not usually sell it, but on request they get it for us. If the skin is cut very thin, I advise you to add it only during the second hour, since it will take much less time to cook than the pigs' feet.

3. If you like, you may add a cup of peeled, diced potatoes along with the cauliflower, or ½ cup of *ditalini*—a small, thimble-size pasta—or the same amount of a type of macaroni called *maccheroncini rigati.*

4. Pecorino sardo is a grating cheese made of ewes' milk and is indigenous to the island of Sardinia.

Egg and Lemon Soup with Tripe
Serves 6

1–1½ pounds cooked tripe
Coarse salt
2 quarts chicken, beef, or lamb broth
1 medium-size onion, peeled
1 knob celery, peeled
1 clove garlic
¾ cup raw rice
2 egg yolks
Juice of 2 ripe lemons
Paprika (optional)

Scrub, scrape and clean tripe. Rub it with coarse salt, then run cold water over it for about 10 minutes. Place in a large pot, cover with water and boil for about 10 minutes. Discard water, then rinse tripe. Cut into thinnest possible slivers.

Return tripe to soup pot with broth, onion and knob celery; if you have to use water instead of stock, add salt to taste. Cook tripe until it loses its rubbery quality and can be chewed easily. Depending on how well cooked the tripe was when you bought it, this step may take 1 to 3 hours. Somewhere along the line, add the clove of garlic for 20 minutes; then remove and discard it.

In a separate pot, mix the rice with 2 cups of water and cook for about 20 minutes over slow heat until rice is tender. Set aside.

Just before tripe is cooked, put 2 egg yolks in a large mixing bowl and whip until they become frothy. Holding container of lemon juice in one hand, continue to whip yolks with the other. Add the lemon juice little by little. When all juice has been added, keep whipping mixture for another 3–4 minutes.

When tripe is completely cooked, remove 1 ladleful and, little by little, whip it into the egg mixture. Keep adding as many as 4–5 ladlefuls of the hot broth. Don't delay; later it will be difficult to make the texture smooth, since there are little tripe pieces in the pot. When you have about 4 cups of this mixture well whipped, add it to the tripe; add cooked rice, sprinkle top with a little paprika (optional), and serve.

NOTES:

1. As with much of the culinary repertoire from this area, it is impossible to determine whether it was the Turkish, Greek, or some other nearby nation that developed this recipe. The Ottoman Empire acted pretty much as the Austro-Hungarian Empire did, amalgamating most of the dishes into a quasi-single cuisine. In any case, this dish is generally called either *Skembe* or *Ishkembeh,* and if lamb's feet are added to it, it's called *Patsas.*

2. In Greece, they use lamb or mutton tripe exclusively, but I think you will find beef tripe tastier and easier to obtain. Although it is possible to buy what is called ready-to-cook tripe that has been cleaned as well, I have never come across a product that did not still have to be cooked—and for at least 1 or 1½ hours. I advise you not to try starting with raw tripe because it's a pretty messy job; moreover it will take about 3–6 hours of cooking time.

3. Many of the recipes I've read call for cornstarch as an extra thickening agent. Make sure you return the cookbook or recipe that suggests it to wherever you got it.

4. I suggest serving the soup with extra lemon, because many people like a more lemony taste than the recipe I've given you will produce.

5. A fine variation on our theme is to use fish broth instead of the chicken, beef or lamb stock in this recipe. In Greece they add lots of extra vegetables to tone down the taste of fish. I, personally, don't think it's necessary.

6. It is something of a shock to a Parisian that his beloved onion soup has an equivalent in the Near Eastern part of Europe. Yet it's true that the egg-lemon tripe soup also stands for nostalgic, bohemian, all-night parties in a different part of the world.

Potée Paysanne

[[PEASANT SOUP]]

Serves 6

---

2 pork knuckles, each split in half
½ pound lean salt pork
3–4 pounds beef flank
Small head of savoy cabbage, cored and
    sliced
A few carrots, peeled and whole
2 small turnips, peeled and halved
2 large, or 3 smaller, leeks—trimmed,
    washed and split lengthwise
About 1 foot-length fresh garlic sausage
3–4 potatoes, peeled and whole
Bouquet garni of parsley, thyme and bay
    leaf

---

*B*ring pork knuckles, salt pork and beef almost to the simmering point in 2½ quarts of water. Delay simmer by adding a ½ cup of cold water 2 or 3 times in order to bring most of the impurities to the top so they can be skimmed. Then cook about 1½ hours, or until meat is almost tender. Remove meats and set aside. Add to the broth all the vegetables except potatoes, and cook 20 minutes longer.

Add the sausage, potatoes and *bouquet garni*. Add 2 cups water if soup seems too thick. Cook 20 minutes more over medium heat.

If all vegetables are properly done— that is, not overdone—turn heat down very low and simmer gently for a few minutes more. Skim off the fat.

TO SERVE: There are many ways to make a fine presentation of POTÉE PAY-SANNE. We arrange the salt pork, pigs' knuckles, sausage and beef in a pile on a serving platter—possibly one that is lined with a wooden board—and surround it with the large vegetables: potatoes, carrots and leeks. The soup, including the savoy cabbage, is served in a soup tureen and accompanied by toasted French bread or simply a good crusty one.

NOTES:

1. If you happen to be a native of any one of certain European countries, you may want to add a much larger piece of salt pork to the *potée*. If it's not completely fresh, boil it separately first for a couple of minutes and discard the water; it's then ready to use. In any case, be sure to skim fat from soup before serving it.

2. The sausage can be Italian *cotteghino,* or a German, Hungarian or Polish type as long as it's not smoked. Depending on the type you choose, it will need a little more or a little less cooking time.

3. You may also use other vegetables, such as whole string beans; other ingredients, too, such as smoked pork shoulder or even preserved goose. Certainly, you may add garlic if you are addicted to it.

4. The family of *potées* is a large one in France and, frankly, I have never found a single source that agrees with another on its definition. I suppose that it could be loosely described as a soup, meat and vegetable dish—all ingredients of which have been cooked together in a special pot and, of course, never puréed, creamed or thickened with anything. Every nation has a dish resembling it—from the Chinese Hot Pot cooked in earthenware to the New England Boiled Dinner, and several hundred varieties in between. Actually, even a *Pot au Feu* is a *potée* of a sort, although Gallic purists would argue with me on that point. Probably the most famous of all *potées* comes from Auvergne. The Auvergnat *potée* generally contains just about anything to be found in a local kitchen, including pickled pork, all kinds of sausages, and the like.

5. The most important thing to remember about all *potées* is that you must cook them as slowly as possible; the water should always be kept at a simmer.

Bográcsgulyás
[[KETTLE GULYÁS (Soup-Stew)]]
Serves 6

---

2 tablespoons lard
2 medium-size onions, peeled and coarsely chopped
2½ pounds beef chuck or round, cut into ¾-inch cubes
½ pound beef heart, cleaned and cut in 1-inch dice (optional)
1 garlic clove
Pinch caraway seeds
Salt
2 tablespoons "Noble Rose" paprika, sweet
1 medium-size ripe tomato
2 green frying or Italian peppers
1 pound potatoes
Hot cherry pepper pods to taste (optional)
LITTLE DUMPLINGS (page 79)

Melt lard in a heavy 6–8 quart flameproof casserole, and sauté onions over low heat so as not to let them brown. When onions become glossy, add beef and beef heart, and, stirring from time to time, cook for about 10 minutes so that onions and meat sauté together, until brown on all sides.

Meanwhile, chop the garlic and, using the flat side of a heavy knife crush it with caraway seeds and a little salt. Remove pot from heat and, stirring rapidly with a wooden spoon, add paprika and garlic mixture. As soon as paprika is absorbed, add 2½ quarts of warm water. (Cold water toughens meat if added while meat is frying.) Replace pot; cover, and cook over low heat for about 1 hour.

While the meat braises, peel the tomato, then cut into 1-inch pieces. Core and seed the peppers and slice them into rings. Peel potatoes, and cut into ¾-inch dice. After meat has braised 1 hour, add tomatoes, green peppers and enough water to give liquid a soup consistency. Add a little salt and simmer slowly for 30 minutes more.

Add potatoes, and cook until meat and

vegetables are tender (tenderness depends on cut), and that's when the GULYÁS is done. Adjust salt. Add cherry pepper pods, if you want the stew spicy-hot. Cook dumplings in the stew. Serve the GULYÁS steaming hot in large, extra-deep bowls. The meat should be tender but not falling apart.

VARIATIONS:

1. Some housewives start with small pieces of smoked bacon instead of lard.

There are many variations, even on the basic ingredients. Some people use different types of meat, including pork, veal and sausages. Some add other vegetables such as carrots, green beans, kohlrabi, and the like.

As far as spicing is concerned, some cooks insist upon adding a small amount of black pepper in addition to paprika; others add marjoram or bay leaf; some use a little more onion and no garlic at all. Particularly in the southern section of Hungary, fresh or dried cherry peppers are added, which puts the crown on this glorious soup for the Hungarians. For a non-Hungarian, however, the crown is white-hot.

2. *Palóc Soup:* The city cousin, a creation of Gundel's, the famous Budapest restaurant, is the *palóc soup.* This is a mutton *gulyás* with lots of green beans and sour cream.

3. *Beer Gulyás:* Make the same way as KETTLE GULYÁS, but use 2½ quarts of beer instead of that amount of water.

4. Strained *Gulyás* Broth (*derített gulyásleves*): For a formal dinner, prepare a rich *gulyás* without potatoes or dumplings. When finished, strain. Serve the broth in soup cups. Use the meat to stuff green peppers.

NOTES:

1. The meat can be an inexpensive cut. It is a waste of money to use steak or tenderloin. The more different cuts you use, the better tasting the soup will be.

2. The paprika must be Hungarian "Noble Rose." Spanish paprika and other types are only coloring agents.

3. The more parts of beef and beef innards used, the better the GULYÁS will be. Lard or bacon and chopped onion are absolute musts.

5. Never use any flour. Never use any other spice besides caraway. Never Frenchify it with wine. Never Germanize it with brown sauce.

6. As I wrote in *The Cuisine of Hungary* (Atheneum, '71), a strange thing has happened to Hungarian *gulyás.* According to a 1969 Gallup Poll, *gulyás* is one of the five most popular meat dishes on the American cooking scene. Of course, what is usually served under this name shouldn't happen to a Rumanian. The origin of the soup can be traced back to the ninth century, when shepherds cut their meat into cubes, cooked it with onion in a heavy iron kettle (*bogrács*) and slowly stewed it until all the liquid evaporated. They dried the remnants in the sun (probably on their sheepskin capes), and then put the dried food in a bag made of the sheep's stomach. Whenever they wanted to eat, they took out a piece of the dried meat, added some water and reheated it. With a lot of liquid, it became a *gulyás* soup (*gulyásleves*); if less liquid was added, it became *gulyás*

meat (*gulyáshús*). Even today this distinction exists, probably to mystify foreigners and foreign cookbook writers.

Coleridge said: a man who refuses apple dumplings cannot have a clear conscience. He must have meant KETTLE GULYÁS.

Soup of the Evening

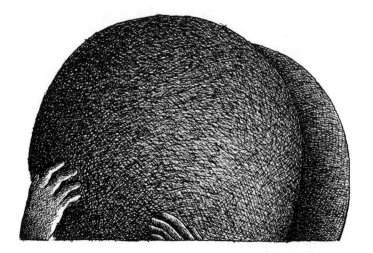

Balkan Yogurt and Cucumber Soup

Serves 6

6 cups plain yogurt
1 cup buttermilk
2 medium-size cucumbers
3 tablespoons finely chopped fresh dill
1 tablespoon finely chopped fresh mint leaves, or ½ teaspoon crumbled Egyptian dried mint
1 teaspoon salt
⅓ small clove crushed garlic, or to taste
¼ teaspoon white pepper, or to taste
1 tablespoon white wine vinegar
1 teaspoon olive oil

Whip the yogurt and buttermilk together for a few minutes until it is smooth and quite liquid. Set aside.

Peel and finely slice, or coarsely grate, the cucumbers. Add them to the yogurt mixture along with the dill, mint, salt, garlic and pepper. Stir for a few minutes. Stirring constantly, add the vinegar, drop by drop. Proceed the same way with the olive oil, making sure to combine it so thoroughly with the soup that, finally, not one drop is visible.

In the summertime, serve the soup very cold in cups with an ice cube in the center of each serving.

NOTES:

1. Pickled vegetables, very finely chopped, may be added to this soup.

2. Although I am certain that no buttermilk is used anywhere in the Near East, the only way I could achieve the correct texture (short of using water, which would have diluted this soup too much) was with buttermilk.

3. This soup is claimed by Turkey, Bulgaria, Greece and several other nations in that part of the world. Generally, it is known as *tzacik.* The last time I made this soup, it suddenly occurred to me that it can be the Near East's answer to Spain's *gazpacho,* with finely chopped green peppers, peeled and chopped onions, chopped pickles and croutons added.

4. By adding more cucumber and eliminating the buttermilk, this serves as an appetizer-dip *pita* with warm bread as an accompaniment.

5. This dish is markedly like the Indian *raita,* which is flavored with freshly crushed cumin seed.

Fourteenth Century Cabbage Soup
Serves 6

1½ quarts oxtail broth (use beef, if
    necessary)
3 leeks, well washed and thinly sliced
2 medium-size onions, peeled and chopped
Small head savoy cabbage (about 1 pound)
    sliced
1 tablespoon salt
2–3 pinches ground allspice
Pinch of saffron

To the broth, add all vegetables, salt and allspice and slowly simmer for about 30–35 minutes, or until cabbage is tender.

Meanwhile, toss a pinch of saffron into a small frying pan and shake it over high heat for a couple of seconds; make sure not to burn it. Add it to the soup.

Adjust salt to taste and serve.

NOTES:

1. This soup tastes much better than its simple preparation would indicate. But the real reason I suggest you cook it one good winter evening is that, as far as I know, it is the first soup recorded in the English language. The anonymous master cook of Richard II wrote a collection of recipes entitled *The Form of Cury.* (The manuscript is in the British Museum.) The exact recipe reads:

CABOGES IN POTAGE

Take Caboches and quarter hem, and seeth him in gode broth, with oynonns y mynced, and the whyte of lekes y flyt, and corve small, and do thereto safronn and salt and force it with powder douce.

Translated into modern English: Take cabbages and quarter them, and boil in good broth with minced onions, the white of leeks slit and cut small, adding saffron, salt and allspice.

2. This really was the age of thick broths (perhaps history should be rewritten, based on this designation), and a *tranche* or a slice of stale bread was used as a thickening agent instead of flour. As a matter of fact, the very first written record we have of a soup in Europe is by Taillevant, who also thickened his milk, saffron and honey soup with bread.

3. I hope you noted the little saffron trick I learned from a chef who came from a village near Marseilles. He showed me the difference between the BOUILLABAISSE he had made, in which the saffron used was "toasted," and another one in which it was used plain.

4. The use of savoy cabbage is wholly arbitrary: it was what I had in the pantry when I was testing this recipe.

5. Fried SOUP PEAS (page 79) go well with this soup.

Beet and Cranberry Borshch
Serves 6

5 or 6 medium-size beets, peeled and cut julienne
1½ quarts beef broth
½ pound fresh cranberries
1½ quarts water
½ small cabbage (about ½ pound), finely shredded
2 medium-size onions, thinly sliced
2 medium-size potatoes, peeled, and cut julienne
Salt
2–4 tablespoons sugar
3–6 tablespoons sour cream

Cook beets very slowly in beef broth; it will probably take about 45 minutes. At the same time, cook the cranberries, separately, in 1½ quarts of water over medium heat for about 10–15 minutes, or until all the skins have popped. Reserve cranberry broth. Put cranberries through a food mill (or *Mouli*), then combine them with their broth. Pour cranberry purée-broth into a soup pot; add shredded cabbage, onion and potatoes. Cook for 20 minutes or longer, until cabbage is tender. Don't be concerned if the potatoes more or less disappear; this aids the soup's purée texture.

Combine the contents of both pots in one pot, and begin the tricky flavoring process. Because beef broth has probably been seasoned, you may need only a little salt. Depending on the sourness of the cranberries, however, you may have to add as much as 4 tablespoons of sugar to give the soup a piquant, well-balanced sweet-sour flavor.

Remove a cupful of broth; mix well with sour cream until smooth; stir back into soup, and serve. Add steamed potatoes in middle of each serving, if you like.

NOTES:

1. The only thing more mysterious than the spelling of this soup is its origin in the dim Russian past. Originally, according to early records, *borshch* was a soup made with blood. Later, beet and beet juice were substituted for blood in order to achieve a similar color.

2. Whenever I eat beef-based *borshch* outside of Russia, I am surprised that it lacks a certain bite. In Russian provinces and even in different households, the soup varies in many aspects, but this rather sharp taste is a characteristic common to them all. Some of the better cookbooks suggest the addition of citric acid (sour salt) or vinegar or lemon juice to approximate it, but the use of cranberries makes this device unnecessary.

3. If you feel you have to be absolutely authentic, perhaps you should try to begin with a *borshch* stock, which can be made in a jar. Place in it 8 or 10 slices of dark (Russian) pumpernickel bread, a sliced onion, 2 raw peeled and grated beets; cover them with warm water and keep in a warm place. In about four days or so, you can strain and use this stock to start your *borshch.* This is actually a form of *kvas,* and may be used for meat and vegetable, or cabbage, *borshch* as well.

4. If you are using freshly made beef broth, you will have some boiled beef, of course; you may dice and add it to the soup to make a more substantial dish.

5. Most recipes suggest cooking the beets whole, peeling and slicing them, then adding them to the soup. I think that in cooking them separately, the beet broth, which is an essential part of this soup, is lost completely.

6. You may also serve this cold, as a summer soup. If you do, pour it into a transparent glass dish and top each serving with a spoonful of sour cream.

Chestnut Soup

Serves 6

THE STOCK:
Cracked veal bones, about 3 pounds
Soup greens
Pot herbs

INGREDIENTS TO COMBINE WITH STOCK:
1½ pounds chestnuts
2 slices bacon, cut into small pieces
2 large, or 3–4 smaller, celery knobs,
    peeled and diced

Salt
1 teaspoon dry sherry
THIMBLE DOUGHNUTS (page 80)

You will need 2½ quarts of stock as the base for the soup. Gauge the amount of water from the beginning; add more hot water, if necessary, during cooking to end up with the required amount.

Make the stock by simmering the bones, soup greens, pot herbs and water for about 2½ hours. Strain it through cheesecloth, then return to pot. Set aside; discard bones, greens and herbs.

Meanwhile, with a sharp knife, score each chestnut crosswise, on flat side, and roast for 10 minutes in a preheated 400 F. oven. Peel and cut each one into 3 or 4 pieces.

Fry the bacon in a skillet until it lets out fat; add the chestnut pieces and cook over medium heat for about 20 minutes, stirring often.

Add chestnut-bacon mixture to strained stock and simmer until chestnuts are almost tender (about 1 hour). The chestnuts must not be mushy. Add diced knob celery, and cook about 15 minutes.

While celery cooks, make THIMBLE DOUGHNUTS. When celery is done, stir in sherry. Add THIMBLE DOUGHNUTS, and serve.

NOTES:

1. Those worthy ladies, Mrs. Leyel and Miss Hartley, in their fine oeuvre, *The Gentle Art of Cookery,* actually wrote an entire chapter on chestnuts. But even they approached the chestnut from the usual, seemingly inevitable angle: purée; and, more often than not, in a somewhat sweetened formula. Nearly everyone adds cream, or cooks chestnuts in milk. It seems to be a traditional shotgun marriage. The above recipe treats chestnuts as a vegetable, and the romance takes place between knob celery and chestnut with surprisingly felicitous results.

2. Cleaning chestnuts is very easy if you first boil them until done, and then peel them. However, the result is good only for dessert purées, not for the type of soup at which I'm aiming. Therefore, I suggested the above method; it permits the chestnut to retain body, which is so necessary for this soup. It does make the shelling a bit difficult, and often the inner skin must be sliced off rather than peeled off.

Palotai Uccai Kalárábé Leves

[PALOTAI STREET KOHLRABI SOUP]
Serves 6

Plenty of cracked veal bones (about 4 pounds) and some chicken giblets (about 1 pound)
2 carrots, peeled
Small bunch parsley, flat (Italian) if possible
1 small onion, peeled
2 parsnips, peeled

6 cups water
1 tablespoon salt
5–6 kohlrabi, peeled and diced
1–2 tablespoons butter
1 tablespoon flour
1 teaspoon sugar
1 cup whole milk
1 tablespoon sour cream

ake a stock of the bones. Be sure to follow all the rules of stock-making, including the addition of cold water to delay the simmering; skim off impurities. Cook 1 hour; then add giblets, carrots, parsley, onion, parsnips, 6 cups water and 1 tablespoon salt and cook ½ hour longer. Be sure, too, that the stock never boils, but stays at a simmer.

While the stock simmers, peel and dice the kohlrabies; be sure to discard all "woody" pieces. In a separate pot, melt the butter and gently sauté the kohlrabies for a few minutes. Cover the pot with a tight lid, and cook very slowly over the lowest possible heat until it is tender but not overdone. When done, sprinkle it with the flour and stir it in rapidly without mashing the kohlrabies. You may need another teaspoon of butter if there is not enough juice. Cook kohlrabies, uncovered, for a few minutes, stirring constantly. Add the sugar and stir another minute or so more.

Strain the finished stock through cheesecloth (reserve vegetables and giblets; discard bones) and pour it into the kohlrabi mixture. Stir gently, making certain that the flour disappears completely in the broth. Mix the milk and sour cream together, and add to it 1 cup of broth from the soup. Mix, then pour the entire mixture back into the simmering soup.

Adjust sugar and salt, and serve it forth. To be served with LITTLE GALUSKA with vegetables and giblets on the side.

NOTES:

1. Kohlrabi is very little known in the United States, although you'll find it in the better vegetable stores in large cities. The vegetable belongs to the cabbage family and it is extremely popular in Middle Europe.

2. I dedicated this soup to the street where I was born in the town of Székesfehérvár, where I tasted it at many evening meals. I am sure that every Hungarian will give you a slightly different recipe but, recalling the taste, this is how I reconstruct the modified mother's milk I was brought up on. I also remember that the carrots and parsnips and chicken giblets were served separately on a gleaming white platter. A bridge to heaven . . .

Chicken Broth in Coconut

Serving per person

Coconut shell cup (see NOTE below)
About ¾ cup strong chicken broth
About 2 tablespoons diced breast of chicken
    per coconut shell

aw off top of coconut shell or have your butcher do it with the electric saw used for sawing bones. Discard the water.

Bring chicken broth to the boiling point and pour it into coconut shell to a little more than ¾ full. Add diced breast of chicken. Place coconut shell (or additional filled shells) in a previously prepared baking dish filled with rock salt (about 2–3 inches high so as to imbed and stand shells up securely). For 6 or 8 shells you will need a large baking dish with sides 2–3 inches high. Place pan in a preheated 500 F. oven for 1 hour. Serve it forth, using coconut tops as lids.

NOTES:

1. This is a Chinese preparation I have eaten in Bangkok. Since they used freshly cut coconut, the taste of the soup was better than the preparation I have made with coconuts obtainable in New York fruit stores. Nevertheless, it's interesting. Candidly, I must admit that although the coconut flavoring of the chicken soup is a nice touch, the only reason for coping with the problems involved is the spectacular service, which is just right for a certain kind of party.

2. The trick is to figure out how to serve the individual coconuts. You can use individual dishes with a bed of rock salt and stand the coconuts in them, or crumpled silver foil will serve the same purpose. If you happen to have hotel-service supreme dishes and remove the rings, I think you will find they will hold the coconuts quite securely. At any rate, you must work this out before you start.

Korhelyleves

[SOUSE'S SOUP]
Serves 6

1 pound sauerkraut
2 tablespoons bacon drippings (from smoked bacon)
2 tablespoons flour
1 small onion, peeled and minced
1 tablespoon paprika
½ pound smoked sausage, sliced thin
3 tablespoons sour cream
Vinegar
Salt

Squeeze sauerkraut thoroughly and reserve the juice. Cook drained sauerkraut in 2 quarts of water over medium heat until it softens.

Meanwhile, heat the bacon drippings in a skillet and add the flour; stir and fry until the mixture is light beige. Add the onion, and cook 5 minutes more. Remove from heat, and stir in paprika; immediately add 1 cup cold water and whip until smooth.

Pour reserved sauerkraut juice into a soup pot; add flour and onion mixture, the sliced sausage and the sauerkraut with its cooking liquid. Cook for 10 to 15 minutes.

In a soup tureen, mix the sour cream with a cup of the hot sauerkraut broth. Add salt if needed. Adjust the taste of the simmering soup with vinegar and salt to be sure it is quite sour (somewhat like hot, sour Szechuan soup), and pour into tureen. Mix with the sour cream, and serve.

NOTE:

This soup is generally served in the wee hours of the morning to revive the guests in a private home or restaurant after an all-night party. Therefore, it really should have its own category as *Soup of the Night*. It is guaranteed to perk up all the tired, dizzy and confused senses more than "prairie oysters." This traditional soup can be made in several different ways; variations must have two things in common: the soup must be slightly fatty, and should have a very sharp taste.

A Few Soup Garnishes

LITTLE DUMPLINGS

Makes 36 tiny dumplings

1 egg
3 tablespoons all-purpose flour
Pinch of salt

Mix the egg with the flour and salt. Spoon the mixture into boiling soup, ¼ teaspoon at a time. Cook in the soup for 2 or 3 minutes just before serving.

FRIED SOUP PEAS

Serves 6–8

1 egg
½ cup all-purpose flour
⅓ cup milk
Pinch of salt
1 cup lard or chicken fat

Mix egg, flour, milk and salt until smooth. Heat lard (to just under smoking point) in a large frying pan, then turn heat to low.

Use a sieve with large holes, and little by little, drip the batter through the holes into the frying pan; make sure the drops fall next to each other, not on top of each other.

Immediately, move the "peas" with a wooden fork, or long-bladed spatula, to prevent sticking. Separate them if they clump together. Turn them until they are light brown, then remove with a slotted spoon onto heavy paper toweling.

NOTE:

1. In Hungary, special equipment is used to make this soup garniture. The batter can be pushed through pastry tubes or separated with demitasse spoons. However, the easiest and fastest method is the one described here.

2. If you make the "peas" hours before serving, reheat them in the oven for a few minutes until they are hot and crisp.

THIMBLE DOUGHNUTS

Serves 6–8

1 cup all-purpose flour (or more if needed)
2 eggs
Pinch of salt
1 cup lard

Make a semihard dough by kneading 1 cup flour, eggs and salt on a floured board. If eggs are extra large you may have to add a little more flour. Roll dough on a floured board until it is knife-edge thin.

Wipe flour from the dough with a barely damp cloth and fold sheet in half. It will stick together.

Press a thimble into the dough, making as many tiny rounds as possible.

Heat lard in a frying pan. Turn heat down to low. (Hot lard will not spatter if you put a bit of salt in it.) Fry the thimbles for 1 or 2 minutes, turning once. Remove with a slotted spoon and drain on a triple-thickness of paper toweling.

Wines for Soup

ALEXIS BESPALOFF

The menu for a formal dinner will often include a consommé or clear broth, and the hostess who wants every course to be accompanied by a different wine would offer a glass of sherry or Madeira. The soups described here, however, are quite different in style, and may be considered, for the most part, as the main dish of the meal. They therefore call for a red or white wine, as would any dish that is made up primarily of meat or fish.

Many of these soups are robust in character and complex in taste, and would overpower a delicate wine. As the wines of a country are usually suited to its cuisine, and as many of these soups are Hungarian in origin, what would be a more appropriate accompaniment than the red and white wines of Hungary? These wines are not available in every shop, but they are interesting enough to look for when you plan to make one of these soups.

The best-known red wine of Hungary is Egri Bikavér, a brisk, full-flavored wine which somewhat resembles a young Bordeaux. Hajosi Cabernet, Villányi Burgundi, and Szeksárdi Vörös are three other interesting Hungarian red wines with enough flavor to stand up to the heartiest of soups.

The white wines of Hungary have an attractive, flowery bouquet and a soft, not entirely dry taste. Debröi Hárslevelu, Csopaki Olaszrizling and Badacsonyi Szürkebarát are three appealing examples available in this country. If these unfamiliar names confuse you, it will help you to know that, generally speaking, the first word is that of the village or region of origin; the second is the grape variety from which the wine is made.

As an alternative to the wines of Hungary, you should look for wines with some flavor to them. Among red wines, Côtes-du-Rhône from southern France, California Zinfandel, and Spanish Rioja are three possible choices. Alsatian Riesling, Mâcon Blanc from southern Burgundy, and a Sauvignon Blanc or Dry Semillon from California are some white wines with character and personality sufficient to complement these satisfying soups.

These suggested wines are meant to accompany the midday and evening soups. Whether or not you want to carry authenticity to the point of having a glass of red or white wine with your breakfast soup will depend on your mood and on your plans for the rest of the day.

Pasta is one of the most misunderstood and perhaps misused of all Italian foods. It is also the most versatile and interesting. Pasta can be a gastronomic delight (who doesn't like pasta?) or unfit for human consumption. It can be a healthy, nourishing food and it can be a useless blob of glue. It all depends on the quality of pasta used and the way it is cooked.

Pasta is made from semolina—a granular, finely ground durum wheat, somewhat yellow in color; it looks very much like fine cornmeal. Semolina, unlike white flour, contains great amounts of vitamins, proteins and minerals. I have noted that imported Italian pasta is far superior to American pasta. One can easily test various American brands of the same type of pasta —spaghetti, for example—and be amazed to discover the difference in taste. Yet all are supposed to be made from hundred-percent semolina. Although there are several good American brands, none can equal a good pasta imported from Italy.

Some American pasta is impossible to cook properly. A good pasta will not overcook easily, and the proper doneness, *al dente,* can be accomplished with no great effort. *Al dente* means firm to the teeth— one should be able to bite into a piece and feel the texture of the pasta. Some American pastas overcook and become gummy before becoming *al dente.*

There is only one way to cook pasta and that is in an abundant amount of rapidly boiling water (about 5 quarts for each pound of pasta). After pasta is added to the water and it is boiling again, salt is added. The pasta must be stirred often. During the entire cooking process, the water should boil. Taste the pasta often to check for doneness. There is no way to time the cooking because different brands and different types of pasta require different cooking times. Pasta should be drained about five seconds before it is perfect (this timing takes some practice) and served immediately. Cold water should not be poured over pasta unless the recipe calls for it.

Certain dishes must be made with certain types of pasta because of the character of the sauce. A thin pasta is used in LINGUINE CON BROCCOLI (page 96), since the cooking time is short and the thin pasta absorbs the sauce more quickly. Linguine is often used with fish sauces because they are also thin and the flat pasta holds such sauces better than a round, spaghettilike pasta does. Penne, on the other hand, is used in the PASTA CON VONGOLE AL BRANDY (page 98) because, being large, penne is sturdier and, therefore, suitable in casserole cooking. Needless to say, homemade pasta is the most interesting and the tastiest. The LASAGNE and CANNELLONI recipes should be made from homemade pasta; the instructions and suggestions are on page 88.

My relatives in Italy have always told me that pasta was not fattening if one drank wine with it. I assumed it was an old wives' tale, although I noticed that, contrary to popular belief, there was much less obesity in Italy than in America. However, I heard the same statement from my wife's cousin, a very sophisticated person who had been living in Italy for several years. I then thought there might be something to it. When I returned to the United

States, I asked a friend who was a biochemist at Rockefeller University if it was possible that wine could have such an effect on pasta. He thought for a few seconds, and said, "Sure, it's very *possible*. The acid in the wine would affect the carbohydrates in the pasta."

I do not know if it is a chemically proven fact, but I would like to believe it might be, because it seemed to work that way with my Godfather Tommaso, who ate two pounds of pasta every day and was slim all of his eighty-odd years.

I still remember with nostalgia the odors of pasta permeating the neighborhood on Sunday mornings, along with the "Italian Program" that all the women turned on while cooking sauce and rolling out the pasta. Carlo Buti was the tenor one often heard on the "Italian Program" in those days. My father would be reading *Il Progresso,* the Italian newspaper printed in America, and, impatiently, looking at the clock; he was waiting for it to strike one—that was when he would complain about his hunger and ask why dinner was not ready. My mother, when behind schedule, would turn the clock back; my father never complained until "the big hand was on twelve and the little hand on one."

I have tried to vary as much as possible the pasta recipes given here. There are pasta salads, pasta recipes with fish, with vegetables and with meat. There are sauces and casserole dishes and a recipe for CANNELLONI (page 88). Many of the pasta recipes have never been published in America before. The bulk of my recipes come from Italians I have met during my travels, from relatives and from friends.

I have avoided the most commonly known recipes and have tried to show how unusual and varied pasta dishes can be. One can expand on many of these recipes, can replace some ingredients that are not available with others that are procurable; the combinations are endless.

About Tomatoes

There are some important facts to remember when one makes a tomato sauce. First of all, it is important to remember that the longer the sauce cooks the more bitter and acid the tomatoes become. The idea of simmering a sauce for hours on end, which some people think makes an authentic Italian sauce, is wrong; it is also a great way to have heartburn for dessert. During my seven years in Italy, or in the homes of relatives and friends, I never saw an Italian cook a meat sauce for more than 2 hours.

The sweetest tomato sauces are those cooked the least amount of time, and my favorite sauce is the raw tomato sauce in the recipe for SPAGHETTINI CON POMIDORI FRESCHI (page 106).

There is no reason to cook a MARINARA SAUCE (page 91) more than 45 minutes, and no reason to cook a meat sauce more than 2 hours. Most Italians—in Italy —make a meat sauce with a few bones, such as chicken feet, pork bones, a veal or beef bone, and, perhaps, a small piece of lard, *pancetta* (pig belly or bacon) or pig skin. It's the bones that make a sauce sweet; the result is a lighter, less fatty sauce.

It should be noted that Italians generally use less sauce on their pasta than Americans. Americans probably drench their pasta with sauce because the pasta is of such poor quality.

In my opinion, the best tomato sauces are made from fresh tomatoes. Tomato paste should be used as little as possible; or, better, avoided altogether. In this book all the recipes that call for tomatoes require either fresh or canned. Unless stated,

the fresh tomatoes do not need to be peeled or seeded. They should simply be cut up coarsely and put through a food mill. The canned tomatoes can be put through the food mill with their liquid.

If the sauce is too thin, instead of overcooking it or adding tomato paste as a thickener, just cook your pasta until about three-quarters done; drain it and add it to the sauce, cooking and stirring constantly. The pasta will absorb some of the sauce and thicken it during the cooking process. This is especially effective in MARINARA SAUCES, such as that used for SPAGHETTI ALLE CIPOLE (page 105).

About Ricotta and Other Italian Cheeses

In America, ricotta is made from pasteurized cows' milk. In Italy, ricotta is made from unpasteurized ewes' milk. Needless to say, there is a difference in flavor. American ricotta is bland and tasteless, and one has to work with it to make it taste like something. Italian ricotta is rather sweet and, although very delicate, has a most distinctive flavor. Anyone who has savored the delight of fresh ricotta in Italy knows what I mean. The Italian ricotta is also looser and has a better texture. One has to use more cheese, more eggs and more seasonings when using American ricotta in a recipe to get close to the taste of the original. Cottage cheese or cream cheese is often used instead of ricotta— but that is a losing battle.

A good imported Grana parmigiano

(Parmesan) is necessary if one wishes to get some sort of accuracy in many of the following recipes, and nothing can replace it. I strongly urge the reader to avoid the packaged grated parmigiano, which tastes more like soap than parmigiano.

Pecorino romano, made from ewes' milk, is a good cheese that is excellent in certain dishes. I use a pecorino made by my relatives in Italy. It is sweeter than the romano. I like it better; but, unfortunately, it is not available in America.

Some people like American-made asiago for grating. I think it is a decent grating cheese, much better than the grated packaged stuff, if imported parmigiano is not available. Sardo is a nice grating cheese, too, but nothing can compare with good imported parmigiano.

About Olive Oil

There are many different qualities and brands of "pure virgin olive oil." Though some are more like kerosene than olive oil, there are several brands that are excellent. The very best canned or bottled olive oils packed in Italy are available in America. There are very delicate ones from the Lucca area of Italy, and heavy, aromatic ones packed in Sicily. Readers will have to experiment with the brands available and discover what pleases them.

Remember that good olive oil is not "greasy." For Italian dishes, buy only olive oil packed in Italy, not Italian olive oil packed in America; use it sparingly. The longer you cook olive oil the stronger it gets—it's best raw. Avoid deep frying in olive oil.

I have some rich, green, heavy olive oil that my cousin packs in Italy. It is an excellent oil that I use only raw. One should remember that the quality of olive oil used can ruin a dish or make it a success. My preferences are the following:

Callistro Francesconi—the lightest olive oil available—excellent in sauces, too light for salads and vegetables. Olio Sasso, packed in Italy—excellent in sauces, a little heavier than Francesconi, better on salads; Berio—not as good as Sasso, a little heavier, good in sauces and salads; Madre Sicilia—heaviest of the four, perhaps best on salads.

At one time, Italians used only freshly pressed olive oil that was sold in bulk. It is difficult to find excellent olive oil sold in bulk in Italy today, just as it is difficult to find an excellent table wine. Most Italians buy tinned olive oil now; the most popular seems to be Sasso. When I was a student in Italy, only bulk oil was sold; it usually was excellent.

Contrary to popular belief, Italian food, if prepared properly, is not heavy, is not saturated with tomato paste and garlic, is not greasy. It is a delightful, healthful experience. One can easily improvise with Italian recipes after becoming acquainted with Italian cooking.

*Pesto**

⟦BASIL SAUCE⟧
2 cups

The original way to make PESTO is with a mortar and pestle. The solids and the olive

* From *Italian Family Cooking*, by Edward Giobbi. Copyright © 1971 by Edward Giobbi. Reprinted by permission of Random House, Inc.

oil are added slowly as the PESTO is worked. The result is a looser PESTO with a rougher texture than that of the blender version below.

5 cups fresh basil leaves, washed, drained, and tightly packed
¼ cup chopped parsley, Italian if possible
¾ cup olive oil
2 tablespoons finely minced garlic
½ cup pignoli (pine) nuts
1 teaspoon salt
½ cup pecorino romano or parmigiano cheese (I prefer pecorino)

*P*lace all the ingredients in the container of an electric blender and blend, stirring down with a rubber spatula as necessary, until a smooth paste forms. Unless the PESTO is to be used immediately, spoon it into a Mason jar or plastic container and cover with about ¾ inch of olive oil. Cover tightly and store in the refrigerator or in a cool place.

PESTO keeps indefinitely and can be used at any time, spooned directly from the jar onto pasta or into a sauce. Use about ½ cup PESTO or less, diluted with about 2 tablespoons of warm water, for each pound of freshly cooked pasta. Toss quickly and serve immediately on hot plates.

Canneloni

[BAKED MEAT-FILLED PASTA TUBES IN SAUCE]
Serves 6

THE PASTA
¾ cup semolina flour (all-purpose flour may be used instead of semolina. If all-purpose flour is used, do not use olive oil)
4 large eggs
1½ teaspoons salt
2 teaspoons olive oil
2 teaspoons warm water

THE FILLING
Have all the following ingredients ready to mix together when it is time to fill the cooked pasta.
¼ pound fresh spinach (boiled, drained, liquid pressed out, then chopped)
3 cups ricotta
¾ cup chopped boiled ham (about ¼ pound)
1 tablespoon chopped Italian parsley

3 large eggs
½ cup grated parmigiano
½ cup grated pecorino romano
½ teaspoon grated nutmeg
Salt and freshly ground black pepper

THE SAUCES:
2 cups MARINARA SAUCE (page 91), or MEAT SAUCE (page 90); (any meat or marinara sauce will do)
1 cup Beciamella (medium white sauce; page 90)
¾ cup chopped mozzarella (dots of butter may be used instead)
Grated parmigiano

*O*n a bread board or countertop make a well in the semolina. Into the center, break the eggs and add the salt, olive oil and water. Beat the eggs with a fork, gradually working in part of the semolina. When half of the semolina is incorporated, start using your hands to blend in the rest, working slowly in a circular motion. Scrape the board occasionally with a pastry scraper or a knife so that all the ingredients are in and thoroughly mixed. If the dough flakes apart, add more water in drips. If too sticky, add a little more semolina.

Sprinkle the board lightly with semolina so that the dough does not stick to it. Knead the dough in a rolling motion, pushing it away from you with the heels of your hands for about 20 minutes or until it is velvetlike and smooth.

Cut dough in half; roll each half into a ball, then flatten each ball into a thick cake and rub with olive oil to prevent drying. Put each cake of dough in a deep dish and cover it—preferably with a soup plate, hollow-side-down like a dome—to insulate the dough from air. Let dough rest for 1 hour.

After 1 hour, cut each cake of dough into quarters. With a rolling pin, roll out one quarter about 1/4 inch thick and run through pasta machine according to machine instructions. (For problems and challenges in rolling out pasta by hand to the necessary thinness and texture, see page 88). Repeat process for each quarter of dough. Cut machine-thinned-strips into 4-inch-long pieces, trim edges, and lay out side by side on a floured board; let dry for 1 hour.

Cook pasta pieces in 5 quarts rapidly boiling salted water until *al dente*. Drain; rinse under cold water. Blot each pasta piece dry with paper towel.

Combine all the ingredients for the filling. Put 2 tablespoons of filling in center of each piece of pasta. Starting at the 4-inch side, roll dough over filling to form a tube enclosing it.

Heat oven to 350 F. Spread a little MARINARA sauce in the bottom of a 3-quart baking dish—about 13½ x 8¾ x 1¾ inches. Cover the whole surface; then gently place the pieces of CANNELONI, side by side, on the sauce. Pour more sauce over CANNELONI, spoon BECIAMELLA over, and sprinkle with chopped mozzarella or butter. Cover dish (you can use aluminum foil), and bake for 20 minutes. Serve with grated parmigiano.

Ed Giobbi's Lasagne

Serves 8–10

MEAT SAUCE

1 pound sweet Italian sausages
1 pound ground chuck
Salt
Freshly ground black pepper
½ pound mushrooms, sliced or chopped
1 teaspoon chopped garlic
6 cups fresh MARINARA SAUCE (page 91)

WHITE SAUCE—BECIAMELLA

3 tablespoons butter
3 tablespoons flour
1 cup milk
1¼ cups heavy cream
Salt and pepper to taste
¼ teaspoon nutmeg

PASTA AND ASSEMBLY INGREDIENTS

1-pound package lasagne (imported, if possible), green or white, preferably green (for homemade PASTA VERDE, see page 92)
½ pound mozzarella cheese, cut in small cubes
½ cup freshly grated parmigiano
6 tablespoons melted butter

Cook the sausages in a 10-inch glass-ceramic skillet over medium heat until brown all over. Remove sausages and set aside. Pour off and discard almost all of the sausage fat; add to the skillet the beef, salt and pepper; cook, breaking up the lumps of meat with the side of a large kitchen spoon. Add the mushrooms and garlic. Stirring frequently, cook until the meat loses its red color.

Then, stirring occasionally, continue to cook until meat starts to brown.

While the meat mixture cooks, skin the sausages and slice them thin. When beef begins to brown, add sausage slices and the MARINARA SAUCE. Lightly mix all ingredients together. Partially cover skillet with a lid, pulled up on one side to allow steam to escape. Simmer sauce about 45 minutes, stirring occasionally. Set aside.

Preheat oven to 375 F. Meanwhile, cook the lasagne in a big pot of salted boiling water until it is *al dente*. (If lasagne is homemade, it will take 5 minutes or so; if packaged, about 10. Also see PASTA VERDE instructions.) Carefully drain off half of the water from the pot, and set pot under cold running water until cool enough to remove each lasagne by hand. Lay lasagne on paper towels (do not let pieces overlap or they will stick together), then blot each one on top with more paper towels.

To make Beciamella: In a saucepan, over low heat, melt the 3 tablespoons of butter and, using a wire whisk, stir in flour until blended. Gradually, stir in the milk with the whisk and keep stirring until thickened. Stir in the cream, and season with salt, pepper and nutmeg. (This white sauce should not sit long or it will become too thick.)

Assemble the dish: Spoon a layer of the meat sauce into an open, 13-inch-long ovenproof roaster; cover the entire surface of the bottom. Over the meat sauce, spoon

3–4 tablespoons of the white sauce; lengthwise on top of the sauces, arrange a layer of lasagne strips. Over the lasagne, spread a thin layer of meat sauce, a few tablespoons of white sauce, and a layer of mozzarella cubes. Sprinkle with a little of the parmigiano. Trickle 2 tablespoons of melted butter over the surface.

Begin again with lasagne, and construct each layer as just described, ending with meat sauce, white sauce, mozzarella, parmigiano and melted butter. Bake about 45 minutes, or until piping hot and bubbling throughout.

NOTE: Ricotta may be included in layers between LASAGNE. If desired, see LASAGNE WITH RICOTTA (page 92).

Marinara Sauce

6–8 *cups*

½ cup olive oil
4 cups coarsely chopped onions
2 small carrots, peeled and cut into rounds
    (about 1 cup)
3 cloves garlic, finely minced
8 cups canned Italian plum tomatoes with
    their liquid (about 2½ 28-ounce cans)
Salt and freshly ground black pepper
1 tablespoon finely minced Italian parsley
¼ pound butter
1½ teaspoons dried orégano
2 tablespoons chopped fresh basil, or 2
    teaspoons dried basil

In a 10-inch glass-ceramic skillet, heat the oil; add the onions, carrots, and garlic. Cook, stirring until vegetables turn golden brown.

Meanwhile, strain the tomatoes through a sieve into a bowl and push the pulp through with a wooden spoon. Discard the seeds.

Add the puréed tomatoes to the vegetables in the skillet; season to taste with salt and pepper. Partially cover the skillet and simmer for 15 minutes.

Set a sieve (conical, chinois type, if possible) into a bowl; pour the sauce into it, and press with a wooden spoon to push the solids through. Pour sauce back into the skillet; add the butter and herbs. Partly cover the skillet, and simmer 30 minutes more, stirring occasionally. This is best freshly made, but it can be stored, tightly covered, in the refrigerator for 2 days.

Lasagne with Ricotta

Serves 8–10

1 pound ricotta cheese
3 eggs
1 cup grated parmigiano (or use half parmigiano, half pecorino romano)
2 tablespoons chopped parsley, Italian if possible
Salt and freshly ground black pepper
1 recipe LASAGNE (page 90)

*C*ombine the ricotta, eggs, cheese and parsley until blended; add salt and pepper to taste. Follow recipe for lasagne exactly, but include layers of the ricotta mixture between the layers of the sauces between each layer of lasagne strips.

Pasta Verde

〚GREEN LASAGNE〛
Makes enough pasta for LASAGNE, 1 *pound green noodles*

2 cups semolina or unbleached all-purpose flour
1 teaspoon salt
2 eggs (room temperature)
½ package (10 ounces) frozen spinach cooked according to package instructions; drained; all water pressed out; spinach forced through food mill or puréed in blender)

OR

½ pound fresh spinach (carefully washed; cooked in ½-inch of water 10 minutes; strained; all water pressed out; spinach forced through food mill or puréed in blender)
2 tablespoons warm water (use more if needed)
Olive oil as needed

*P*lace flour and salt together on a bread board or countertop and make well in center. Break eggs into well. Beat eggs lightly with a fork, gradually working in part of the flour. Add spinach and water. Work in remaining flour with hands. Continue to blend the eggs and flour, working slowly in a circular motion. Scrape board occasionally with a pastry scraper or knife so that all the ingredients are thoroughly mixed into a firm dough. If dough is too sticky, stir in a little more flour.

Sprinkle work surface lightly with flour so that dough does not stick, taking care not to use too much. The dough must remain soft and pliable. Knead dough in a rolling motion, pushing it away from you with heels of your hands for about 20 minutes or until dough is velvetlike and smooth. It may be necessary to flour work surface lightly from time to time; use as little flour as possible.

Cut the pasta in half and roll each

half into a ball. Flatten the balls so that each resembles a cake of cheese. Rub each with a little olive oil to prevent drying. Put each cake into a soup plate; cover with another soup plate—like a dome—and let rest at room temperature for at least 1 hour.

TO ROLL PASTA

To Hand-Roll Pasta: The cakes of dough can be rolled out by hand, but it is very difficult to get the pasta paper thin, and it takes a great deal of practice. In fact, I think it is not likely that one can do it perfectly without having lived in a "pasta-making environment" and learned it by imitation from childhood, much as one learns language. My advice to the newcomer is to buy a pasta-making machine. However, if you wish to roll out your own pasta, use a lightly floured surface and a lightly floured rolling pin. Roll each cake of dough to 1/4 inch thickness. Let rest 1 minute; then roll again to 1/8 inch thickness. Let dough rest 1 minute, then roll to paper thinness. The thinner the better. Between each rolling, let dough rest 1 minute; the dough stretches more easily this way. Cut dough into 2-inch wide strips, long enough to fit your casserole.

To Roll With a Pasta Machine: Cut each cake of dough into 4 pieces. With a rolling pin, roll one piece out 1/4 inch thick (dust with flour while rolling), then place it in the largest opening of the pasta machine. Put through according to machine instructions. Cut machine-rolled lasagne into lengths to fit your baking dish. Repeat until all pasta dough is used. Spread machine-made or hand-rolled lasagne strips on tabletop and dust with flour.

To Cook Pasta: Boil salted water; add one sheet of lasagne to the water at a time. Cook until tender. Homemade pasta cooks more quickly than commercial brands; 5 minutes should be sufficient.

Carefully drain off half of the water from pot. Add cold water to pot until cool enough to remove lasagne from it by hand. Place each sheet on absorbent towels; blot. Lasagne is now ready for baking dish. The pasta can be drained 1 hour ahead of time, if desired, but be careful it does not dry out.

NOTE: This dough can also be cut into noodles of varying widths to be used in other pasta dishes. Let noodles dry in a single layer on a lightly floured surface for several hours or overnight, then store and cook as necessary.

Gramigna in Salsa Bianca con Salsiccia

[GRAMIGNA IN A WHITE SAUCE WITH SAUSAGES]

Serves 6

1 pound Italian-style sweet sausage, or
    1 pound lean ground pork
2 tablespoons butter
1 tablespoon olive oil
1 cup chopped onions
1 cup dry white wine
1 teaspoon dried thyme
2 cloves
¾ pound gramigna pasta *
1 cup (½ pint) heavy cream
4 tablespoons (¼ cup) grated parmigiano
½ teaspoon grated nutmeg
Salt and freshly ground white pepper to
    taste
Butter

Sauté sausages in a 10-inch glass-ceramic skillet, uncovered, over moderate heat. Poke holes in them with a fork to let out fat. As sausages cook, split them open with a knife; cook until well done. Drain sausages, discard the fat, and chop sausages coarsely. Return chopped sausages to skillet, add butter and oil. When butter melts, add onions. When onions soften, add wine, thyme and cloves. Cover; simmer over low heat until wine cooks away—about 30 minutes. Meanwhile, cook pasta rapidly in salted boiling water until *al dente*. While pasta is cooking, add cream, parmigiano, nutmeg and salt and pepper to sausage mixture in skillet and, mixing often, cook over moderate heat until cream thickens (3–5 minutes).

Drain pasta and pour into 2½-quart bowl. Add several pats of butter to it. Serve sausage mixture on each portion of pasta.

NOTE: I first tasted this recipe in a wonderful Bolognese restaurant in Rome, and I have had it a number of times since elsewhere. The recipes vary according to tastes, but this recipe is quite close to my first introduction to GRAMIGNA IN SALSA BIANCA CON SALSICCIA.

---

* Gramigna is the name of a pasta a little thicker than spaghetti with a small hole running through its length. Each piece of the pasta is about 2 inches long and it is always used in this dish. Unfortunately, it is rarely found in America, although I have found it occasionally in New York. A short tubular pasta, such as elbow macaroni, can be used.

Insalata di Rigatoni

[RIGATONI SALAD]

Serves 6–8

½ pound rigatoni (imported, if possible)
1 cup fresh string beans * (julienne; that
    is, cut lengthwise into strips)
Salt
6 tablespoons good olive oil
Salt and freshly ground black pepper
Optional: 2 tablespoons PESTO (p. 87)
3 cups sliced tomatoes (red tomatoes that
    are still partially green)
½ cup chopped green onions (scallions)
2 6½-ounce cans tuna fish, packed in
    olive oil **
3 tablespoons chopped parsley

* Cooked zucchini or peas may be substituted for string
beans—do not boil with pasta; add along with tomatoes.

** If American-style canned tuna is used, drain liquid and
discard. Mix tuna with 1 tablespoon olive oil; then add to
pasta.

Cook rigatoni and string beans together in rapidly boiling salted water. When pasta is cooked *al dente,* drain. Pour cold water over pasta and beans, drain well, and place in 4-quart bowl. Add 4 tablespoons of the olive oil and salt and pepper to taste; add PESTO if desired; mix gently. Add tomatoes, green onions, the tuna in chunks, parsley and the rest of the olive oil. Toss gently (taste for salt and pepper).

Prepare the dish ahead of time, if desired. Do not refrigerate. Serve at room temperature.

NOTE: I was introduced to this recipe in Rome. It is an excellent summer dish and can be prepared ahead of time, if it is kept and served at room temperature.

Insalata di Riso

[RICE SALAD]

Serves 6–8

1½ cups rice, preferably Italian (avorio)
    or long grain
1 jar artichoke hearts (6 ounces), packed
    in olive oil
1 can tuna (7 ounces), packed in olive oil,
    drained (use at room temperature)
2 hard-cooked eggs, sliced
2 tablespoons capers (drained)
4 tablespoons (¼ cup), or more, good
    olive oil
Juice of 1 lemon

2 tablespoons chopped fresh parsley
Salt and freshly ground white pepper
    to taste
1 tablespoon fresh basil, or 1 teaspoon dried

Cook rice until tender but firm—*al dente.* Drain; rinse in cold water. Drain artichoke hearts and chop coarsely. Mix all ingredients together in a 2½-quart bowl. Let stand at room temperature for 1 hour and serve.

Linguine con Broccoli

[LINGUINE WITH BROCCOLI]

Serves 6–8

---

1 bunch fresh broccoli or 1 pound broccoli
    di rapè (see note)
8 tablespoons olive oil
2 tablespoons coarsely chopped garlic
Hot pepper flakes (optional), or freshly
    ground black pepper
2½ cups water (approximately)
½ pound linguine or spaghettini (im-
    ported, if possible), broken into 2-inch
    lengths
Salt

Cut off broccoli flowerets. Peel the stems. Cut flowerets into 2-inch lengths, cutting large ones in halves or quarters. Wash and set aside.

Put olive oil, garlic and hot pepper flakes (or freshly ground black pepper) in a large skillet or shallow pot. Turn up heat. When oil begins to get hot, add broccoli, one cup of water and, all at once, the uncooked pasta. Mix well to combine ingredients. Add salt; mix. Cover, and cook over moderate heat, mixing often and taking care that pasta does not stick to the bottom of pot. Add more water if needed. Cook about 10 minutes. Serve hot, *al dente*. No cheese is used in this dish.

NOTE: This recipe was given to me by an Italian I met on a train in Germany. He was from the area of Napoli. The recipe calls for *broccoli di rapè* instead of broccoli. Since *rapè* is a vegetable rarely seen in most parts of America, I substituted broccoli. If the reader can find *rapè*, by all means use it instead of broccoli.

To clean *rapè,* remove the tough leaves from the stem. Peel the stems, and cut up the tender leaves; cook with *rapè* flowerets in the same way as described for broccoli.

Broccoli di rapè is such an unusual vegetable that I strongly urge the reader to attempt to find or order it. It is an elegant green that is a kind of cross between broccoli and turnip greens. Moreover, it is a winter green that I have had success growing in my own garden. I plant the seeds in August and harvest the *rapè* after the first frost in October and November. It is a vegetable that delights my family and my friends.

Maccheroni alla Campagna

[MACARONI COUNTRY STYLE]
Serves 6–8

1 pound tubular pasta (such as penne,
    elbow, ziti, etc.)
2 cups peeled and diced raw potatoes,
    ½-inch cubes
3 cups sliced green cabbage
3 tablespoons olive oil
5 tablespoons butter
1 cup chopped onions
½ pound slice of boiled ham (½-inch
    thick), cut into ½-inch cubes
Salt and freshly ground black pepper
¾ cup dry white wine
1 tablespoon chopped parsley, Italian if
    possible
1 teaspoon dried marjoram
Grated pecorino romano cheese
    (parmigiano will do), about 1 cup

In a large pot, bring about 5 quarts of water to a boil. All at once, add the pasta, potatoes, cabbage and a generous amount of salt. Bring to a rolling boil; stir often.

Meanwhile, heat the olive oil with 2 tablespoons of the butter in a 10-inch skillet until the butter melts, add the onions and cook until soft. When onions begin to brown, add the ham cubes. Combine well, stir in salt and pepper to taste; cook for a few minutes, and add the wine, parsley and marjoram. Cover, lower heat, and simmer until most of the wine cooks away—about 15 minutes.

While sauce cooks, check the pasta often for doneness. Stir often. When the pasta is *al dente,* drain the pasta mixture and place in a bowl. Add the sauce to the pasta mixture, tossing well. Add remaining butter, mix and serve hot with an abundant amount of grated cheese.

Pasta con Trippa alla Parmigiana

[PASTA WITH TRIPE AND PARMESAN CHEESE]
Serves 6

1 pound honeycomb tripe, cut into strips
    about 3 inches long and ¼-inch wide
3 tablespoons olive oil
1 cup chopped onions
1 cup dry white wine
1 bay leaf
1 teaspoon dried rosemary
Pinch of hot pepper flakes (optional)

1 clove garlic, minced
Salt
1½ cups tomatoes (preferably fresh), put
    through a food mill
1 pound tubular pasta, such as penne,
    elbow, ziti, etc.
Freshly ground black pepper
Grated parmigiano, about 1 cup

ash tripe under cold running water. Place in cold water to cover; bring to a boil for 1/2 hour. Drain; blot dry with paper towels. Warm olive oil in a 10-inch glass-ceramic skillet and sauté tripe over low to medium heat. Stir often so that tripe will not stick to the bottom of the skillet. When liquid begins to evaporate, add the onions and cook, mixing often, until the onions soften—about 1/2 hour. Add wine, bay leaf, rosemary, hot pepper, garlic and salt. (If you prefer, use freshly ground black pepper instead of hot pepper flakes.) Cover, and simmer over low heat until wine cooks away—about 10 minutes.

Meanwhile, bring tomatoes to a boil in a flameproof casserole. Add tripe mixture, cover, and simmer over lowest heat for 2 hours. Stir occasionally; add a little water if sauce sticks.

Cook pasta in a large pot of salted boiling water. Drain when pasta is *al dente*. Place in serving dish; mix with tripe sauce (seasoned with salt and pepper to taste). Also pass an abundant amount of grated parmigiano.

Pasta con Vongole al Brandy *

[PASTA WITH CLAMS AND BRANDY]
Serves 6

6 tablespoons olive oil
1 cup chopped green pepper
2 tablespoons finely chopped parsley
   (Italian if possible)
2 cloves garlic finely chopped
1 cup tomatoes (perferably fresh), put
   through a food mill
1 tablespoon finely chopped fresh basil or
   1 teaspoon dried basil
1 teaspoon dried orégano
1 teaspoon dried mint—or 1 tablespoon
   fresh chopped mint
Salt and hot pepper flakes or freshly ground
   black pepper
1 1/2 dozen small fresh clams, in shell,
   scrubbed
1 pound short, tubular pasta, such as penne,
   rigatoni, etc.
1 pound fresh shrimp, shelled, deveined
   and cut into 1/2-inch pieces
1/4 cup brandy (or bourbon)
3 tablespoons butter

ut olive oil, green pepper, parsley, garlic, tomatoes, basil, orégano, mint, salt and hot pepper to taste in a medium-size saucepan. Cover and cook gently for 20 minutes. Add clams; re-cover; raise heat and cook until clams open. As soon as clams open, remove them from the sauce. Continue cooking the sauce, covered, for 5 minutes over moderate heat. Preheat oven to 450 F.

Remove the clams from shells; discard shells and cut each clam into 2 or 3 pieces; using scissors may be the easiest way.

Bring 4 quarts of salted water to a boil. Add pasta and stir with a wooden spoon. As soon as water comes back to a boil, drain pasta. Put drained pasta in 4-quart ovenproof glass casserole or baking

* From *Italian Family Cooking*, by Edward Giobbi. Copyright © 1971 by Edward Giobbi. Reprinted by permission of Random House, Inc.

dish approximately 3″ high by 10″ in diameter. Add sauce, clams, shrimp, brandy or bourbon and butter; mix. Cover tightly and place in oven. Bake, stirring often, until pasta is tender but firm to the bite, *al dente*. About 15 minutes.

NOTE: Sauce may be made a day ahead of time; refrigerated and gently reheated before using.

Penne con Cavolfiore

[PENNE WITH CAULIFLOWER]
Serves 6–8

1 medium-size cauliflower
3 cloves garlic, chopped
¾ cup finely chopped onions
5 tablespoons good olive oil
2 cups tomatoes (preferably fresh), put through food mill
1 teaspoon orégano
2 tablespoons chopped parsley (Italian if possible)
Salt and freshly ground black pepper
2 cups sliced mushrooms
2 cans (6½-ounces each) tuna fish packed in olive oil, drained and broken up with fork
¼ cup white raisins
¾ pound penne, rigatoni, or any tubular pasta (imported if possible)

Cut off cauliflower flowerets. Wash them and cook in boiling salted water for not more than 5 minutes. Drain and set aside.

Sauté garlic and onions in 4 tablespoons of the olive oil. When onions are translucent, add tomatoes, orégano, parsley, salt and pepper. Cover and simmer over low heat.

In another pan, sauté mushrooms in the remaining tablespoon of olive oil until they are tender; add to the simmering sauce. Cook several minutes, covered; add tuna, raisins and cauliflower, cook 10 minutes more, covered. Check salt and pepper.

Preheat oven to 350 F. Meanwhile, cook pasta in boiling salted water for about 8 minutes (it should not be completely cooked); drain, but reserve about ¼ cup of the pasta water. In a deep, 4-quart oven-proof glass casserole, toss pasta with the sauce and the reserved ¼ cup of pasta water. Cover and bake about 10 minutes, depending upon type of pasta used. Do not overcook.

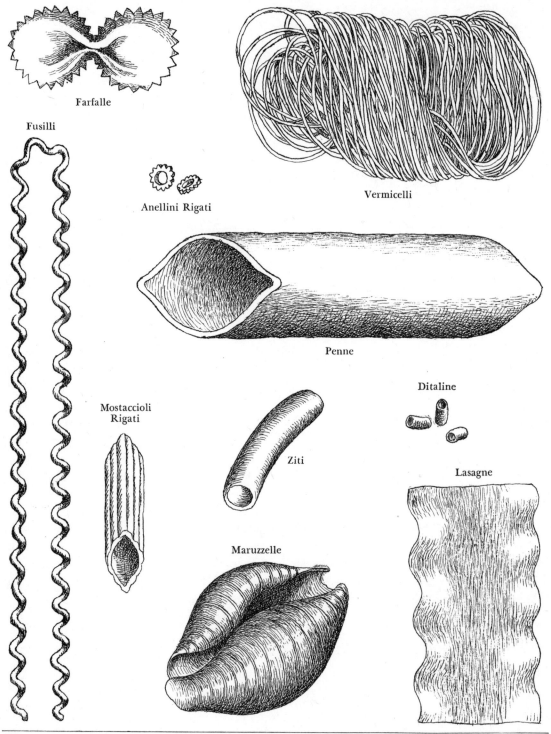

Farfalle

Fusilli

Anellini Rigati

Vermicelli

Penne

Mostaccioli
Rigati

Ditaline

Ziti

Lasagne

Maruzzelle

THE GREAT COOKS COOKBOOK

Penne con gli Asparagi

[[PENNE WITH ASPARAGUS]]
Serves 6

1½ pounds fresh asparagus, or 1 (10-ounce)
    package frozen asparagus
3 tablespoons butter (only 1 tablespoon if
    using frozen asparagus)
2 tablespoons olive oil
2 cloves garlic, chopped
2 cups tomatoes (preferably fresh),
    put through food mill
2 tablespoons chopped fresh parsley
Salt and freshly ground black pepper
1 pound penne (or other tubular pasta)
2 whole fresh eggs and 1 extra yolk
Grated pecorino or parmigiano cheese

Cut asparagus into 1½-inch pieces; discard any tough, fibrous stem ends. Sauté in 2 tablespoons butter until tender but firm to the teeth. Set aside. (If frozen asparagus is used, cook in rapidly boiling salted water for about 3 minutes. Drain, and set aside.)

In a skillet, melt the remaining one tablespoon butter with the olive oil and sauté the garlic. When garlic begins to brown, remove it with a slotted spoon and discard. To the skillet add tomatoes, parsley, salt and pepper. Cover, and simmer for 10 minutes. Add asparagus, and cook with tomatoes for 5 minutes.

Meanwhile, cook pasta in salted boiling water until *al dente*. As pasta cooks, in a small bowl beat eggs and yolk with 3 tablespoons of grated pecorino or parmigiano. When pasta is cooked, drain; immediately mix the beaten eggs lightly into the pasta. Add tomato sauce with asparagus. Toss; add salt and pepper if needed and serve hot, accompanied by grated pecorino or parmigiano.

Penne con Pomidori Verdi alla Parmigiana

[[PENNE WITH GREEN TOMATOES AND PARMESAN CHEESE]]
Serves 6–8

2 small fresh eggs
Salt and freshly ground pepper
2 pounds green tomatoes (medium to
    large), cut into ½-inch slices
Flour
Vegetable oil
½ recipe MARINARA SAUCE (page 91)
Grated parmigiano
1 pound penne or rigatoni (imported if
    possible)

Beat eggs; add salt and pepper. One side at a time, dip tomato slices into beaten egg; and then lightly into flour; set aside.

Pour vegetable oil about ¾-inch deep into a medium-size skillet. Heat oil, and check for correct temperature by flicking a few specks of flour into it. Oil should boil violently when flour goes in. With a slotted spoon, place tomato slices into the hot oil a few at a time. Be careful; this spatters. Brown slightly on both sides, remove and place between paper towels to drain. Repeat process until all tomato slices are used.

Put ¼ of the MARINARA SAUCE in the bottom of a deep, ovenproof glass casserole. Place a layer of tomato slices on the sauce, then pour a little sauce on the tomatoes and sprinkle with grated parmigiano. Repeat process until all tomato slices are used. Pour sauce over top layer of tomatoes and sprinkle with parmigiano. Preheat oven to 350 F. and bake, covered, for 20 minutes. If there is too much liquid, remove cover so some can cook away.

Cook pasta in rapidly boiling salted water until *al dente*. Drain. Heat remaining MARINARA SAUCE and put into a serving bowl. Toss pasta in the sauce, add freshly ground black pepper and grated parmigiano. Serve sauced pasta and casserole of baked tomato slices separately, but spoon onto the same plate to complement each other.

NOTE: This recipe was given to me by an old friend from the Abruzzi. It is an excellent way to use green tomatoes. The baked green tomatoes can be frozen in the casserole, then reheated when ready for use.

Rigatoni con Salsa di Gorgonzola alla Romana
[RIGATONI WITH GORGONZOLA SAUCE, ROMAN STYLE]
Serves 6

1 cup (½ pint) heavy cream *
½ pound imported gorgonzola,** chopped
Salt and freshly ground black pepper
1 pound rigatoni (imported if possible) ***
2 tablespoons butter
½ teaspoon nutmeg
½ cup grated parmigiano
Grated parmigiano to pass with pasta

* For a lighter sauce, use either half-and-half or milk, instead of heavy cream.

** If gorgonzola is not available, a Roquefort cheese—or other good blue cheese—will do; but it will not be the same dish.

*** Penne, ziti, or any long tubular pasta will do. The secret of the success of this recipe is the excellence of its ingredients.

Heat cream in a saucepan. When hot, add the gorgonzola; alternately crush it into the cream with the back of a spoon and stir it thoroughly. Add salt and pepper, stirring with a wire whisk to combine well, and cook until cheese is smoothly blended with cream.

Meanwhile, have the rigatoni cooking in rapidly boiling salted water until *al dente,* then drain. While pasta drains, heat butter in a big skillet. Add the drained pasta, then the cream and gorgonzola mixture. Cook for several minutes over moderate heat, stirring constantly; add nutmeg; then add the ½ cup of grated parmigiano. Serve immediately on hot plates accompanied by additional grated parmigiano and black pepper.

NOTE: I tasted this dish for the first time in the home of a prominent Roman. The gorgonzola gives the sauce a unique "bite."

Risotto con Fagioli

[RISOTTO WITH BEANS]
Serves 6

BEANS

¾ cup dried beans (navy or cannellini; if navy, soak in cold water for 2 hours; if cannellini, soak overnight in cold water)
4 cups fresh cold water
1 bay leaf
1 medium carrot
2 celery ribs
1 medium onion
1 teaspoon rosemary
Salt and freshly ground black pepper

RISOTTO

2 tablespoons butter
2 tablespoons olive oil
    (or use butter—4 tablespoons in all—instead)
1 cup rice (preferably imported Italian avorio, but Carolina long grain will do)
1 medium onion, chopped
Salt and freshly ground black pepper
1 cup dry white wine
⅓ cup grated parmigiano
Extra butter or oil for topping
Extra grated parmigiano to pass

Drain the soaked beans. Pour the fresh cold water into a deep 2-quart pot, and add the next six ingredients. Cover, and bring to a boil. Lower heat; add beans and boil gently until beans are tender—from 2 to 3 hours. Drain beans, reserving the liquid. (It will yield about 2 cups.) Remove and discard the bay leaf, carrot, celery and onion. Set beans and reserved liquid aside.

For the risotto: In a shallow pot, heat butter and oil. Add the rice, and cook, stirring constantly. In a few minutes add the onion, salt and pepper. When rice begins to color, add the wine. Mix often. When the wine cooks away, add the bean stock a little at a time, mixing constantly. Continue adding and stirring in the stock until the rice is tender but firm. (Use warm water or meat stock if bean stock is not sufficient, but there will probably be enough.) Add drained beans to rice. Stirring, cook together for 5 minutes. Add cheese, and combine well. Put a pat of butter or several drops of olive oil on each portion as you serve, and pass the grated parmigiano.

NOTE: I read, recently, that a perfect health dish, which is both nourishing and economical, is a rice and bean combination. It is interesting that practically all poor Western nations have some sort of traditional rice and bean dish.

Risotto con Frutta di Mare alla Genovese

[RISOTTO WITH SHELLFISH GENOESE STYLE]

Serves 6

2 pounds mussels (well scrubbed and beards removed), and 1 dozen small clams (well washed and drained), or 2 dozen clams (well washed and drained)

2 cups broth (preferably the clam and mussel broth; a fish or chicken stock will do)

2 cloves garlic, sliced

4 tablespoons olive oil

3 cups peeled and coarsely chopped fresh tomatoes

2 tablespoons chopped parsley (Italian if possible)

Hot pepper flakes or freshly ground black pepper

2 tablespoons PESTO (p. 87)

1 tablespoon butter

1 cup chopped onions

2 cups rice (if possible, Italian avorio, but Carolina rice will do)

1 cup dry white wine

Salt and freshly ground black pepper

3 tablespoons grated pecorino or parmigiano

Steam mussels and clams open. Set aside and, when flesh cools, remove from shells and chop coarsely. Save broth. Measure. If there is not 2 cups, add enough fish or chicken stock to make 2 cups.

In a skillet, sauté garlic in 2 tablespoons of the olive oil. When garlic browns, remove it with a slotted spoon and discard it. To the hot oil, add the tomatoes, parsley, salt and either hot pepper flakes or freshly ground black pepper. Cover, and simmer over moderate heat for about 10 minutes. Add chopped shellfish and cook, uncovered, over moderate heat for 5 minutes. Add PESTO; mix well. Turn off heat.

Put the remaining 2 tablespoons of olive oil and the butter in a fairly deep pot. When butter melts, add onions and sauté until they are limp; add rice; cook over moderate heat mixing constantly. When rice begins to color, add wine, salt and freshly ground black pepper; continue to cook over moderate heat, stirring constantly, until liquid is absorbed. Still stirring constantly, add the broth a little at a time and, using more as needed, cook until rice is tender but firm to the bite. You should use just enough liquid at any time to keep the rice boiling; all the liquid should be absorbed when the rice is cooked. Turn off heat and mix in the grated cheese.

To serve, put a mound of rice on each plate; make a well in the mound with the convex side of a soup ladle or large serving spoon; then, pour a generous amount of shellfish and sauce into the well.

NOTE: Any variety of shellfish may be used in this dish.

Spaghetti alla Salsa di Pepperoni

[SPAGHETTI WITH PEPPER SAUCE]
Serves 6

1 medium onion, thinly sliced
2 cloves garlic, chopped
2 tablespoons olive oil
2 tablespoons butter
1½ large green peppers, stem end removed; seeded and thinly sliced
Salt and freshly ground black pepper
1 pound spaghetti
4 canned anchovy fillets, drained and cut into ½-inch pieces
¾ cup dry white wine
1½ cups tomatoes (preferably fresh), put through a food mill, or canned, drained
2 tablespoons chopped parsley (Italian if possible)
Hot pepper flakes or freshly ground black pepper
Pecorino romano cheese

Over low heat, sauté onion and garlic with oil and butter. When onions begin to soften, add green peppers, salt and freshly ground black pepper; continue cooking, mixing often. When peppers are almost tender, add the anchovies. Cook for a few minutes, and add the wine. Cover, and simmer for several minutes; turn up heat and cook away most of wine.

Add the tomatoes and parsley; boil gently for about 25 minutes. Serve hot with freshly grated pecorino romano.

Spaghetti alle Cipole

[SPAGHETTI WITH ONIONS]
Serves 4–6

1 pound spaghetti
2 tablespoons olive oil
3 tablespoons butter
2 cups thinly sliced onions
2 cups tomatoes (put through a food mill, or peeled, seeded, and puréed in a blender)
⅔ cup milk
Salt and freshly ground black pepper
Grated parmigiano

Set a large pot of water to boil for the spaghetti. Meanwhile, heat the olive oil and butter, and sauté the onions over low heat until they are limp. Add tomatoes, milk, salt and pepper, and boil gently for ¼ hour.

Add salt to the boiling water, then add the spaghetti, and cook it until it is almost *al dente*. Drain; add to the sauce and finish cooking spaghetti in the sauce over moderate heat, tossing constantly. If sauce becomes too tight, add more milk. Add salt and pepper to taste—a generous amount of freshly grated parmigiano—and serve.

NOTE: The starch in the pasta keeps the milk from curdling, and the result is a velvety, creamy sauce.

Spaghettini con Pomidori Freschi
[SPAGHETTINI WITH FRESH TOMATOES]
Serves 4–6

3 cups fresh tomatoes, coarsely chopped, and kept at room temperature
2 cloves garlic, peeled and sliced
2 tablespoons chopped parsley, Italian if possible
4 tablespoons (¼ cup) chopped fresh basil
4 tablespoons (¼ cup) good olive oil
Salt and freshly ground black pepper
1 pound spaghettini (imported if possible)

*P*ut all ingredients, except spaghettini, into a blender and blend to a purée.

Cook the spaghettini in rapidly boiling salted water until *al dente*. Drain well, then toss with the fresh sauce. Serve without cheese.

NOTE: All ingredients in this recipe must be fresh and of the best quality. It is a delightful summer dish when fresh tomatoes and basil are available.

If a creamy sauce is preferred, add 2 tablespoons of imported gorgonzola cheese to the rest of the ingredients in the blender.

Torta di Riso con Fegatini di Pollo
[RICE WITH CHICKEN LIVERS]
Serves 6

4 tablespoons butter
1 tablespoon olive oil
1 pound fresh chicken livers (washed in cold water and drained)
Salt and freshly ground black pepper
1 jigger brandy (bourbon will do)
1 teaspoon dry sage
1½ cups rice (imported Italian rice, avorio, or long grain Carolina rice)
4 cups thinly sliced onions

2 fresh eggs
¼ cup milk
⅔ cup grated parmigiano
Bread crumbs, dry

*I*n a 10-inch skillet, heat 2 tablespoons of the butter with the olive oil until butter melts; add livers and cook uncovered over high heat. When livers change color, add salt, pepper, brandy and sage. Cover, lower heat and cook for 5 minutes. Let livers cool. Remove livers from pan. Dice them into ½-inch cubes; return to sauce in pan and set aside.

Cook rice in boiling salted water until *al dente*—20–25 minutes. Drain; place in a bowl. Add remaining butter and set aside. While rice cooks, put onions in salted boiling water and boil until tender, drain and set aside until cool.

Meanwhile, thoroughly mix eggs and milk together. Combine cooled onions with this egg-milk mixture, and set aside.

Preheat oven to 450 F. Butter a 3-quart, deep, ovenproof casserole and place in it half of the diced livers and half of their juices. Add half of the onion mixture. Stir the parmigiano into the rice, combining well, and spread half of it on top of the onion mixture. Put the remaining livers and sauce over the rice, top with the remaining onion mixture, and then the remaining rice, sprinkling bread crumbs over it. Cover and bake in oven for 15 minutes. To serve, spoon out of casserole.

Wines for Pasta

ALEXIS BESPALOFF

Italian wine is the logical accompaniment to Italian dishes, especially as there is now a greater variety of Italian wines available here today then ever before. In matching up wine and food, the simplest guide, of course, is whether the dish is based on meat or fish. When you prepare dishes flavored with vegetables—tomatoes, onions, peppers, and so on—choose either red or white depending on your over-all preference. Nevertheless, you may find that, given a choice, red wines stand up to robust sauces better than white wines. It would be a mistake, however, to choose a fine red wine to accompany dishes that include tomatoes, as their acidity will diminish the wine's quality.

The most popular Italian red wines are the lighter wines of Valpolicella and Bardolino, and the somewhat sturdier wines of Chianti. The straw-covered *fiasco*

has always been associated with Chianti, but nowadays more producers are putting their better Chianti into high-shouldered bottles similar to those used in Bordeaux. Lambrusco, a fruity, more or less sweet wine with a very slight sparkle, has become very popular in the past few years. Those who prefer wines that are not altogether dry will find it an excellent accompaniment to very rich dishes.

Barbera and Grignolino, each named after the grape variety from which it is made, are distinct and appealing wines from the Piedmont district in northern Italy, and provide interesting change from Valpolicella and Chianti. Barolo, a classic and comparatively expensive wine from the same district, is the wine many Italians would bring out for special dishes and fine occasions.

The most popular white wine of Italy

is Soave, and good examples are among the most appealing of fresh, light-bodied wines. Frascati and Verdicchio are two other dry white wines that are readily found in this country. Orvieto, from central Italy, can be vinified to produce both a dry wine, labeled *secco,* and a semisweet one, *abboccato.* The *abboccato* is especially attractive, and is an interesting alternative to a Vouvray or a Graves.

The most readily available alternative to Italian wines are those from California. Remember that red wines labeled California Chianti, and those bearing Italian-sounding proprietary brand names are generally sweeter than California wines labeled Burgundy and Chablis. Dry and full-flavored California reds include Barbera, Petite Sirah, and Zinfandel; Riesling and French Colombard are California dry whites with some refreshing acidity.

About Fish and Seafood

Nature has been wonderful and charitable to us. From the mother—*mare*—sea has evolved, as did primitive life itself, a marvelously bounteous and varied crop of food. Largely uninterfered with by man until caught and brought to table, seafood is a natural and healthy food. Uncontaminated by additives, it requires only clean water to be splendid and pure. Compared to meat, it is less fattening and richer in minerals. One oyster compares favorably with a sirloin steak.

America, with its vast seacoasts, lakes and rivers, its changes in climate and terrain, spawns forth perhaps the world's most multitudinous catch of fish, crustaceans and bivalves. It ranges in color from blue to red to yellow to gray and green, touching all the tints in between. It runs in size from the tiny Olympia oysters of the Pacific Northwest to giant tunas. Some are beautiful, like mountain trout; and some are strange, like crabs and octopuses. They reflect the complex, mysterious and relatively unexplored life under the sea and in the rivers' depths and shallows.

Beyond all other foods, fish, in order to be great, must be very fresh. This is something that you can determine for yourself when selecting a fish. Its flesh should feel firm—not retaining any marks when pressed—and should be solidly attached to the skin and the bone. The scales should be shiny and tightly attached to the skin. The gills should be red or clear pink—not brownish. The fish must be clean and fresh-smelling; the eyes must be absolutely clear and bulging. Remember, fresh fish does not have a strong, unpleasant fishy odor. Trout and carp are best bought alive.

The way to be sure of fresh lobsters or crabs is to buy them live, choosing those that have come from the coldest waters. All cold-water fish and seafood tend to have a better texture than their warm-water relatives.

If live lobster is not available and you must buy fresh-boiled, look for a deep red color and a tightly curled-under tail. Oysters, clams and mussels should have well-closed, intact shells. When you knock two of the shells together the sound should be solid, not empty. American oysters and clams, when opened, should have a fresh color and plenty of liquid. The shells should be filled with meat, having absolutely no odor.

Fish spoils easily. Place it in a dish; cover with plastic wrap and refrigerate. If you intend to keep fish more than one day, make sure it is perfectly clean and then freeze it.

About Cooking Fish

Fresh fish is beautiful. I think that to cook it overly ornately, changing its character, is sacrilegious. All seafoods have distinctive and delicate flavors, along with their health-giving properties. To assault these with artificial seasonings and other foods and flavors is to destroy something beautiful. This beauty remains only with simplicity of cooking. The less you fuss with the cooking the better the results.

The only rule in cooking fish is not to overcook it; remember, much fish and seafood—clams in America, tuna in Japan and scallops in Mexico—is eaten raw. "Fish is cooked to develop the flavor, not to make it tender," cautions the Fishery Council of New York. Fish is cooked as soon as the flesh can be easily flaked or separated from the bone, or when the translucent raw flesh turns opaque. Aside from this, there are no rules; all the kinds of cooking that man has invented—boiling, steaming, baking, broiling, sautéeing, deep frying, braising, pickling, marinating and smoking—can be used inventively to match the varieties of fish itself.

Pickled Shrimp
Serves 4

SHRIMP
24 medium-size raw shrimp

MARINADE
¾ cup olive oil
3 cloves garlic, peeled and crushed
2 onions, peeled and finely sliced into rings
½ cup wine vinegar
½ teaspoon dry mustard
2 tablespoons chopped parsley
2 tablespoons chopped fresh dill
Freshly ground black pepper and salt
1 teaspoon sugar

Bring 3 quarts of salted water to boil. Add shrimp and cook for 6 to 8 minutes—until they turn pink. Remove shrimp from fire and put under running water until thoroughly cooled. Drain, shell and devein. In a large bowl, combine the marinade ingredients; add the cooked shrimp. Mix well and marinate in the refrigerator overnight. Serve the shrimp on greens with a little (about 2 tablespoons) of the marinating liquid poured over each portion.

Cold Shrimp Rémoulade

Serves 4

2 pounds shrimp
1 bay leaf
1 rib celery
2 sprigs parsley
10 black peppercorns
Salt

*P*eel the shrimp, make a small incision down the back and remove dark vein. Wash under cold water.

Place the shrimp in a saucepan with the shells, bay leaf, celery, parsley, peppercorns and salt. Add water to cover. Bring to a boil and simmer about 6–7 minutes. Drain the shrimp; place in a covered bowl and chill. Add generous amounts of RÉ-MOULADE SAUCE, mix well and chill for 5–6 hours.

RÉMOULADE SAUCE

2 cups MAYONNAISE (see page 36)
1 teaspoon dry mustard (English)
4 anchovies chopped very fine
1 teaspoon very finely chopped capers
1 teaspoon very finely chopped parsley
1 clove of garlic, peeled and very finely chopped
1 hard-boiled egg, chopped very fine
Juice of one lemon
White wine (optional)

Mix all the ingredients thoroughly before using sauce. (If the sauce is too thick dilute with a little dry white wine.)

Mussels Marinière

Serves 4

2 quarts mussels
4 shallots (or 1 onion), finely chopped
3 sprigs Italian parsley
Green leaves of 1 stalk of celery, coarsely chopped
½ cup chopped parsley
1½ cups dry white wine
½ cup water
Freshly ground black pepper
4 ounces butter (½ cup)
1 lemon, cut in half

*W*ash and scrub mussels very well with a stiff brush; remove beard. (The gatherings of beard are like vegetation on the shell.) Be sure to discard any mussels that are not firmly closed. Place well-cleaned mussels in a heavy saucepan, add shallots, Italian parsley, celery leaves, ¼ cup chopped parsley, wine, water, black pepper and ½ of the butter. Cover saucepan securely and let it steam over a low flame until the mussels open. (If any of them do not open, discard.) Remove mussels to large tureen or bowl.

Strain broth through a doubled cloth (a dish towel or napkin—not cheesecloth). Return broth to saucepan over high heat for 2 minutes. Add the rest of the butter and the rest of the parsley to the mussels; squeeze the juice of the lemon over them and pour the hot broth over all. Toasted French bread is great with this dish.

Fresh Mussels Marinara (Cold)

Serves 6–8

Even though the names sound the same, this dish, spicy and tomatoey to serve cold as a first course or for *hors d'oeuvre,* is very different from the preceding.

2 quarts of mussels
2 cloves garlic
8 black peppercorns
½ cup dry white wine
½ teaspoon dried orégano
¾ cup olive oil
2 tablespoons wine vinegar
2 tablespoons chopped parsley
¼ cup tomato paste
Salt and pepper

Wash the mussels in cold water and scrub them with a brush; remove the beard. Discard any mussels with shells not tightly closed. Place the good ones in a pan with the garlic, peppercorns, wine and orégano. Cover and cook until the shells open—about 8 to 10 minutes. Discard all unopened shells. Remove the rest of the mussels from the shells, cutting them away with a small, sharp knife; discard the shells.

Strain the broth through a double cloth (a dish towel or napkin) placed in a sieve and wrung out in cold water. Add the remaining ingredients to the broth and pour over the mussels. Cover and place in the refrigerator to marinate for 4 hours before serving.

Lobster Bisque

Serves 6

2 1½-pound lobsters
2 tablespoons vegetable oil
¼ pound butter
3 tablespoons Cognac
2 tablespoons tomato paste
1 cup finely chopped celery
1 cup peeled and finely chopped onion
1 cup peeled and finely chopped carrots
Touch of dried thyme
1 bay leaf
2 leeks, washed and chopped fine (only white part)
3 large ripe tomatoes, peeled, cored and chopped
1 cup dry white wine
1 cup clam broth (you can use canned)
3 cups chicken broth (or fish stock)
¾ cup raw white rice
Salt and pepper to taste
½ teaspoon Tabasco sauce
2 cups heavy cream

Kill the lobsters by plunging a knife into the thorax. Break off the tail and leave it intact. Cut the claws off and split the main body in two. Discard the sac over the eyes; remove the liver and coral and keep them for later use, *or* you can ask the seafood market to do the job for you—but only at the last minute.

Over high flame, heat the oil and butter in a large kettle and add the tails, claws and carcasses of the lobsters. Toss around with a wooden spoon until the shells begin to turn red. Add the Cognac and ignite. Add the tomato paste, and, mixing constantly, continue to cook for another 3 minutes. Add the celery, onion, carrots, thyme, bay leaf, leeks, fresh tomatoes, wine, clam broth, chicken broth, and rice. Stir and simmer, covered, for about 35 to 40 minutes. Remove the tails and claws from the soup and set aside one tail and one claw. (Refrigerate the rest to be used for appetizer or salad.)

Pour the soup mixture, with the remaining parts of the lobster carcass, into a food mill and push through the liquids, and as much of the solids as can be extracted. Pour the resulting broth through a very fine sieve set over a large pot, again pushing the solids through; season to taste with salt, pepper and Tabasco. Press the reserved liver and coral through a sieve into the soup. Stir in the heavy cream; cut the meat from the claw and tail into small cubes and add; bring the soup to a boil for 1–2 minutes. Serve hot.

Fresh Oysters Ambassadeur

Serves 2 at lunch or 3 for appetizers

12 large oysters on the half shell
3 shallots, finely chopped
½ cup finely chopped parsley
1 teaspoon chopped fresh chervil, or a
   pinch dried
Dash Tabasco sauce
1 teaspoon Worcestershire sauce
5 ounces (⅔ cup) butter
6 ounces lump crabmeat, picked over

BÉCHAMEL *
2 tablespoons butter
2 tablespoons flour
2 cups milk
¾ cup grated Gruyère cheese (about 3
   ounces)
Fresh lemon

* You can use FISH VELOUTÉ (page 124) instead if you like
a fishier taste.

Preheat oven to 450 F. Arrange oysters on the half shell in an ovenproof glass baking dish. Mix the shallots, parsley, chervil, Tabasco sauce, Worcestershire sauce and butter, and top each oyster with a teaspoonful of the mixture. Arrange some fresh crabmeat over each oyster.

To make the Béchamel: Melt butter over moderate heat; whisk in flour; allow to cook for 2 minutes. Whisking constantly, gradually add milk. When all the milk has been added, allow to cook for approximately 5 minutes longer, or until thickened. Cover each oyster with this sauce Béchamel. Sprinkle the grated cheese over the oysters and bake for about 8–10 minutes, or until golden brown. Squeeze fresh lemon juice over the baked oysters, and serve hot.

Fresh Deviled Lobster and Crab

Serves 4 as a first course

½ pound fresh lump crabmeat, picked
   over
½ pound fresh lobster (cooked meat cut
   into very small cubes—or use lobster
   tail meat)
2 tablespoons minced parsley
1 teaspoon dry mustard
2 teaspoons Kikkoman soy sauce
Juice of one lemon
1 teaspoon salt

1 cup fresh bread crumbs made in blender
¾ cup very finely chopped celery
2 tablespoons very finely chopped green
   pepper
2 tablespoons butter and 4 teaspoons melted
   butter
2 tablespoons grated onion
3 egg yolks
2 tablespoons heavy cream

In a large bowl, combine the crab and lobster meats; add the parsley, dry mustard, soy sauce, lemon juice, salt, and half of the bread crumbs.

In a heavy pan over low heat, sauté celery and green pepper in 2 tablespoons butter for about 10 minutes; add the onion; continue to cook for another 4 minutes. Pour these vegetables over the lobster and crabmeat mixture; fold in well.

Heat oven to 375 F. Lightly beat egg yolks with heavy cream and pour over sea-food mixture; stir very thoroughly. With hands, form into desirable rounds—about the size of a lemon. Lightly butter a low, heat-resistant glass baking dish and place the rounds on it. Dust with the rest of the bread crumbs, pour one teaspoon of melted butter over each. Place them in the oven until nicely browned, and serve hot with TARTAR SAUCE,* fresh squeezed lemon juice or FISH VELOUTÉ (see page 125).

* For each cup of MAYONNAISE (see page 36), add 3–4 finely chopped, drained sour pickles, parsley, dash of dry mustard.

Rainbow Trout Sauté Meunière

Serves 4

4 trout, ¾ pound each
Salt and pepper
2 cups all-purpose flour
1 cup yellow cornmeal
1 cup vegetable oil
¾ cup butter
½ cup dry white wine
Juice of 1½ lemons
Beurre manié (2 tablespoons) *
2 tablespoons chopped parsley

* Make BEURRE MANIÉ by kneading butter and flour together in one to one proportions.

Season trout with salt and pepper. Combine flour and cornmeal; roll trout in them. In a heavy iron skillet large enough to hold all of the fish, heat mixture of oil and butter; sauté fish on *medium heat* until golden brown (about 5 minutes per side, turning once). Place fish on heated platter. Discard all oil mixture from skillet. Return skillet to the heat. Add wine and bring to a boil. Pour lemon juice in it and add BEURRE MANIÉ a little bit at a time, mixing well with a wooden spoon until slightly thickened; pour over fish; sprinkle with parsley and serve.

Poached Rainbow Trout au Bleu

Serve 1 trout per person

Even if you cannot move directly from stream to pot, you must try for trout no more than a few hours out of the water for this recipe to work.

COURT BOUILLON
3 quarts water
1 onion, cut in half
1 bay leaf
1 tablespoon salt
1 cup white vinegar
6 peppercorns

THE FISH
1 live trout, about 1 pound
Melted butter
Lemon wedges
Chopped parsley

In a large pot, bring the water, onion, bay leaf, salt, vinegar and peppercorns to a boil. Give the trout a blow on the back of the neck. Wash trout, cut it open and clean thoroughly, but leave head and tail on. Plunge trout into the boiling court bouillon and poach for about 4 minutes.

Put fish on a hot plate, and serve immediately with melted butter, SAUCE HOLLANDAISE or SAUCE MOUSSELINE (see this page), lemon wedges and chopped parsley.

Makes ¾ cup

SAUCE HOLLANDAISE
2 egg yolks
2 teaspoons water
½ cup melted butter
Dash of cayenne
Pinch of salt
Lemon juice or white wine vinegar

In the top of a glass double boiler, over simmering water, combine the egg yolks and water. Whisk until the eggs are well mixed and slightly thickened. Continue to whisk, making sure the water does not boil underneath, and gradually add the butter, a dribble at a time. If the sauce becomes too thick, dilute with a little warm water. If it curdles, add a little boiling water, and mix it briskly. When it turns thick and creamy, add cayenne, salt and lemon juice or vinegar to taste.

SAUCE MOUSSELINE: If you wish a very delicate sauce, combine the Hollandaise with an equal amount of whipped cream after you remove it from over the hot water. This sauce must be served immediately.

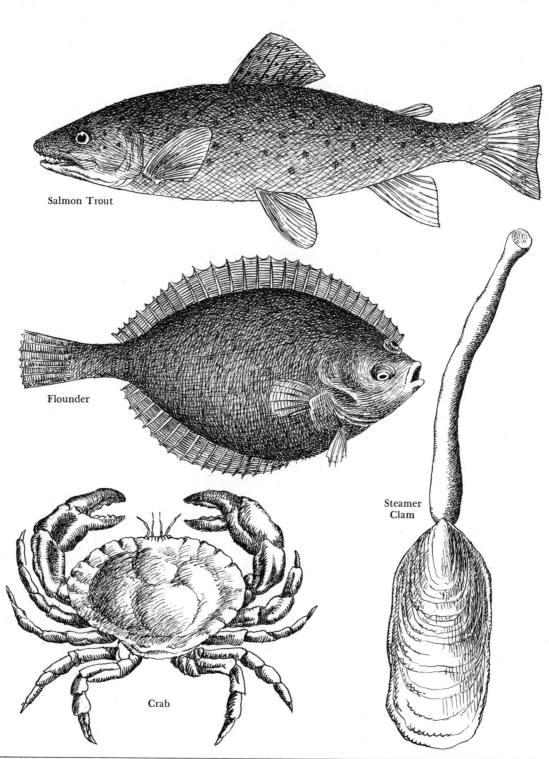

Salmon Trout

Flounder

Steamer
Clam

Crab

THE GREAT COOKS COOKBOOK

Fresh Whitefish au Beurre

Serves 4

Lake Superior whitefish is one of the most delicate and delicious fishes in the world. Have your fish market clean and fillet 2 whitefish of 4 pounds each.

FISH:
4 fillets of whitefish
2 tablespoons butter, melted for brushing, plus 2 tablespoons for sautéeing
Salt and pepper
1 cup flour
4 tablespoons SAUCE AU BEURRE

---

*T*o Broil: Brush fillets on both sides with butter, and season them with salt and pepper. Broil under medium flame about 8 to 10 minutes.
To Sauté: Season fish with salt and pepper, flour them well and sauté in medium flame in hot butter 5 minutes on each side.

When done, remove fish to a warm platter, discard remaining butter from pan, place the SAUCE AU BEURRE in the pan and when it is just about melted, pour over the fish and serve.

SAUCE AU BEURRE
¾ cup butter (6 ounces), room temperature
1 tablespoon very finely chopped parsley
1 teaspoon very finely chopped chives or scallions
1 teaspoon Worcestershire sauce
½ teaspoon celery salt

In a bowl, cream the butter very well with the remaining ingredients; keep in refrigerator until you are ready to use. This will prevent the sauce from being greasy.

Striped Bass à la Grecque

Serves 4

---

1 4-pound striped bass, cleaned and left whole
4 lemons
Salt and pepper
2 medium onions, peeled and finely chopped
4 scallions, white part only
2 carrots, peeled and thinly sliced
1½ cups drained, canned plum tomatoes

2 cloves garlic, peeled and chopped
2 bay leaves
1 teaspoon dried orégano
½ cup fresh parsley, chopped
½ cup dry white wine
½ cup olive oil
8 cherrystone clams, washed and scrubbed
8 shrimps, back of shells split lengthwise to devein, but not removed

---

*S*plit bass, lengthwise, down the middle of each side. Rub well on each side and inside with the juice of 2 of the lemons and salt and pepper.

Place fish in the center of a glass roasting pan. Spread vegetables and herbs over and around the fish. Sprinkle with the juice of 1 lemon and pour over the wine and olive oil. Slice the remaining lemon into rounds, removing the seeds, and place the slices over the fish.

Preheat oven to 450 F. Place fish in it for 25 minutes. Remove fish from oven. Arrange clams on one side of it and shrimp on the other; return to oven; reduce heat to 375 F. and continue to bake for another 15–20 minutes, or until the clams have opened. Serve 2 clams and 2 shrimp per person with a portion of fish and the natural sauce that has formed in the pan.

Lobster Tails Skorpios

Serves 4 at dinner for a main course and 8
as an *hors d'oeuvre* or luncheon dish

3 tablespoons olive oil
1 cup finely chopped onion
1 clove garlic, peeled and finely chopped
2 cups fresh or drained canned plum
    tomatoes, peeled and chopped
½ cup canned tomato sauce
¼ teaspoon dried orégano
¼ teaspoon sugar
⅛ teaspoon dry mustard
Freshly ground black pepper
¼ cup finely chopped parsley
8 baby lobster tails, preferably fresh—if
    frozen, thaw
3 tablespoons butter
Flour
¼ pound feta cheese

*I*n a saucepan, heat the olive oil and sauté the onion without browning. Add garlic, tomatoes, tomato sauce, orégano, sugar, mustard, freshly ground black pepper and parsley. Cook the combined ingredients, uncovered, for about 30 minutes or until they are reduced to a moderately thick sauce.

Heat oven to 425 F. Shell the lobster tails, taking care to remove the meat in one piece. In a skillet, heat the butter. Dust the lobster tails with flour and sauté briskly, stirring them for about two minutes or just until firm. Transfer the lobster tails to a shallow glass baking dish. Pour the prepared sauce over them. Cover them with thin slices of feta cheese and bake for about 10 minutes, or until the cheese melts. Serve with rice pilaf and green salad.

Crab with Prosciutto

Serves 6

24 thin slices prosciutto
¾ pound lump crabmeat, picked over
    well (about 1½ cups)
¾ cup butter
1 teaspoon Worcestershire sauce
½ teaspoon Tabasco sauce
Juice of 1 lemon
2 tablespoons finely chopped parsley
Freshly ground black pepper

*A*rrange 4 slices of prosciutto on a flat surface, each slice slightly overlapping the next one. In the center, place 1 tablespoon crabmeat. From a narrow end, roll up prosciutto to form a tube with crabmeat filling. Repeat with remaining prosciutto and crabmeat to make 6 rolls. Heat oven to 180 F.

In a large skillet, melt the butter; place the prosciutto rolls in the butter and cook over medium heat. When heated, the ham will cling to the crabmeat. Turn over only once, and cook until ham begins to brown and crisp. Transfer rolls to a warm platter or ovenproof glass casserole and keep hot in oven.

To the juices remaining in the skillet, add Worcestershire sauce, Tabasco sauce and lemon juice. Heat, stirring with a wooden spoon; pour over prosciutto rolls. Sprinkle with parsley and pepper.

Fish Soup of the Islands

Serves 5

¼ cup olive oil
2 onions, finely chopped
1 leek, carefully washed and finely chopped
    (white part only)
5 baby squid, cleaned and cut into 1-inch
    pieces, including (optional) tentacles
2 ribs celery, finely chopped
3 cloves of garlic, peeled and finely chopped
10 black peppercorns
1 bay leaf
1 teaspoon saffron threads
1 can (# 2½) plum tomatoes

2 large fresh tomatoes, peeled, cored and
    chopped
1 teaspoon dried orégano
1 cup dry white wine
3 cups water *
Dash of Tabasco
2 pounds firm-fleshed fish, such as striped
    bass, sea bass or carp, cut into steaks
2 dozen mussels, scrubbed and washed well
2 dozen clams, scrubbed and washed well
1 tablespoon Pernod (optional)
¼ cup finely chopped parsley

* FISH STOCK (page 124), used instead of water, will make a richer dish.

eat half of the oil in a large, heavy skillet. Add the onion, leek, squid, celery, garlic, peppercorns, bay leaf and saffron. Cook, stirring, until most of the moisture evaporates. Add canned and fresh tomatoes, orégano, wine, water, and Tabasco. Bring to a boil; cook uncovered for 40 minutes. Add the fish, mussels and clams. Cover and boil briskly for another 20 minutes. Add the remaining oil, Pernod and parsley. Shake well to combine and serve hot over toasted GARLIC BREAD (see page 124).

Bouillabaisse

Serves 5–6

3 tablespoons olive oil
2 onions chopped
2 leeks finely chopped (white part only)
3 cloves garlic peeled and finely minced
3 large tomatoes, peeled, cored and chopped
1½ teaspoons thyme
1 bay leaf
2 sprigs fresh parsley
1 cup dry white wine
3 cups water *
1 teaspoon saffron threads, crushed
Dash of Tabasco
¼ pound butter and 1½ teaspoons flour
2 1¼-pound lobsters
2 pounds fresh striped bass, red snapper or sea bass, cut into serving pieces
1 quart mussels, well scrubbed and washed
2 dozen medium-size, hardshell clams
1 tablespoon of Pernod

eat the olive oil in a deep, large skillet, and add onion, leek and garlic and let them cook for a few

* FISH STOCK (page 124), used instead of water, will make a richer dish.

minutes until wilted. Add the tomatoes, thyme, bay leaf, parsley, wine, water, saffron and Tabasco, and simmer for about 12 minutes.

Either have your fish store prepare the lobsters as described below or prepare by separating the tail from the carcass. Cut the tail into four round pieces, with the shell on. Split carcass in half lengthwise; remove the liver and coral and place them in a bowl. Remove the tough sac near the eyes and discard. Break off the claws with a heavy knife. Add the carcass to the tomato mixture. Cover and cook for 30 minutes. Blend the butter and flour with the fingers, and mix with the coral and liver. Set aside.

Strain the tomato mixture through a medium sieve, pushing through as many solids as possible. Pour broth into a deep pot and bring to a boil, adding the fish, mussels, clams, lobster pieces and claws; cover. Simmer for about 15 minutes or until mussels and clams open. Stir in the butter mixture; bring to a boil, add the Pernod and serve hot with GARLIC BREAD.

Seafood à la Méditerranée

Serves 4–5

12 large shrimp
12 cherrystone clams
4 lobster tails, preferably fresh—if frozen, defrost
½ cup olive oil
3 cloves garlic, peeled and finely minced
2 cups drained, canned plum tomatoes
¾ cup dry white wine
1 bay leaf
½ teaspoon dried orégano
Salt and pepper
2 tablespoons parsley, finely chopped

Slit the shells of the shrimp lengthwise down the entire back; devein and dry. (Do not remove the shells.) Scrub and wash the clams. Wash the lobster tails, and, with a large kitchen knife, cut them, unshelled, into one-inch slices—crosswise.

In a large, deep skillet over medium heat, heat the olive oil with garlic and cook for 1 minute, taking care that the garlic does not brown. Add the shrimp and lobster-tail slices and cook for 2 minutes. Stir in the tomatoes and wine. Add the bay leaf, orégano, salt and pepper. Increase the heat and cook briskly for about 5 to 6 minutes. Add the clams; cover the skillet and continue to cook briskly—shaking and stirring—from 10 to 12 minutes or until the clams open. Remove from fire; sprinkle with the chopped parsley and serve hot. It is great with pasta or rice and a crispy green salad.

Salmon with White Raisins or Currants

Serves 4

½ cup of butter
2 onions sliced in thin rings
2 stalks of celery, thinly sliced
2 carrots, thinly sliced
1 bay leaf
3 sprigs of parsley
Salt and pepper
2 cups of white dry wine
4 cups of water or fish stock *
1 fresh salmon (5 to 6 pounds)
4 egg yolks
* See page 124.

1 cup (½ pint) heavy cream
2 tablespoons white raisins or currants
The juice of 1 lemon
2 tablespoons *beurre manié* **
1½ tablespoons chopped parsley

** See page 116.

In a large fish poacher, place the butter; add the onions, celery, carrots, bay leaf, the 3 sprigs of parsley, salt and pepper to taste and, stirring with a wooden spoon, cook over medium flame for about 5–6 minutes. Add the white wine and water and bring to a boil.

Salt the salmon well inside and out. Wrap it in a long piece of cheesecloth and place in the boiling broth, tying the long ends of the cheesecloth to handles at the end of the pot. Cover and simmer over medium heat for about 35–40 minutes or until salmon can be easily flaked. Remove (lifting it in the cheesecloth) to a warm platter. Peel off the cheesecloth and remove the skin and bones. Keep warm by covering the fish with a warm, moist towel.

Strain the vegetables and discard them. Return broth to pot and, over high heat, reduce it to half (about 2½ cups). Beat the egg yolks for about 5 minutes; add heavy cream and continue to beat for another 4 minutes. Add a few spoons of the hot broth to the egg mixture while continuing beating. Pour the egg mixture into the broth; beat; add raisins or currants; add lemon juice; heat almost to boiling point; reduce fire to lowest point and, stirring constantly, add *beurre manié*, a little at a time. The sauce will thicken. Pour sauce over the salmon; sprinkle with parsley, and serve hot.

Garlic Bread

This is for fish soups, not to serve on the table. As such it serves 8.

8 slices crusty, day-old French or Italian bread
1 clove of garlic split
½ cup melted butter

Preheat oven to 400 F. Rub the bread on both sides with the garlic. Brush both sides generously with butter. Place on a rack or baking sheet, and bake until golden, turning over if necessary. (Be sure not to burn. It would spoil the taste of the soup.)

Fish Stock

This may be used instead of water or clam broth in fish soups.

2 pounds fish bones and heads
1 stalk celery with leaves, coarsely chopped
1 onion, peeled and coarsely chopped
1 clove garlic, unpeeled and flattened with a knife

¼ teaspoon dried thyme
1 bay leaf
10 black peppercorns
5 sprigs parsley
1 leek stalk (just white part), well washed and coarsely chopped
Salt to taste
1 cup dry white wine
4 cups water

ombine all the ingredients in a saucepan and simmer for 45 minutes, skimming the surface if necessary. Strain through a fine strainer. Fish stock can be frozen.

Fish Velouté

This simple sauce does well on poached fish. It can be used as an optional sauce on the FRESH DEVILED LOBSTER AND CRAB during baking or used in the FRESH OYSTERS AMBASSADEUR instead of BÉCHAMEL.

4 tablespoons butter
¾ cup all-purpose flour
2½ cups hot FISH STOCK (see page 124)

elt the butter in a saucepan, and stir in the flour with a wire whisk. Cook briefly, without browning, over medium heat. Pour in the fish stock all at once, stirring very rapidly with the wire whisk until the mixture is smooth. Continue to cook over low heat, stirring constantly for about 30 minutes. Strain the sauce through a fine sieve.

Wines for Fish

ALEXIS BESPALOFF

Since many of the recipes in this chapter evoke those wonderful dishes that are served informally in seaport restaurants around the world, the accompanying wines can be chosen in the same casual way. An obvious possibility is to set out carafes of jug wines from California or New York State. Delightful and inexpensive as they are, many of these wines lack the crisp acidity that so effectively sets off the flavor of fish. There are, however, a number of light-bodied and refreshing white wines that are particularly attractive with light dishes, outdoor luncheons and shellfish.

Muscadet from the Loire Valley and Sylvaner from Alsace are two French wines; Soave and Verdicchio, two examples from Italy. California Chablis can be found everywhere, and California Riesling (actually the Sylvaner) and French Colombard are also easy to find. If you want to try light dry wines that are less frequently seen, Vinho Verde from Portugal is a possibility; so are any number of Swiss wines, such as Neuchâtel, Fendant, Aigle and Yvorne.

Rich foods will overpower delicate wines, however, and call for wines with body, flavor and character. Burgundy is the classic choice—Pouilly-Fuissé, Chablis, Meursault, and Puligny-Montrachet—but these wines are now as expensive as they are delicious. You may want to try less expensive examples of Burgundy, such as Bourgogne Blanc and Mâcon Blanc, some of which are also labeled Pinot Chardonnay, after the name of the grape from which they are made. Full-flavored dry wines are also made in Bordeaux—Graves and Bordeaux Blanc are the most often seen—but some producers market white Bordeaux that are slightly sweet. Sancerre and Pouilly-Fumé, from the Loire, both have enough body and intensity of taste to accompany even the richest foods. Among the wines of California, Pinot Chardonnay, Pinot Blanc, Sauvignon Blanc and Dry Semillon are distinct and flavorful dry wines. Another possibility is white wine from Greece. Retsina is an unusual wine, flavored with pine resin, that will not appeal to everyone; but there are also several non-resinated Greek white wines that are comparatively inexpensive.

Semisweet white wines include those from the Rhine and Moselle such as Bernkasteler, Piesporter, Johannisberger, Niersteiner and so on; some examples of Graves; Vouvray; many New York State wines; and such California wines as Chenin Blanc and Johannisberg Riesling. There are some who insist that a rich seafood dish is best accompanied by a semisweet white wine, others who prefer the balancing acidity of dry wines. This controversy is one that you and your guests will enjoy resolving for yourselves.

Fish stews and soups are a staple of villages along the Mediterranean, and are often served with a dry rosé, such as those from Provence and the village of Tavel. A full-flavored rosé, well chilled, comes into its own with, for example, bouillabaisse. If you don't want to pay the price for Tavel, try a dry pink wine from California, such as Grenache Rosé or Gamay Rosé or one of the many wines simply labeled Vin Rosé.

THE GREAT COOKS COOKBOOK

Poultry and Game

Since the term poultry covers all the barn-yard fowl, and "game" speaks to us of wild animals killed in the hunt, the distinction seems clear. In culinary practice, however, the terms fuse slightly. Of all the birds we eat, only the chicken is always and only domestic. Although most of us think of duck and goose as domestic, to the hunter they are superior game. The beautiful ring-neck pheasant is now farm-raised. In this case, it is not only domestic, but it also has a less-pronounced flavor due to the difference in its feeding, among other things. Among the game animals, of course, are the four-legged ones. Of these, only deer are farm-raised and hence domesticated. In this chapter, I will deal with the different kinds of animals usually considered poultry and game. Since game is relatively less familiar, I will begin with some general notes about it.

About Game

I love to hunt. But what a poor shot I am! The beauty of wild animals over-whelms me, and my bullets are always late. There was a time when man lived only by hunting for his food. I guess I would have starved. When civilized man no longer had to hunt to obtain his food, hunting became a sport. As time passed, man forgot the original purpose of the hunt; he became destructive, often killing only for the sake of killing. However, in America, Europe and in many other parts of the world, hunting is seasonal; this provides protection for game species. Now, with more understanding and, of course, fewer animals, we have come to what I call the "double-barreled" pleasure of game hunting which, indeed, combines not only the challenge of the hunt but also the enjoyment of eating.

The term "game" applies to any animal hunted for the purpose of eating it. We have all heard the expression "gamey taste," which, in my opinion, describes the slightly stronger flavor of wild-animal meat as compared with that of domesticated animals. Many dislike the taste, and many have a passionate love for it. But one way or the other, the fact remains that it is there. The exciting flavor depends only on what is done with it. If you treat your animal or bird correctly, this "gamey" flavor can be either very delicate or completely neutralized while still retaining the particular quality of game. Of course, game has little or no fat. Anytime you work with it, you should consider adding some; this will keep your meat moist and juicy.

The handling of game is an important factor in getting the best results with its texture and taste. (And a little extra information about its handling before hunting begins will help you a bit to understand and deal with your favorite catch.) Hanging the meat is the first and most important procedure in handling game; it acts as a tenderizing process and, of course, also improves the flavor of the meat. In camp, the animal, eviscerated, or the whole bird should be hung high in a tree, or on a pole about 16 feet above the ground; this will keep insects from sniffing around your game for the 1 or 2 days needed.

The flavor of your animal or bird may vary, depending upon its age, diet and handling and, especially, what it had eaten just before having been shot. If your game bird or animal has been badly shot up, it is a good idea, before cooking and after hanging, to clean it thoroughly, then soak in salt water for several hours.

Game birds keep very well when stored at zero or below. They should first be plucked and cleaned, then wrapped individually in vapor- and moisture-proof material, foil or plastic wrap. Meat should be cut into pieces or sections, actually ready to cook, and wrapped individually. It is also a good idea to label your packages when storing. The meat stores very well without losing its qualities for 6 to 12 months. However, the edible organs (heart, liver, etc.) should be used within 6 months.

Frozen meat should be at least two-thirds thawed before cooking. But, for best results, it must be well thawed at room temperature (this allows the meat to retain the greatest amount of its moisture content), used quickly and never refrozen. Ready-to-cook frozen poultry or game is available in most markets, and the quality is generally good.

For some reason or other, we seem to panic when we decide to serve game, and we are in doubt as to what to serve with it. Actually, game is like any other meat and should be accompanied by simple, basic dishes. With the use of a little imagination, it should not be a problem. Game will always go with mushrooms, turnips, onions, peas, cabbage, beets, sweet potatoes (preferably puréed) or winter or summer squash.

And speaking of squash, zucchini can be presented in a most glamorous way, and with very little effort. Just shred zucchini (about 1 medium zucchini per person) and remove all water by squeezing the zucchini dry in a clean cloth. In a skillet, melt a generous amount of butter, then add garlic, sage and chopped truffles. When the butter mixture is bubbling hot (do not allow to brown), add zucchini. Toss just long enough to heat the zucchini through. Season with salt and freshly ground pepper, and serve immediately.

The basic lentil will make your game dish quite special. Of themselves, lentils are one of the most interesting of all legumes and one of the most nutritious. What a meal I can make of them! I simply combine cold, cooked lentils with onions and shredded lettuce. Season them with good olive oil, vinegar, sweet basil, salt and freshly ground black pepper, and it is a smashing salad! When dealing with lentils, it is important not to overcook them, or they will lose all their flavor and nutrition. They should be cooked for only a short length of time, just until they are slightly tender. Commercially processed lentils can be cooked in approximately 25 minutes, and are sold labeled in that way.

Some breads go better with certain food than with others. That is why I like to serve game with a good sourdough bread, for example. Sourdough and game were made for each other. Cornbread in its many varieties, blueberry or cranberry muffins, pumpernickel or just plain French bread are always desirable with game.

An excellent method of flavoring and handling game is to smoke it. Smoking acts as a preservative and, properly done, adds an interesting taste. There are several ways to do it. Cold smoking, which I prefer for its delicate flavor, is a slow process, but does produce a subtle quality. Cold smoking uses temperatures between 90 and 120 F., and can take 48 hours or more. Hot smoking, which uses temperatures between 140 and 170 F., takes approximately 6 hours, depending on the size and thickness of the meat, and it is important to keep the temperature constant throughout the entire smoking period. Hot smoking both cooks and cures the game at the same time.

Smoked meats can also be frozen, if first thoroughly dried then double-wrapped in freezer paper. Bear in mind that the wood you use will determine the flavor of the finished game. You have several varieties from which to choose. Dry hardwoods or sweet woods, such as hickory, apple, maple, buttonwood, mangrove and orange, lend excellent flavor. Even ground corn-cobs will produce very good results.

In the atmosphere and ritual of hunting, the movement and beauty of an animal excites the eye; our senses sharpen and every movement counts. Meanwhile, the imagination sneaks away in a hundred directions, planning the feast—"What an entrance my catch is making!"—even if I haven't yet caught it.

The cooking of game requires basic understanding and love. In return it gives you a succession of pleasures which start with the catch and how you treat it. Preparing, presenting and serving it in order to delight the palate is what dining on game is all about.

About Seasonings

In flavoring game feel free to pick and choose among almost any herbs you have handy. Your choice must be added moderately, however, so as not to overpower the natural taste of the meat. Some herbs suitable in cooking game are tarragon, thyme, rosemary, sage, bay leaf, fennel, dill, basil and maybe a touch of orégano.

Fresh herbs are much better than dry ones, and there is a world of difference between them. It is nice to season freely with fresh herbs; dry herbs, because they are much more concentrated, have to be added with discretion. Dry herbs keep well in tightly closed jars stored in a cool, dry place, but do not keep them too long; try to cook with them frequently because they lose their bouquet. Any herbs you prefer when preparing your meals are fine.

Salt and pepper are, of course, called for in most recipes. It is good to use coarse (non-chemical) salt in cooking. If you are going to use pepper, it should always be freshly ground black pepper.

THE GREAT COOKS COOKBOOK

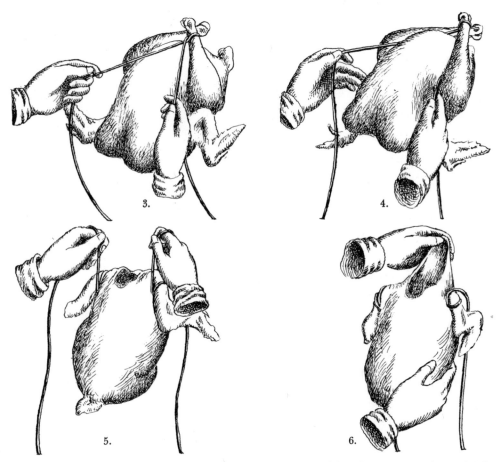

1.,2.,3.,4. with bird on back, wings toward you, take a good length of cotton twine and follow steps. At 5., flip bird onto breast, wings are now away from you. After step 6., turn page.

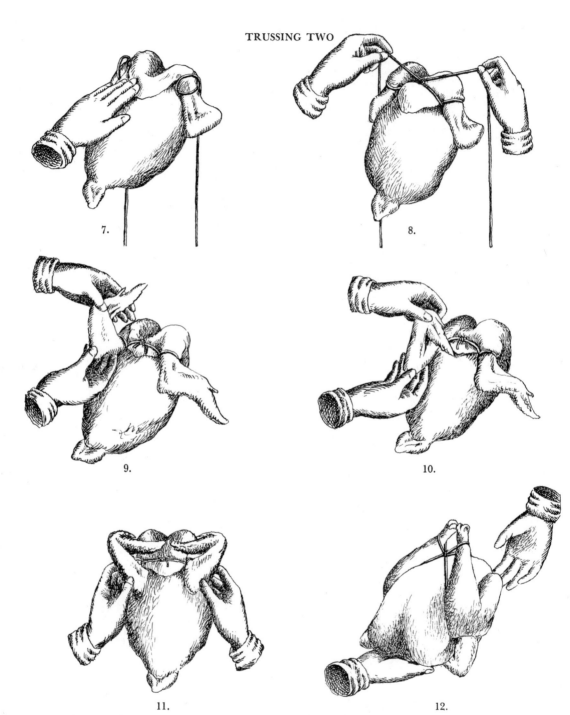

7.

8.

9.

10.

11.

12.

After completing steps 1.–6. on the previous page, follow steps on this page, cutting off the string at 9. and turning bird after 11.

THE GREAT COOKS COOKBOOK

About Chicken

The most commonly available and perhaps the most versatile of the poultry and game animals is the chicken. Primitive man was familiar with the chicken even before he discovered fire and cooking. The Chinese began to use chicken as early as 1400 B.C. And with the help of man, chicken traveled around the world. It is a bird with excellent qualities, and in relation to cooking is quite forgiving. . . .

Today, as a result of modern technology, not only is chicken available in great quantities but there are many varieties from which to pick and choose. When you shop, you should select a chicken for the specific purpose you have in mind. Allow about ½ pound per person.

BROILER chickens are young and plump. Typical broilers are 13–18 weeks of age and weigh 1–2 pounds. They can be used split in half lengthwise, quartered, or cut in pieces. The fryer is an all-purpose bird which can be fried, sautéed, baked or braised. ROASTING chickens are heavy-breasted, tasty birds 5–9 months of age and 3–5 pounds. A roasting chicken generously serves 4 or more. A CAPON is actually a gelded rooster which is at its best when roasted, but often is cooked in many other ways. If you want a larger bird for roasting than the chicken, I suggest you choose a capon. (Allow 1 pound per person.)

Roast Chicken or Roast Capon

Wash the bird inside and out, dry well and remove any pinfeathers. Heat oven to 375 F. Rub the cavity with the cut side of a lemon and sprinkle with salt and freshly ground black pepper. You may add to the cavity any flavoring you wish—rosemary or thyme, for example. Place in it an onion (whole, peeled), a few cloves of garlic, some fresh sprigs of tarragon (or 1 tablespoon dry) and truss * tightly. Rub entire surface with generous amounts of softened butter. Place on a rack set in a roasting pan and, allowing 20 minutes per pound, roast in a preheated 375 F. oven, basting frequently with melted butter or any other basting liquid you prefer. If the bird is browning too quickly, cover it with aluminum foil or buttered wax paper. In checking for doneness, the legs should move easily and the juices run clear yellow with no trace of pink when you prick the skin with the point of a knife.

* See TRUSSING (page 131).

Variation: Prepare chicken as just described (including seasoning of cavity). Lay strips of bacon on a rack set in a roasting pan. Place chicken breast-down on top of bacon and, basting frequently with pan drippings (or any basting you prefer), roast for ½ of cooking time. Turn chicken breast-up, spread generously with butter, and finish roasting. Cooking time and temperature as for ROAST CHICKEN OR ROAST CAPON.

Stuffing a Roasting Chicken: Allow 1 cup stuffing for each pound, ready-to-cook weight; always stuff chicken just before roasting. Fill neck cavity with stuffing, or skewer neck skin to back. Spoon stuffing into cavity of bird lightly (never pack), close opening with skewers, or sew it closed with needle and thread. Truss bird tightly.*

* See TRUSSING (page 131).

Chicken Tandoo

Putting flavor under the skin of the chicken is an idea I find very interesting. Begin by running your fingers between the skin and the flesh of the whole breast section, leaving the skin attached only at the bone (it prevents the skin from shrinking). You can go on, if you like, separating skin from flesh along the sides and the legs of the chicken as well. Then work under the skin, covering the flesh of the breast, sides, and legs entirely with DUXELLES.

DUXELLES is a mushroom paste used in many ways. To prepare it, chop very finely 2 pounds of fresh mushrooms that have been wiped clean. Place in a dish towel and squeeze out all liquid. (Save liquid; it is suitable for other sauces in place of, or combined with, broth.) Chop 1 clove garlic (or substitute 1 tablespoon finely chopped shallot). In a skillet, melt ½ pound butter. Add garlic and mushrooms. Stirring now and then, cook over low heat until all liquid has evaporated and mushrooms form a dark, dense mass. Taste, and season with salt and freshly ground black pepper. Mix well and place under skin as described above. Any extra DUXELLES can be refrigerated for future use.

For another version of CHICKEN TANDOO use a good amount of wilted * fresh spinach (or defrosted, frozen spinach) drained, then squeezed dry and sautéed in plenty of butter. Allow 1 stick of butter for every pound of cooked spinach. Season with nutmeg, salt and freshly ground black pepper, and place under the skin.

For both versions of CHICKEN TANDOO, truss ** chicken after stuffing, then place on a rack set in a roasting pan. Roast in a preheated 375 F. oven, allowing 20 minutes per pound (weight before stuffing),

* To wilt fresh spinach, wash it well, then place in a large pot. Cook covered, but without water, over low heat. Toss twice while cooking to wilt all leaves. Remove from heat immediately and remove cover.
** See TRUSSING (page 131).

and baste frequently with pan drippings or melted butter.

I have also had marvelous results with bacon. I sprinkle one or two slices of bacon generously with freshly ground rosemary or thyme, and freshly ground black pepper, then place them flat, right under the skin, covering the flesh of the breast entirely. I find that bacon used in this way makes the meat of the chicken juicy and tender, and gives it a most unique and delicate flavor.

Chicken Provençale
Serves 4–6

4–5 pound roasting chicken (preferably boned)
½ pound ground pork
1½ pounds fresh spinach (1 cup, wilted *), drained, squeezed dry and chopped; or 2½–3 (10 ounces each) packages frozen spinach, defrosted, drained, squeezed dry and chopped
1 teaspoon sage
1 teaspoon thyme
2 tablespoons pistachio nuts
Salt and freshly ground black pepper
1 egg, beaten
1 boiled egg, medium hard, shelled
2 cloves garlic, crushed
1 teaspoon ground turmeric (optional)
2 tablespoons olive oil

Wash the chicken inside and out; dry well and remove any pinfeathers. In a bowl, place the ground pork, chopped spinach, sage, thyme, pistachio nuts, 1 teaspoon salt, ½ teaspoon pepper and beaten egg. Mix well together. (This
* See page 134.

recipe includes raw pork; if you wish to taste to correct seasoning, you must first sauté a little of the mixture until done.) Sew the neck skin to the back of the chicken. Line cavity of the chicken by packing in half the stuffing; place boiled egg carefully in center of it, and add rest of the stuffing. Sew the cavity closed.

Preheat oven to 375 F. Crush the garlic—preferably in mortar with pestle—add salt, pepper, turmeric and olive oil. Mix, combining well. Rub the entire surface of the chicken well with this mixture. If you have some left, save for basting.

Place chicken on a rack set in an ovenproof glass roasting pan and roast for 1½ hours, basting frequently; use olive oil if you have no more of the rubbing mixture. If chicken is roasting too quickly, cover with aluminum foil or greased brown paper. Serve hot as a main course, or cold—cut in thin slices—as an appetizer. Garnish with watercress and sprigs of mint.

Vegetable Chicken Casserole

Serves 4–6

1 fryer chicken, washed and dried
½ cup peanut oil
½ pound butter
2 onions, sliced
⅓ cup carrots, peeled and sliced lengthwise
2 tablespoons chopped celery
1 red pepper, seeded and sliced (optional)
1 green pepper, seeded and sliced
1 teaspoon dried rosemary
¼ teaspoon dried sweet basil (2
    tablespoons fresh)
Salt and freshly ground black pepper
½ cup spinach, wilted *
½ cup mushrooms, sliced
½ cup black olives
½ cup chicken broth
1 small (6-ounce) can tomato paste
1 garlic clove, peeled and cut in half
1 cup sliced romaine lettuce (or iceberg)
1 tablespoon chopped fresh mint or parsley
Chopped peanuts

Cut chicken into serving pieces. Heat peanut oil in a frying pan and fry chicken pieces 1 layer deep, until golden brown, turning with tongs

* See page 134.

from time to time. Remove chicken and place on paper towels to drain.

In a skillet, melt the butter, add the onions, carrots, celery, red and green peppers, rosemary, sweet basil, salt and pepper. Over medium heat, sauté until vegetables are just tender (4–5 minutes). Add the spinach, mushrooms and black olives. Stir, then cook a minute or two. Combine the chicken broth with tomato paste and pour over the vegetables. Stirring, bring to a boil and cook 2 minutes longer. Set aside.

Preheat oven to 375 F. Rub the inside of a lidded ovenproof glass casserole—about 2 quarts—with garlic; using both halves, rub strongly with the cut sides. Arrange sliced lettuce on bottom of casserole and sprinkle with mint. Lay half the chicken pieces on the lettuce and cover with half the sautéed vegetables. Place remaining chicken pieces on the vegetables and, over them, the rest of the vegetables and juices. Cover casserole and put into oven for 35 minutes. To serve, garnish with sprinkling of chopped peanuts.

Chicken Panné

Serves 4–6

4 boned whole chicken breasts, cut in half
Flour, seasoned with salt and freshly ground
    black pepper
2 eggs, beaten lightly
1 cup soft bread crumbs
5 tablespoons butter
1 tablespoon oil
¼ cup Cognac
1 cup cream combined with 2 raw egg yolks

Place each breast between 2 pieces of wax paper; pound each one quite flat with the side of a heavy cleaver —or use a pounder. Dip one by one in the seasoned flour, then in beaten egg, and, finally, in the bread crumbs, coating both sides. Place each piece between 2 sheets of wax paper and chill in refrigerator until ready to use.

To cook, heat the butter and oil together in a skillet over high flame until bubbling, but do not allow to burn. Add chicken breasts and brown quickly on both sides. Cook an additional minute on each side and remove from heat. Warm Cognac in a small saucepan, set aflame, and pour, flaming, over chicken. When flame dies out, remove breasts to hot platter (preferably ovenproof glass), and keep warm. To the skillet, add the cream-egg mixture and, over low heat, stir until just thickened, making sure it does not boil. Correct seasoning; serve over chicken.

Aji de Gallina

[HOT-PEPPER CHICKEN]
Serves 4–6

This dish calls up many pleasant memories. After all, I was born in Lima, Peru, where AJI DE GALLINA is a traditional dish. Naturally, it is very popular there. It is really marvelous that I can make it in New York, dreaming nostalgically about my childhood. Of course, quite often I run into difficulties finding the exact ingredients for it, but there are substitutions that work very well in this recipe. Sometimes, when I cannot find fresh hot peppers, I dash to a gourmet shop in a research state of mind, and I always find a little can (around 4 ounces) of green chilies, or diced green chilies. I drain them and use them instead—with amazingly good results.

And speaking of fresh hot peppers, I volunteered my services one day in our kitchen back in Lima where the chef, a wise guy (I loved him), gave me the job of cleaning the hot peppers. But he forgot to tell me to dip my hands continually in salt or to use rubber gloves when cleaning the insides of these peppers. And, believe me, the next day I thought I was about to die. I couldn't touch anything without saying, "Ouch!" my skin burned so much. I certainly learned something about fresh peppers!

I enjoy this dish so much that I make it any time I have a chance—taking the necessary precautions—and give myself, as well as my friends, a luscious Peruvian treat. I usually start the day before I want to serve the meal so as to have time to prepare the peppers.

---

8 hot green peppers (or 4 ounces canned, seeded green chili peppers; or 2 tablespoons canned, diced chili peppers)
¾ cup olive or vegetable oil
Medium-large (5–6 pounds) chicken
1 thin slice commercial white bread
½ cup milk
¾ cup walnuts (preferably skinned), chopped
½ cup olive oil
2 cloves garlic
2 onions, chopped (1½ cups)
1 bay leaf
1½ teaspoons chili powder
2 tablespoons chopped parsley
1 teaspoon sweet basil
1½ teaspoons salt
½ teaspoon freshly ground black pepper
¼ cup chopped walnuts for garnish (optional)
Boiled potatoes
Hard-boiled eggs, shelled and halved

TO COOK CHICKEN
1 teaspoon salt
2 celery stalks
1 medium onion, peeled

2 cloves
1 bay leaf
4 sprigs parsley
6 peppercorns

---

*T*o prepare the peppers: If you use fresh hot peppers, roast 3 of them over open flame until some of the skin darkens. Allow to cool; cut lengthwise and remove all seeds. Cut the remaining 5 unroasted peppers lengthwise, remove all seeds; then, generously salt inside all the peppers. Place in a bowl and let stand 5–6 hours at room temperature, or, preferably, refrigerate overnight.

Wash peppers under cold running water, soak in a bowl of cold water for at least 1 hour. Drain, dry well and cut into small pieces. Pour ¼ cup of the olive oil into container of electric blender, add pepper pieces, and blend 1 to 2 minutes until they turn to a paste. Remove paste to a bowl and set aside.

If you use canned chilies, take right from the can; chop fine and set aside.

To cook the chicken: Put it into a large pot with water to cover, add salt, celery stalks, onion, cloves, bay leaf, parsley and peppercorns. Bring to a boil, reduce heat, cover and simmer until chicken is tender—about ½–¾ hour. Remove the chicken and reserve 1 cup of the broth. Separate the flesh from the bones; chop the skin finely; shred the meat and set it and skin aside.

Soak bread in milk. Place in container of electric blender and blend, gradually adding the ¾ cup walnuts. When all the walnuts have been added and blended, turn off blender and set mixture aside.

THE GREAT COOKS COOKBOOK

In a heatproof glass pan or skillet, heat the olive oil over medium heat. Add garlic, chopped onions, bay leaf and chili powder. Sauté until onions are soft. Add hot pepper mixture, parsley, sweet basil, salt, pepper, chopped chicken skin and shredded chicken. Stir ingredients together lightly as they cook for a few minutes, still over medium heat. Add reserved 1 cup chicken broth and, stirring now and then, cook uncovered for 10 or 15 minutes more. Add walnut mixture, combining well, and cook 3 to 5 minutes longer. Taste for additional salt.

Garnish with ¼ cup chopped walnuts. Serve over boiled potatoes, accompanied by halved, hard-cooked eggs.

Turkey

America's national emblem is the eagle. Perhaps it should have been the turkey. I am sure that he, himself, suffered great disappointment (maybe he wasn't handsome enough) and settled instead for the place of honor at the American table.

For many of us, it wouldn't be Thanksgiving or Christmas if the turkey did not make its corpulent appearance. Actually, this marvelous bird can be enjoyed at any time of year.

The turkey, wild or domestic, is a bird of excellent quality, and there is little difference between them. They differ mostly in size—the domestic turkey being larger—and in fat content; the wild turkey has minimal, if any, fat. The treatment of both birds is exactly the same when it comes to cooking them, but the wild turkey will cook faster.

Roast Turkey

For ample servings, allow 1 pound per person. (Cold turkey yields more servings per pound than hot turkey, since it can be better sliced, with less waste.)

Rub turkey inside and outside with cut side of a halved lemon, salt and freshly ground black pepper. The turkey can be stuffed or plain. Stuffings can be moist or dry, but must always be light and well seasoned.

There is a traditional family bread stuffing, that I, myself, am not crazy about. If you desire this kind of stuffing, do not use soggy bread. Sausage meat, sauerkraut or fruit can make excellent stuffings. Whatever stuffing you choose, always bear in mind these precautionary measures: for moist stuffings, prepare the liquid ingredients and refrigerate them; prepare the dry ingredients and store them at room temperature. Combine the two just before stuffing and roasting the bird.

Whether your turkey is stuffed or not, truss * it tightly before roasting. Rub with a generous amount of butter. Place on a rack in a roasting pan, breast-up. Allow 20 minutes per pound, roast in a preheated 350 F. oven; baste frequently with melted butter.

Or how about this for basting? In a saucepan, place 2 teaspoons of apricot jam and 1/3 cup pineapple juice and cook over low heat, stirring frequently, until jam is completely dissolved and sauce is well blended. Add 1/2 cup melted butter, stir well and remove from heat. It is then ready for use. A tablespoon of rum will also lend interest to this basting liquid; add it with the pineapple juice. Actually,

* See TRUSSING (page 131).

THE GREAT COOKS COOKBOOK

you can use any basting liquid you prefer, but baste frequently.

If your turkey is not stuffed, place 4–6 sprigs of parsley and 1 large onion in the cavity. If the turkey is browning too quickly, cover it either with aluminum foil or buttered wax paper. When the bird is done, remove from oven and allow to rest 20 to 30 minutes before carving, which makes carving easier.

VARIATIONS

1. Preheat oven to 425 F. Prepare turkey as just described (stuffed or plain). Butter turkey generously and lay strips of bacon across the breast. Place, breast-up, on a rack set in a roasting pan and roast for 15 minutes. Reduce heat to 375 F. and continue roasting, allowing 13 minutes per pound from the time the heat is reduced.

2. Preheat oven to 400 F. Prepare turkey as described (stuffed or plain). Truss * tightly and place slices of pork fat or bacon on breast, covering entirely. Wrap completely with cheesecloth soaked in melted butter. Place turkey breast-down on a rack set in a roasting pan, and roast for 20 minutes. Turn over. Continue roasting, turning the bird from side to side every 20 minutes; baste often with pan drippings or extra butter. Finish roasting breast-up. Allow 15 minutes per pound, over-all time.

* See page 131.

Roast Wild Turkey *
Serves 6–8

8–8½ pound turkey, cleaned and
    eviscerated
½ lemon
1 teaspoon salt

STUFFING
4 tablespoons butter
1 medium onion, finely chopped
½ cup finely chopped celery
1 cup raisins (soaked in warm water 5–10
    minutes, then drained)
¾ cup shelled, coarsely chopped pecans
4 cups soft bread crumbs
¼ cup chopped parsley
2 eggs
⅓ cup milk
½ teaspoon salt
¼ teaspoon freshly ground black pepper

* This can be done as happily with domestic turkey.

BASTING LIQUID
6 tablespoons butter, melted, then
    combined with 2 tablespoons white
    wine or vermouth

*R*emove all pinfeathers. Pass turkey over flame to singe off hairs. Wipe turkey inside and out with a wet cloth; dry thoroughly with paper towels. Rub cavity with the cut side of the lemon, then with salt. Set aside.

To prepare the stuffing: Melt the butter in a skillet, add onion and celery. Sauté over moderate heat, stirring occasionally, until vegetables are tender—about 5 minutes. Stir in the drained raisins and chopped pecans, tossing to moisten them in the butter. Transfer to large mixing bowl; add bread crumbs and parsley. In a small bowl, beat together the eggs, milk, salt, pepper; toss into ingredients in mixing bowl, lightly but thoroughly.

Preheat oven to 350 F. Fill cavity of the turkey with the stuffing (don't pack tightly); close by inserting a piece of aluminum foil, or sew the skin together with thread. If there is enough stuffing left (and there should be), fill the cavity of the neck, too, folding over the neck skin and securing it with a skewer. Cut away any excess skin.

Truss * the turkey. Brush the entire surface with BASTING LIQUID. If the skin browns too fast, cover with a piece of buttered brown paper or aluminum foil, but remove it 10 minutes before the bird is done.

Test for doneness by cutting into leg section where it joins breast; it should cut easily and the juices should run clear. Remove from oven, cut away trussing strings and let rest for at least 10 minutes—or for as long as 20 minutes—before carving.

* See page 131.

Turkey Florentine
Serves 4–6

5 tablespoons butter
3 tablespoons flour
1 cup milk
Drop or two of Tabasco
Salt and freshly ground black pepper
½ cup heavy cream
2 pounds fresh spinach, wilted; * or 3
    packages frozen spinach
¼ teaspoon nutmeg or cayenne
4 to 6 slices cooked turkey, breast meat
½ cup grated Gruyère or Swiss cheese
    (about 2 ounces)

* See page 134.

To MAKE SAUCE: Melt 3 tablespoons of the butter in a saucepan over low heat. When bubbling, add flour, stir with a wire whisk until well blended, and cook a second or two more. Warm the milk, add all at once to the butter-flour mixture. Stir vigorously with a wire whisk until sauce is thickened and smooth. Add the heavy cream, stirring well. Season with Tabasco, salt and pepper. Remove from heat and set aside.

Preheat broiler; put rack 5–6 inches from heat. Drain, then press all water from wilted fresh spinach and squeeze dry. (If using frozen spinach, defrost, drain and squeeze dry.) Heat remaining 2 tablespoons butter in a skillet; add spinach, nutmeg, salt and pepper to taste. Sauté for a few minutes. Add ½ cup of sauce; stir well. Remove from heat and, with a spoon, transfer sautéed spinach to a 10-inch ovenproof glass dish. Lay turkey slices on spinach, cover with remaining sauce. Sprinkle entire top with grated cheese and place in preheated broiler for 3 minutes or until cheese is slightly browned. Serve immediately, accompanied by white rice.

Duck

Duck is the most popular game bird, and understandably so. There are many varieties. Domestic ducks should be treated in the same manner as wild ducks.

I do prefer the wild duck; it is smaller and tastier. My favorites are the greenhead or mallard, teal, spoonbill, shoveler duck, the pintail and several others among this most varied species of game bird.

Duck, as opposed to other game, has remarkable amounts of fat. No fat should be added, and, in fact, during cooking you should try to release some of it.

Of course, crispness of the skin is one of the ideals cooks hope to achieve when cooking duck. It may sound like a big job, but it isn't. If you have planned long enough in advance on having duck, leave it washed and well dried in a warm spot in the kitchen overnight. The skin will tighten and feel like dry paper.

There are other ways of gaining the same result, such as putting the duck in direct sunlight, or blowing air over it with an electric fan until the skin dries to the texture just described. Either process will take approximately 2 hours, and the duck will be ready to cook.

Glazed Indian Duck

Serves 4–6

1 or 2 small ducks, cleaned and eviscerated
    (4–5 pounds total)
½ lemon
½ teaspoon thyme
Salt and freshly ground black pepper
4 tablespoons honey
1 tablespoon curry powder

ash duck and dry well. (See above.) Rub inside and out with cut side of lemon, dry thoroughly. Rub cavity of duck with thyme, and inside and out with salt and pepper. Place on a rack set in a roasting pan and roast in a preheated 325 F. oven for 35 minutes. With a fork, prick the entire surface to release fat, and continue roasting for 25 minutes.

Mix honey and curry powder until well combined. Remove duck from oven and brush well with some of honey-curry mixture. Return to oven and roast ½ hour longer, brushing with mixture every 10 minutes or so. (For well-done duck, roast 2 hours in all.) Serve at once, with rice.

Pepper Duck

Serves 4–6

2–3½ pound duck, cleaned and eviscerated
½ lemon
Salt
¼ cup freshly ground black pepper

Wash duck and dry well. Rub inside and out with cut side of lemon. Dry thoroughly.* Heat oven to 350 F. Sprinkle inside and out with salt, then rub salt in gently. Place duck on a rack in a roasting pan, and roast for 30 minutes, turning occasionally so that it browns evenly on all sides. Turn carefully so juices in duck do not run out. Prick breast of duck with fork to release the fat.

Spread ground black pepper over a sheet of wax paper. Remove duck from rack, and turn oven to 375 F. Pour off juice from inside duck and reserve for making sauce later. Breast-side-down, press duck firmly into pepper spread on wax paper. Return to rack, breast-side-up, and roast for 30 minutes, or longer, until duck skin is crisp.

While duck roasts, make the sauce.

SAUCE
1 orange
Reserved duck juice. Add enough chicken broth to make 1 cup

* See page 143.

1 teaspoon cornstarch
2 tablespoons brandy
Salt to taste

Without peeling orange, grate rind into bowl to make 1 teaspoonful; set aside. Peel orange; scrape away and discard all white pith. Section the orange; cut away and discard all white pith and pits. Set orange sections aside.

In a saucepan, combine reserved duck juice mixture with cornstarch, stirring until cornstarch is dissolved. Add brandy and cook over low heat, stirring frequently until thickened. Add grated orange rind and season with salt to taste. Bring sauce to boiling point, add orange sections and remove from heat. Keep warm. Serve on the side. Duck should remain crisp.

Along with duck, serve some boiled potatoes and something I like very much— PURÉE OF CELERY ROOT. Cut off and discard tops of celery roots. Peel and then wash roots. Cook in boiling salted water until tender. Drain; mash until smooth. Add hot melted butter. Taste; season with salt and a pinch of nutmeg. Keep warm in a double boiler.

Spit-Roasted Wild Duck

Serves 2

1 mallard duck, approximately 2½ pounds,
    cleaned and eviscerated
2 cups fresh orange juice
¼ cup olive oil
1 small onion, peeled and thinly sliced
¼ teaspoon dried thyme
¼ teaspoon freshly ground black pepper
⅛ teaspoon salt
1 teaspoon brandy

BASTING BUTTER
2 tablespoons melted butter
¼ teaspoon soy sauce
⅛ teaspoon salt
2 teaspoons brandy

Thoroughly wipe duck dry and re-move any long piece of neck skin. In a bowl wide and deep enough to hold the duck, combine the orange juice, olive oil, onion, thyme, pepper, salt and 1 teaspoon of brandy to make a marinade. Place the duck in it and, turning fre-quently, let it marinate at room tempera-ture for 1 hour (placing some of the marinade inside the duck, too). Remove duck, and let it drain, placed upright in a colander. Dry duck thoroughly. Reserve the marinade.

Preheat a rotisserie for 10 minutes or use a barbecue with a good bed of coals. Place duck on the spit, securing it with clamps, and set aside.

Prepare the BASTING BUTTER by com-bining in a small bowl the butter, soy sauce, salt and 1 teaspoon of the brandy. Brush entire surface of duck with the bast-ing butter. Set the duck into the rotisserie, placing a pan underneath to catch the drippings. As the bird turns, baste it fre-quently with the butter. Roast for 1 hour and 10 minutes, or until the skin is brown and glistening. If you have no more bast-ing butter, use the pan drippings to baste until the end of the roasting period.

About half an hour before the duck is done, pour the reserved marinade into a saucepan. Cook over moderate heat until it thickens and there is only ⅓–½ cupful left. Add remaining teaspoon of brandy; heat for a moment and strain the sauce (discarding the onions) into a heated sauceboat. Pass the sauce with the duck.

Goose

Goose always reminds me of Christmas back home in Peru. It's nice to have a little Christmas anytime, and goose is available all year round. In preparing goose, always consider the age of the bird. Young goose is tender and delicate, and excellent when roasted. On the other hand, an older goose—excellent in flavor—is rather tough, and should always be braised to tenderize it.

In Europe, older geese are exposed to winter cold before being cooked; this freezes the flesh and makes it tender. A goose is a very large bird, but don't let its size fool you. When cooked, goose releases tremendous amounts of fat. You should save the fat because it works beautifully in the preparation of many other dishes. It's great for sautéeing vegetables. As a matter of fact, it is good in many recipes where you would like to add a little extra flavor to the cooking oil.

A favorite French delicacy involves the use of goose neck. After removing the bones, the neck skin, which resembles hollow sausage casing, is tied at one end and stuffed with *pâté de foie gras* (goose liver pâté), then tied again. It is then sautéed in goose fat or sage butter, and served warm or at room temperature. Wow! What an experience!

Braised Goose

Serves 6–8

8–9 pound goose, cleaned and eviscerated
Salt and freshly ground black pepper
Goose neck, gizzard, liver and heart,
    chopped
2 cloves garlic
½ teaspoon dried sage, crushed
Salt
2 cups dry white wine
5–6 cups beef stock or bouillon, as needed

Heat broiler. Wash goose and wipe dry, inside and out. Pull lower fat from inside goose. Rub cavity with salt and pepper. Place goose in heat-resistant glass baking dish and slide into hot broiler not too close to the flame. Broil approximately 15–20 minutes, turning frequently to brown on all sides. Remove from broiler; save the fat drippings.

Heat oven to 350 F. Put 2 tablespoons of the fat drippings into a roasting pan large enough to hold the goose. (The pan must have a cover.) Add the gizzard, neck and heart, and sauté over moderate heat until lightly browned. Add garlic, sage, salt and wine. Stirring, over low heat, bring just to the boiling point. Put goose into the mixture in roasting pan; immediately, add enough beef stock to cover goose ¼-way-up. Still over low heat, bring to a simmer. Cover and place in preheated 350 F. oven for 2–2½ hours. While it cooks, either rotate from time to time or turn over at least twice. Goose is done when leg moves easily at joint and juices run clear yellow. Strain pan juices, skim off fat and serve juices as gravy.

Danish Roast Goose
Serves 6–8

1 goose liver, chopped
2 tablespoons Cognac
6–8 pound goose (ready to cook)
½ lemon
Salt and freshly ground black pepper
1 teaspoon ground sage
½ pound prunes
¼ cup (4 tablespoons) butter
½ cup chopped onions
3 cups tart apples peeled, cored and sliced
4 cups cooked chestnuts, chopped
½ cup coarsely chopped dried apricots
1 tablespoon chopped parsley
6–8 slices bacon

Place chopped liver in a small bowl and add the Cognac. Marinate 15 minutes, or until ready to use. Rub goose inside and out with the cut side of ½ lemon. Sprinkle inside and out with salt and pepper, but only inside with the sage. Set aside.

Plump prunes in a bowl of hot water

—15–30 minutes, drain, remove pits, chop prunes coarsely, measure out ¾ cup and set aside.

In a skillet over medium heat, heat butter, add onions and sauté until they are limp. Add goose liver and Cognac, cook 1 minute or less, stirring. Remove skillet from heat and add apples, chestnuts, apricots, prunes and parsley. Mix together well. Taste and correct seasoning with salt and pepper. Stuff goose with mixture. Close the cavity, and truss.*

Heat oven to 325 F. Put bacon in a saucepan and cook over low heat until it releases all of its fat. Discard bacon; soak cheesecloth in the bacon fat. Wrap fat-soaked cheesecloth entirely around the goose; place goose on a rack set in a roasting pan. Roast in preheated oven (basting frequently with any remaining bacon fat and the pan drippings) for 2½–3 hours, or until goose is tender and the joints move easily.

* See TRUSSING (page 131).

Pheasant

The most common type of hunting is probably for game birds. The pheasant, since ancient times, has been considered an exquisite and superb animal. Of the various types—the common pheasant, the silver pheasant, the golden pheasant and the China pheasant—the ones usually eaten are the common and China pheasant; the others are mainly ornamental.

Imaginative cooks and chefs everywhere have developed fantastic creations with pheasant. Consequently, there are a number of approaches to preparation and cooking of the bird. One, for example, is waiting to cook and eat it for at least one or two days after it has been killed. As a matter of fact, people who are really "into" pheasant will hang it, without eviscerating, for as long as a week or more. They claim this allows the bird to reach its peak in quality and develop a unique taste which they describe as a cross between poultry and venison. Another claim is that pheasant should not be plucked immediately because the oil in the feathers, when absorbed by the skin, adds flavor.

Baked, braised, or cooked in any other way, served hot or cold, pheasant is always exciting. Even commercially frozen birds are a treat, and can be cooked like any domestic bird with excellent results.

Pheasant with Grapes
Serves 4

2 pheasants, each about 2½ pounds
½ teaspoon salt
¼ teaspoon black pepper, preferably freshly ground
¼ pound sliced bacon, cut in 1-inch pieces
¼ pound (½ cup) butter
1 yellow onion, peeled and finely chopped
1 clove garlic, peeled and crushed
1½ cups white seedless grapes (just less than ½ pound), stems removed
1 tablespoon brandy
Watercress

Rinse pheasants inside and out and dry thoroughly. Rub both birds inside and out with salt and pepper. Loosely tie together the legs of each bird. (If legs are not tied, they stick up as they begin to brown, which makes it very hard to brown lower part of breast.)

In a large skillet, place the cut-up pieces of bacon and, over moderate heat, stirring occasionally, let them cook until crisp. Remove the bacon bits from the pan with a slotted spoon and place in a large mixing bowl. Pour off all but 2 tablespoons of bacon fat from the pan; add 4 tablespoons or half of the butter and, when it sizzles, add the onions and garlic and sauté for about 5 minutes or until onions become translucent. Remove onions with slotted spoon, combine with bacon in mixing bowl. Thoroughly toss the grapes with onions and bacon; set aside.

At this point you divide the fat remaining in the skillet, pouring half of it into another skillet, so that you can brown both birds at the same time, turning the birds frequently with a spatula or tongs until they are evenly browned all over. This will take about 10 minutes. If you have only one pan, you'll find it's easier to brown one at a time, setting the first bird aside while you brown the other.

Preheat the oven to 375 F. for 15 minutes. When the birds are cool enough to handle (a matter of about 5 minutes), cut away the string from the legs; divide the onion-garlic-grape stuffing in two equal parts and fill the cavities of both birds. Then truss * each bird. Handle them carefully or the stuffing will fall out. If trussing is too difficult, at least tie the legs together.

Quickly melt the remaining 4 tablespoons butter in a small saucepan and stir in the brandy. Place the birds breast-side-up on a rack set in a glass-ceramic roaster, and brush them with the brandy-butter. Basting frequently, roast the pheasants for 45 to 50 minutes. (To baste, I first use a brush and later a bulb-baster.) After 45 minutes, insert a thermometer into the breast; when it reads 160 F., the pheasants are done. Remove trussing strings. Scoop out some of the grape stuffing onto dinner plates; halve pheasants with carving knife or poultry shears, and lay each half alongside stuffing. Garnish with watercress and serve at once. Each pheasant serves two.

* See TRUSSING (page 131).

Pheasant in Madeira Sauce

Serves 2—amply

One 2–3 pound pheasant, cleaned and eviscerated, washed and dried thoroughly
1 pheasant liver, washed and dried
½ lemon
Salt and freshly ground black pepper
1 bay leaf
1 clove garlic
4–6 sprigs parsley
4 slices bacon
Melted butter, approximately 1 pound
1 teaspoon cornstarch

1 cup chicken broth
3 tablespoons butter
¼ cup (approximately) Madeira
Salt

Preheat oven to 350 F. Rub pheasant inside and out with cut side of ½ lemon, then sprinkle inside and out with salt and pepper. Place in cavity the bay leaf, garlic and parsley. Truss * very tightly.

* See page 131.

Chop pheasant liver fine. Set aside to use in sauce preparation.

Cover breast with the bacon slices. Cut cheesecloth large enough to wrap the bird entirely. Soak it thoroughly in melted butter, then either wrap it completely around the bird (the cloth will adhere to itself), or just spread over the bird. Place pheasant, breast-up, on a rack set in a roasting pan and roast for 30 minutes, or 13 minutes per pound. Baste frequently with melted butter while it roasts; when done, remove cheesecloth, trussing strings and bacon strips. Transfer bird to heated platter and keep warm.

To prepare the sauce, dissolve corn-starch in ½ cup of the chicken broth. Set aside. Skim excess fat from roasting pan; place it with its juices over low heat and add the 3 tablespoons butter. When butter melts, add the chopped liver and, stirring, sauté for a second or two. Don't overcook. Add the remaining chicken broth, bring to a boil, scraping up and stirring in all the browned bits from the bottom of the pan. Lower the heat and add the cornstarch-chicken-broth-mixture, stirring constantly until thickened. Stir in Madeira, bring to boiling point and serve along with the pheasant. If desired, serve pheasant on a bed of rice, accompanied by sauce.

Quail

Squabs, pigeons and guinea hens are all relatives of the quail, varying in size but having similar qualities; all can be handled in the same fashion.

Quail Flambé

Serves 2–4 depending on appetite

½ lemon
4 quail, each about 6 ounces, cleaned and eviscerated; wiped with a damp cloth
1 teaspoon salt
Freshly ground black pepper (about ¼ teaspoon)
2 tablespoons butter
2 tablespoons pork fat
⅓ cup brandy
1 tablespoon pistachio nuts, shelled and chopped

Cut the ½ lemon into 4 pieces; use a separate piece to rub the inside of each bird. Rub inside of each one with salt—about ⅛ teaspoon per bird. Finish seasoning by rubbing the outside of each quail with salt (again, about ⅛ teaspoon, or less, per bird) and the pepper. Tie the legs of each quail together and, if possible, turn the wings back and over themselves. Set aside.

Preheat oven to 375 F. In a large skillet or sauté pan, heat the butter and pork fat together until it foams. Place the 4 birds in the pan and, over moderate heat, sauté on all sides, turning them frequently until the skin is a uniform golden brown. This will take about 10–12 minutes.

Place the browned birds on a rack set in a small roasting pan and roast for 20 to 25 minutes, basting often with the fat from the skillet. (You will probably not use all the fat for the basting, but leave it in the pan; you'll need it to make the sauce.) After roasting for 20–25 minutes, the breasts will feel firm. If the first time you prepare the dish you feel you must test, do so by cutting into one of the quail where the legs join the breast; it should cut easily and there will be no trace of pink. However, I don't think it will be necessary to test! Take pan from oven, remove trussing strings, and keep birds warm.

On top of the range, over medium heat, cook the fat remaining in the skillet along with any juices from the roasting pan. Place the quail in the pan; add the brandy; heat for a moment, then ignite the liquid. Shake the pan so the flames rise dramatically over the birds. When the flame dies out, serve the birds on a small heated platter. Pour the pan juices over them, and sprinkle evenly with chopped pistachio nuts. Depending upon appetites, these serve two or four.

Broiled Quail

Serves 4

4 quail, cleaned, eviscerated; wiped with a
    damp cloth
½ lemon
1 teaspoon lemon rind
½ teaspoon dry mustard
Salt and freshly ground pepper
Softened butter

With a sharp knife or poultry shears, cut quail open down the back. Spread out, skin-side-up, and press down on breast bone, flattening into butterfly shape. Preheat broiler. Turn wings back and over themselves. Rub birds inside and out with cut side of ½ lemon; sprinkle with lemon rind, then the mustard, salt and pepper. Spread generously with softened butter, and place birds, skin-side-down, in broiling pan. Broil about 5 inches from flame for 5 to 6 minutes. Turn birds over; quickly dot surface with bits of softened butter and continue to broil for 5 to 6 minutes, or until tender and browned. Garnish with chopped parsley. Serve with wild rice, if desired.

THE GREAT COOKS COOKBOOK

Hare or Rabbit

Wild hare or rabbit, or domestic rabbit, can all be cooked in the same way. They are at their best when 7–8 months old, when they are tender, plump and fully grown. The rabbit is a very popular game food in Europe, Canada, Mexico and South America. Squirrel, which is a cousin, should be treated and prepared in the same fashion.

Braised Hare or Rabbit
Serves 4–6

5–5½ pound hare (or rabbit) skinned and eviscerated; washed and dried

MARINADE
2 cups dry white wine
1¼ cups oil (I use corn oil)
1 medium-size yellow onion, peeled and thinly sliced
1 carrot, peeled and thinly sliced
1 clove garlic, peeled and crushed (or finely minced)
1 teaspoon salt
½ teaspoon dried tarragon, crushed or crumbled
1 bay leaf, broken into small pieces

BRAISING LIQUID AND SAUCE
2 tablespoons vegetable oil
6 tablespoons butter
2½ cups chicken broth
2 tablespoons flour
½ cup heavy cream
2 tablespoons finely chopped parsley

Cut up the hare in the following manner: with a sharp boning knife —or with a cleaver, if you wish— cut the hare in half lengthwise. Either remove the backbone completely, or leave it attached to one side of the hare. Leaving all four legs intact, disjoint and then sever them from the trunk of the hare. Slice apart the loin and rib sections of each side of the hare. You will have 8 pieces in all. Set aside.

In a large glass bowl (preferably with a cover), combine the marinade ingredients. Place the hare in the bowl; toss the pieces in the marinade; cover, and marinate for at least 1 hour, or as long as 4 hours, whichever is convenient. Turn the pieces every once in a while—when you think of it or at half hour intervals. When marinated, remove the pieces, scrape off any seasonings adhering to them, and dry thoroughly. Discard the marinade.

In a large frying pan (it must have a cover), heat the oil and butter until it sizzles. Add as many pieces of hare as you can without crowding the pan; turn them over after a few minutes, and continue sautéeing until the skin on all sides is light brown. (You may have to brown the hare in 2, or even 3, batches depending on the size of the pan; or use 2 pans, dividing the fat between them.) When all the pieces are browned, return to the pan—or put them into a heavy 4–5-quart ovenproof glass casserole which has a cover. Pour in 2 cups of the chicken broth; cover with lid and, over low heat, let the hare braise (just simmer) for 1 hour and 45 minutes, or even 2 hours, until the meat is tender when pierced with a fork. Transfer the pieces to a heated platter.

Quickly, combine a little of the remaining 1/2 cup chicken broth with the flour until it dissolves; add rest of broth, pass through strainer and stir into the juices in the pan. Continue stirring until the sauce thickens and all taste of flour is gone. Stir in the cream and continue to cook for a minute or so until the cream is just heated through. Pour sauce over the hare, sprinkle with parsley and serve immediately.

Hare or Rabbit with 40 Cloves of Garlic

Serves 8

5–5½-pound hare or rabbit, skinned and eviscerated, sectioned into 8 serving pieces
¾ cup peanut oil
2 tablespoons butter
2 medium onions, sliced
6 stalks celery, cut in *julienne* *
2 large carrots, peeled and cut in *julienne* *
1 fennel, cut into 8 slices
6 to 8 sprigs parsley
½ cup Madeira or dry white wine
40 cloves garlic, peeled
2 teaspoons salt
1 teaspoon dried tarragon
1 bay leaf
Pepper, freshly ground, to taste
Dough

* Thin, matchlike strips.

Wash and dry rabbit well. Place peanut oil in shallow dish or a plate, and turn hare or rabbit in it until well coated on all sides. Set aside.

In a heavy casserole which has a lid (preferably glass-ceramic, and large enough to hold the rabbit and vegetables), put the butter, onions, celery, carrots, fennel, parsley, Madeira or white wine, and 10 cloves of the garlic. Place pieces of rabbit or hare in a layer over the vegetables; sprinkle with some of the salt and tarragon, and 10 more cloves of the garlic. Layer again with rabbit; season with more salt and tarragon, some of the pepper, and 10 more cloves of garlic. Repeat process with remaining rabbit and seasonings, ending with rabbit, salt, pepper, tarragon and garlic. Place the bay leaf on top.

Heat oven to 375 F. Cover tightly, and seal together the edges of casserole and lid with a paste made of flour and enough cold water added to make it soft and pliable.

Bake for 1½ hours without removing lid throughout cooking time.

Serve from casserole with French bread.

Venison

Venison, the meat from any kind of deer, is, like beef, aged or hung at least 2 to 4 weeks before cooking. Roast of venison made with the tough part of the deer—the leg or thigh, for example—must be larded with strips of pork fat or salt pork and marinated. In fact, for best results, all less tender parts of venison should be marinated before cooking.

If you are going to make steaks, cook them in generous amounts of butter or oil. But the saddle of young venison—which I prefer because of its delicacy and tenderness—should be roasted quickly in a very hot oven, and to have it at its best, cooked only to the rare stage.

Saddle of Venison
Serves 4–6

5–6 pound saddle of venison
½ teaspoon dried thyme
Salt and freshly ground black pepper
Salt pork, cut into 8 or 10 thin slices
¼ cup fresh orange juice
3 tablespoons currant jelly
2 tablespoons Cognac

Heat oven to 450 F. Wipe the meat well with a damp cloth. Rub the entire surface of the saddle with thyme, salt and pepper. Place on a rack set in a glass-ceramic roaster and cover the entire top of the saddle with the slices of salt pork. Put into oven and roast, uncovered, for 45 minutes to 1 hour, or until a thermometer inserted into it reads 145 F.

Remove and discard salt-pork strips remaining on the meat and transfer roast to a heated platter. Keep hot. With a spoon, skim off and discard excess fat in the roasting pan. Place pan over heat and add the orange juice, scraping up and stirring in any drippings adhering to the bottom of the pan. Still stirring, bring to a boil, and add the currant jelly, mixing in well. Pour in the Cognac and flame the sauce. Serve immediately with the venison. If you wish, you may serve the roast saddle with sautéed mushrooms.

Roast Venison

Serves 6–8

MEAT

6–7 pound rump of venison
½ pound pork fat, cut in strips about
⅓ x 6 inches long (lardons)
½ pound salt pork, thinly sliced

MARINADE FOR THE PORK FAT—LARDONS

½ teaspoon salt
½ teaspoon pepper
1 clove garlic, crushed
1 tablespoon parsley
2 tablespoons rum

MARINADE FOR THE VENISON

2 cups beef bouillon or stock
2 cups red wine
⅓ cup vegetable oil
1 large onion, peeled and sliced
1 carrot, peeled and sliced
2 ribs celery, including green tops, sliced
2 cloves garlic, peeled and crushed
1 teaspoon salt
10 peppercorns, crushed
Salt and pepper

SAUCE

1 cup beef stock
⅛ teaspoon dried thyme
1½ tablespoons flour
1 cup heavy cream

Prepare the marinade for the larding fat by combining all ingredients in a small bowl. Toss the strips (lardons) in the marinade and leave for an hour—or for as long as 4 hours, if it is convenient. Remove the lardons from the marinade and chill in refrigerator for 20 minutes to facilitate the larding.

To lard the roast: Place a chilled lardon in the groove of a larding needle and insert the tip of the needle into the meat. Moving the needle with a rolling motion of your wrist, gradually penetrate the meat. Place your thumb on lardon and hold it there as you withdraw needle, leaving lardon in its place. Repeat this procedure with the remaining lardons, studding the rump at 1-inch intervals. (The more larding the better the taste, and the more attractive the roast.)

Prepare the marinade for the venison, combining all the ingredients in a large glass bowl, just large enough to hold the meat and marinade. Place the larded venison in the marinade. Cover with plastic wrap and marinate in refrigerator for at least 48 hours—even another 24 hours, if possible—turning the meat about in the marinade at least several times each day.

Preheat oven to 400 F. Drain the meat and dry it thoroughly. Drain the marinated vegetables and make a bed of them in the bottom of a glass-ceramic roasting pan just large enough to hold the meat. Salt and pepper the roast; place on the vegetables; then, cover with the strips of sliced salt pork, securing them with toothpicks if they won't stay in place. Roast the meat for 20 minutes; reduce heat to 325 F., and continue roasting for about 50 minutes more, or until thermometer placed in center of meat reads 140 F., or until roast is browned on the outside and pink when cut. After the first 15 minutes of roasting, baste with the fat accumulated in pan. Continue to baste (about every 15 minutes) until roast is done. Remove the roast; let it rest on its serving platter for about 10 minutes while you prepare the sauce.

Pour off all but 2 tablespoons of the fat from the roasting pan. Add the beef stock and the thyme and stir to combine the brown bits that cling to the pan and the vegetables. Cook for 2 or 3 minutes, or until the stock boils. Strain the sauce, pressing the vegetables against the strainer to get all the juices before discarding them. Pour sauce back into pan.

Quickly combine the flour and cream; mix thoroughly and stir into strained sauce. Return to stove and, over moderate heat, whisk without interruption until the sauce thickens. Pour into heated sauceboat. Serve the venison immediately, spooning some sauce over each serving; accompany with red currant jelly.

Wines for Poultry and Game

ALEXIS BESPALOFF

A familiar wine and food rule is "white wine with chicken, red wine with game." This rule is not universally acknowledged, however: in Burgundy, chicken would more likely be accompanied by a red wine; and along the Rhine, a rich white wine is the traditional partner of game dishes. Certainly, if you prefer white wine to red, you will want to serve a light white wine with something as simple and delicate as a poached chicken, and a bigger white wine with a dish that is spicy or otherwise distinctly flavored. (A number of light and full white wines are described after the chapter, ABOUT FISH AND SEAFOOD.)

On the other hand, many wine enthusiasts would claim that nothing sets off the flavor of a fine and subtle red Bordeaux as well as roast chicken. Even if you normally serve red wine with poultry, you may nevertheless prefer wines more robust than Bordeaux to accompany chicken prepared with tomatoes or highly flavored.

Game, which has a distinct flavor of its own, calls for wines with body and character. Even more important than the style of wine, however, is the quality. Game dishes are rather special, not served often, and add a measure of excitement to any dinner. You should therefore plan to bring out as fine a bottle of red wine as you can afford. Traditionally, this would be a bottle from Bordeaux or Burgundy, although nowadays there are also some remarkable wines to be found from California, as well as from Italy and Spain.

In Bordeaux, there are about eighty vineyards which have achieved a special reputation for producing some of the very best wines of the world. These vineyards —always referred to as châteaux—are situated in the districts of St. Emilion, Pomerol, Graves and the Médoc, which in turn includes the communes of Margaux, St. Julien, Pauillac and St. Estèphe. Among the best known of these châteaux are Mouton-Rothschild, Latour, Haut-Brion, Ducru-Beaucaillou, Pichon-Lalande, Léoville-Lascases, Lascombes, Montrose, Palmer, Talbot, Beychevelle, Figeac, Vieux-Château-Certan, and Haut-Bailly. The label of each of these wines will bear—along with the name of the château—that of one of the districts or communes of origin listed above.

There are excellent Burgundies made in such villages of the Côte de Nuits and Côte de Beaune as Gevrey-Chambertin, Chambolle-Musigny, Vosne-Romanée, Nuits-Saint-Georges, Aloxe-Corton, Pommard and Volnay. Even finer and more expensive Burgundies come from individual vineyards. Among the most famous are Chambertin, Musigny, Clos Vougeot, Romanée-Conti, La Tâche, Richebourg, Grands-Echezeaux and Corton. Wines from the best vineyards of Bordeaux and Burgundy are quite expensive, of course; but there are occasions when you may be tempted to try one of them to complement the food you have prepared.

The finest red wines of California are those labeled Cabernet Sauvignon, which is the name of the grape from which they are primarily made. More than fifty wineries market a Cabernet Sauvignon wine, so that there is a wide range of quality and price. Some of the best examples, produced in limited quantities, are even harder to find than a fine Bordeaux or Burgundy.

Another possibility to consider when you are looking for a fine bottle of red wine is a Barolo, Gattinara or Barbaresco from the Piedmont region, in northern Italy. Some Chiantis labeled *riserva*—which means they have been aged for at least three years—are also excellent, and quite different in style from the lighter wines available in straw-covered *fiaschi*. The specially aged *reservas* produced in the Rioja district of Spain can also be excellent, and are often good value as well.

Most of us cannot drink the world's finest wines often; but game dishes do offer one opportunity to bring out a very good bottle.

About Meat

Man is a meat-eating animal, and meat is the very staff of life to most of us. When we plan a meal, whether simple or elaborate, the very first thing we consider is the meat course. Other courses—soup, vegetables, salad, dessert—are then chosen to complement the *pièce de résistance*. Most families feel that it just isn't dinner if meat in some form is not included. Meat has better flavor and texture than many other protein foods—soybeans, for instance.

The primary definition of meat, as given by lexicographers, is "food in general; anything eaten for nourishment." We speak of nutmeats, sweetmeats, the meat of various fruits, and so on. This usage can only have come to be because of general acceptance of the fact that man has become to a great extent dependent upon meat.

Meat seems (and is) expensive because it costs more to produce. It takes plenty of room to raise animals for meat, and as population density increases, meat production decreases, and so does meat consumption. In America, North and South, we eat considerably more meat than the inhabitants of Europe and Asia, simply because we have more room. In Australia, where there is plenty of room but little grass, sheep are the natural source of meat, for they can survive and prosper where beef cannot. Consequently, Australians and New Zealanders consume more lamb than anyone else; they also have a surplus which they ship to America and Europe. In Argentina, there are miles of lush grasslands upon which beef may fatten, so beef is a great export as well as being the most popular food. In the U.S.A., we raise much beef and lamb, but we are the number-one pork eaters, and pork is usually cheaper than other meats, for hogs are omnivorous and do not require vast stretches of pasture land. As our open spaces fill up—as indeed they must—we will become even more dependent upon pork as a source of meat protein.

Scientific breeding and feeding have pretty well streamlined meat production. The grower knows the exact moment when his steers, lambs or hogs have achieved their optimum size and weight and are ready to go to market. Generally, animals have less fat in proportion to lean meat and are uniform in size. Any variation in this pattern costs more and is more difficult to market, whether it is young white veal or those old-time, enormous T-bone steaks, tiny lambs or real mutton, or pork tenderloins weighing 3 or 4 pounds as called for in many recipes in older cookbooks. Such gustatory delights have been driven out of the market by a passion for standardization.

Travelers to France, Germany, Italy and Spain are regaled with veal dishes which are glorious. Upon their return they wonder why real, honest white veal cannot be found except for a price resembling that of diamonds. In Europe, young animals are used because there is a shortage of pasturage, and the milk of the mothers is needed for cheese and *crème fraîche*. Here there is still room to bring the calves up to beef size, which means more profit per pound of feed. So while the demand for veal exists, the supply is limited to a few specialty producers. Most of that veal ends up in the restaurant trade.

Since the nineteenth century, beef producers have been improving the breed to produce a higher ratio of meat per animal. The famed Texas longhorns, the prototypes of American cattle, have become progressively shorter of leg, thicker of body, by crossbreeding with English Herefords, Scottish Angus, French Charolais, Italian Chianina, and other fast-growing varieties. They are range-raised up to a point, then given the final finishing fattening in pens until they have reached the optimum weight. Consequently, when dressed, there is little or no variation, and a million strip steaks will vary by less than an ounce in market weight. Progress? I suppose so, but I often long for one of those platter-filling steaks of yore. The same holds true for lamb and pork—lambs are neither tiny ones, nor are they mutton; pork is so uniform that even so-called suckling pigs are all but impossible to find under 20 pounds. Despite my complaining, Americans in general have the best meat available anywhere. It is so superior that we ship it to many other countries and we can never ship enough to satisfy the demand of those gastronomes who demand the very finest.

About Beef

Beef is by all odds the most popular of all meats, no matter what it may cost. During the great meat crisis of 1973, although other meats were available, the customers demanded beef, and a sort of black market immediately came into being. For no matter what the cut—tenderloin or chuck—beef has flavor and texture that appeals to almost everyone, and it is easy to cook. The classic cuisine lists literally hundreds of ways to prepare steaks, for example; but the differences in the various dishes exist in their garnishes and sauces, rather than in the cooking of the meat itself. The same holds true with the so-called "lesser" cuts. The actual preparation of stews and pot roasts is generally the same—it is what goes along with the meat that makes the difference. The basic rule is: simplicity for the meat, any amount of complexity for the seasonings and sauces.

Broiled Flank Steak

Serves 3–4

Let's begin with FLANK STEAK, a long, lean, thin piece of muscle from the belly of the steer. It weighs about 1½ pounds from today's uniform animals, and has very little fat; its average thickness is about ½ inch. To my way of thinking, it is best broiled quickly, until brown on the outside, rare and juicy within. Under a hot oven broiler or over a hot bed of coals, it will take about 3 minutes on each side—more than that and it may become dry, tough and stringy. When done properly, it is moist and tender, and is the famous dish, London broil. Before broiling, it may be brushed with a little oil or melted butter; before carving, a good piece of butter should be melting on top.

To carve, use a thin-bladed, very sharp slicing knife, and cut across the meat with the blade at a 20-degree angle to the surface of the meat. The slices will be about 3 inches in width, and should be very thin, and there will be enough for three slices for each of 3 to 4 guests. Spoon over some of the prolific juices that will have accumulated in the well of the carving platter or board. Salt and pepper, the only seasonings required, may be added by the diners at their own discretion. It is one of the best cuts of beef imaginable, and as more and more people have found out about it, its price has risen considerably; but flank steak is still one of the best buys in beef. It can also be prepared the old-fashioned way:

Stuffed Braised Flank Steak

Serves 3–4

1 flank steak, about 1½ pounds
½ medium onion, finely chopped
4 tablespoons butter
1 teaspoon dried orégano
½ teaspoon salt
Freshly ground black pepper
½ cup finely chopped cooked ham
1 cup fresh, soft bread crumbs
1 egg
½ cup chopped parsley
Flour, seasoned with salt and pepper
2 tablespoons butter

1 cup beef broth
1 cup dry red wine
1 clove whole garlic, peeled

Score flank steak, or pound with a tenderizing mallet and set aside. Over medium heat and in a flame-proof casserole that has a cover, sauté the onion in 4 tablespoons butter until soft but not colored; add seasonings, ham and crumbs and mix well. Take off the heat. Beat egg lightly and add, along with the parsley, combining well. Spread the mixture over the flank steak and roll up from the long side, like a jelly roll, fastening with skewers or tying with white string. Dredge lightly with seasoned flour.

Over high heat, melt 2 tablespoons butter in the casserole (cleaned, first, if necessary) and quickly brown the steak roll on all sides. Add the broth, wine and garlic; bring to a boil; turn heat down; cover and simmer until meat is tender—about 1 hour.

To serve, remove string or skewers and cut into slices about ½-inch thick. Pour sauce remaining in pan into a serving boat or bowl and pass separately.

About Round Steak

As its name indicates, ROUND STEAK is round in shape; it is cut from the hind leg of the steer, just below the hip joint. When "full-cut," it contains a round section of the leg bone; when divided into "top" or "bottom" round, the bone is discarded. Although customarily cut 1 to 2 inches thick, it also is often cut into roasts, 5 or more inches thick, which go by a variety of names—Denver, Omaha, Diamond Jim and so on, at the whim of the meat dealer. In nearly all cases, cuts from the round are most suited for braising—long, slow cooking with plenty of moisture. Perhaps the most popular of all dishes made with round steak is what we call Swiss steak, where flour and seasonings are pounded into both sides of the meat, which is then browned, and finally simmered slowly with liquid and vegetables. The famous Flemish CARBONNADE is, for me, the best version of this dish.

Carbonnade of Beef
Serves 4

2 pounds boneless round steak
½ cup flour
1 tablespoon salt
Freshly ground pepper
1 teaspoon dried thyme
2 large onions, sliced
6 tablespoons butter or

oil (or 3 tablespoons each)
1 clove garlic, crushed
1½ cups beer
½ cup tomato juice
1 bay leaf
Minced fresh parsley

ith the back of a cleaver or the edge of a plate, pound into both sides of the steak a mixture of the flour, salt, pepper and thyme; cut steak into cubes.

In a deep glass-ceramic pan with a cover, cook the onions in 4 tablespoons of butter and/or oil until they are soft; re-

move from casserole and reserve.

Add remaining butter or oil to casserole; add meat and garlic, and brown thoroughly. Add the onions, beer, tomato juice and bay leaf. Bring to a boil, lower heat, cover, and simmer until tender—about 1½ hours. Discard bay leaf, correct seasoning; sprinkle with minced parsley.

About Rump

Moving onward and upward, we come to the rump, a very lean piece of meat, roughly triangular in section. If it is Prime Grade and well aged, it may be roasted rare, or steaks cut from it may be broiled. If Choice Grade, as most market rump is, it is better braised—as a pot roast, boiled beef—or cut up for a most delightful stew. Being very lean, it should have fat added, either as larding (strips of fat

pushed through the meat) or as barding (a blanket of fat tied around the outside), and even then great care must be taken lest it become dry in the cooking. Like other less tender cuts of beef, rump has superb flavor; unlike many others, it is close-grained and firm in texture, making it admirable for serving cold. For a splendid addition to a cold buffet try:

Sliced Beef with Oranges
Serves 8–10

4 pounds boneless rump
1 tablespoon salt
1 bay leaf
2 cloves garlic, crushed
1 onion, quartered
1 teaspoon coriander seeds
2 juice oranges, washed
½ cup orange juice
½ cup olive oil

ut beef in a pot (it must have a cover) just a little larger than the piece of meat. Cover with cold water, add the salt, and bring to a boil. Skim carefully; add bay leaf, garlic, onion and coriander seeds, lightly crushed. Reduce heat; cover and barely simmer until meat is tender—about 2 hours. Remove from stove; let cool in the stock.

When cool, slice thin and arrange on a

deep platter. Slice oranges very thin, skin and all, and lay over meat. Mix orange juice and olive oil and pour over (if there is not enough to cover the meat, add more of both ingredients). Marinate for 24 hours in the refrigerator before serving.

About Loin

Forward we go, to the sirloin and the short loin, the sources of the great steaks which are the most sought-after of all beef cuts. Many people regard the top sirloin as the king of steaks (I am one of them). Others prefer the loin strip and/or the tenderloin. These cuts should be cooked and served rare for best flavor and texture, and when properly prepared there are no better cuts of beef. Because they are in great demand they are expensive and, for that reason, are often reserved for special occasions. My friend James Beard has come up with a great recipe for reducing the cost and adding interest to the final product. I serve it often, but only to those who love rare beef. It is called

Stuffed Butterfly Steak
Serves 4–8

4 boneless loin strip steaks cut ¾-inch thick (or 2 boneless top sirloin steaks)
1 pound very lean ground beef
1 cup finely chopped parsley (1 bunch, fresh)
1 cup chopped shallots or green onions
1½ teaspoons salt
1 teaspoon freshly ground black pepper
1 tablespoon capers (optional)
Cognac, 1 jigger (optional)

Lay the steaks flat on a board and carefully, cutting parallel to the board, split them in half almost all the way through so that they may be opened to look like the outstretched wings of a butterfly. Mix together the ground beef, parsley, shallots, salt, pepper and capers. Thickly spread one opened side of each steak with this mixture, then press the two sides together evenly. Sauté, pan-broil or grill the steaks quickly so that the filling is just heated through—the meat should be brown on the outside. The steaks will grill, but it will be easier to sauté or pan-broil them, using a spatula and fork to turn them over. When done, they may be flamed with Cognac, if you like, and served with a Sauce Bordelaise. Or simply top the hot steaks with Maître d'hôtel butter, and serve. Depending upon what accompanies them, they may be cut in two (the sirloins in four) for ample servings.

About Porterhouse and T-Bone

Farther up the line, we encounter the Porterhouse and T-bone steaks, which are among the favorites in this country, and which need no admonitions from me except that, for best results, they should be cooked simply and rare. A nice presentation is to grill the steak—about 3 inches from meat to heat in oven broiler; cut both sides from the bone and slice them thin (allow ½ pound per serving); then reconstruct the steak before presenting it. For a real old-fashioned American touch, cover the cooked steak with smothered onions or mushrooms.

About Prime Rib

Before reaching the shoulder (or chuck) of the critter, we come to the king of roasts, the Prime Rib. This great piece of meat has been the legendary holiday cut in England for generations, and is rapidly achieving the same status here. When you buy one for a dinner party, a 10-pound prime rib will amply serve 10; for a family-size roast, allow ½ pound per person. Have your butcher remove the feather bone and the "strap" (the tendon which lies just below the top); the large end of the chine bone should be cut off. Then the exposed end of the meat should be covered with a blanket of fat, tied in place.

To properly roast a standing rib, a meat thermometer is a necessity. Preheat the oven to 450 F., put in the roast and cook for 15 minutes. Reduce the heat to 350 F. and cook until done to your liking —my liking is 115 F. internal temperature, with the thermometer inserted into thickest part of meat—but not touching bone. If your roast is taken out of the refrigerator just before you put it into the oven, it is going to take longer to cook than if you had let it come up to room temperature beforehand.

If you prefer your beef well done, you're wasting your money buying a standing rib roast; you'd be better off with rump or chuck.

Carve the finished roast in thin slices, having the meat either standing on the ribs or lying on its side. I prefer the latter.

BEEF CUTS

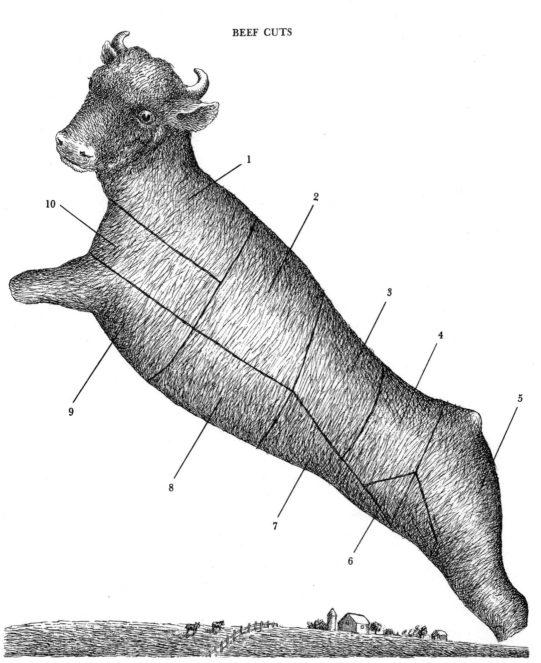

1. Chuck: stew, pot roast, ground beef; 2. Rib: roast, steaks, short ribs; 3. Short Loin: steaks and tenderloin (filet mignon and Chateaubriand) ; 4. Sirloin: steaks; 5. Round: steaks, rolled roast, cubed steak, eye of round roast, ground beef; 6. Tip-kabobs, stew; 7. Flank: steak, ground beef; 8. Plate: short ribs, stew, ground beef; 9. Shank and Brisket: stew, soup meat; 10. Shoulder: pot roast, chuck and short ribs.

Serve it with horseradish sauce (1 cup sour cream mixed with 2 or more tablespoons of prepared white horseradish, drained, a teaspoon of salt) and/or with red currant jelly. Yorkshire pudding is good also.

About Lamb

In today's market, it is difficult, if not impossible, to find a leg of lamb weighing under 5½ or 6 pounds, for it is not economically feasible to slaughter smaller animals. However, the leg you buy will usually have the sirloin (large loin) chops at the big end; these may be cut off for another meal. (When boned and skewered, they are sometimes called "Saratoga Chops.") Not long ago, leg of lamb was the favorite Sunday dinner in many American households, sharing honors with roast chicken. Nowadays, even Sunday dinner has become an informal meal, instead of the great feast of the week as it once was. However, a leg of lamb is still a splendid entrée for a dinner—one that nearly everyone loves. An especially good way to serve it is

LAMB CUTS

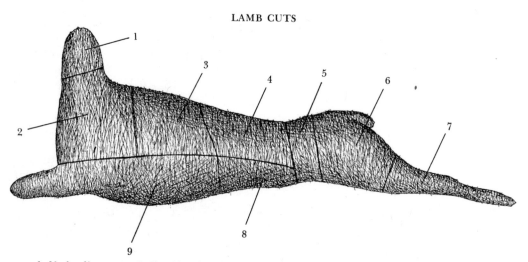

1. Neck: slices, stew; 2. Shoulder: boneless roast to stuff and roll, blade chop (with or without bone, saratoga); 3. Rib: chops, roast (rack), crown roast; 4. Loin: chops, saddle; 5. Sirloin: chops, roast; 6. Leg: roast, chops or steaks; 7. Shank: stews; 8. Flank; 9. Fore Shank and Breast: spareribs, boned and rolled breast, roast, stews

THE GREAT COOKS COOKBOOK

Roast Lamb with Garlic and Olives

Serves 10–12

5½–6-pound leg of lamb
12 large cloves garlic (or more, if small),
    peeled
1 bottle dry white wine
2 cups pitted ripe olives
Salt and pepper
A few sprigs fresh rosemary

Have your butcher bone the lamb. Some butchers are dextrous: without cutting the leg apart, they can remove the bone and leave only a pocket. Have the lamb boned with a pocket, if possible; if not, tie it together in several places. (With the bones make stock.*)

In a shallow pan, put lamb on a rack over the lightly crushed garlic cloves, and pierce meat well all over with the tip of a sharp knife, or use an ice pick so that the lamb will absorb the lovely steam from the wine. Pour the white wine over, and put in a preheated 350 F. oven. Roast, basting with the pan juices every 10 minutes or so until a meat thermometer inserted in the lamb reads 135 F. (Do not cover the pan.)

Remove meat to a warm platter and keep warm. Strain stock and add to pan juices. By this time, the sauce should be slightly thickened by the garlic; if not, add a little *beurre manié*** or some other thickener such as a mixture of arrowroot or cornstarch with water, and finally, stir in the olives, either whole or sliced.

Arrange the meat on a serving dish, garnish it with rosemary sprigs and surround it with small new potatoes dressed with parsley and butter. Pass the sauce separately.

* *To make stock:* Put bones in a saucepan, cover with water, add a teaspoon of salt, and bring to a boil. Skim; then add half an onion stuck with 2 cloves; a small carrot, sliced; a few celery leaves; a sprig of parsley; and a few peppercorns. Cook covered until vegetables are completely soft, 35–40 minutes. Strain and reserve.

** *Beurre manié* is composed of slightly softened butter and flour in a one-to-one proportion, worked together to make a smooth paste.

Weeping Leg of Lamb

Serves 10–12

5½–6-pound leg of lamb, boned
2 or 3 cloves garlic
Salt and freshly ground black pepper
½ tablespoon dried rosemary, crushed
6 medium russet potatoes
Butter
1 good-sized onion
1 cup lamb broth
Parmesan cheese, freshly grated (optional)

Have the lamb boned but not butterflied. Make broth with the bones.* With a sharp, pointed knife, make

* Stock from preceding recipe.

slits in the lamb. Cut garlic into slivers and insert into the slits. Rub meat well with salt and pepper and half of the crushed rosemary.

Heat oven to 325 F. Peel the potatoes and slice them thin (⅛ inch or thinner) into a large bowl of cold water. Turn and wash the slices well to remove starch. Butter a glass baking dish that can come to the table; it must be wider and longer than the leg of lamb. Arrange the potatoes in it in layers. Salt and pepper each layer,

adding a little of the remaining rosemary. After two layers, add a thin layer of very thinly sliced onion. Pour on the cup of broth. Set a rack in the baking dish of potatoes and place the lamb on it (or place the lamb directly on the oven rack above the dish of potatoes). Roast in oven until a thermometer inserted in the lamb reads 135 F., and the potatoes have a nice, brown crust. The potatoes may be sprinkled with Parmesan cheese a few minutes before serving, if desired.

Lamb Steaks

Serves 4

For the dedicated outdoor cook, this recipe is ideal. It is unusual, and delicious as well. Besides, it's easy.

Have your butcher cut a leg of lamb into 1½ to 2-inch slices, across the bone. (This will yield about 6 slices. Serve 1 slice per person; save the loin end and the shank end for other meals.) Crush a clove of garlic and let it rest in ½ cup of olive oil, along with a teaspoon of rosemary (fresh, if possible). Grill the steaks over a hot charcoal fire or under the broiler, basting now and then with the oil and garlic mixture. When nicely browned on the outside, and still pink and juicy within, serve them forth.

Lamb Loin

Serves 4

Lamb loin is best known for those succulent small loin chops, so good simply broiled and served with salt and pepper as the sole embellishment. But the loin makes a splendid little roast too, with the bones removed and the tail wrapped around the eye of the meat and tied or skewered in place. It should weigh about 2–2½ pounds. Put it on a rack in a roasting dish and cook in a preheated 400 F. oven until the exterior is crisp and brown, the center quite rare—about 15–20 minutes or until inserted thermometer reads 130 F. Beforehand, make stock with the bones, cooking

THE GREAT COOKS COOKBOOK

it down until you have a cup (see page 169). Add a cup of white wine and cook at high heat to reduce to 1 cup in all. Meanwhile, cook 2 finely chopped mushrooms and 2 peeled and minced garlic cloves in 2 tablespoons of butter until soft. Stir them into the reduced stock and wine mixture. Season with salt, pepper, and a little tarragon, and serve over the meat.

Rack of Lamb

The rack is the rib section (8 ribs), with the ends of the bones "Frenched"—that is, the meat and fat are cut away, leaving the bones exposed. Excess fat is trimmed off, and the blade bone is removed, as is the chine bone. This recipe is the way it is prepared at the renowned Quo Vadis Restaurant in New York.

Rack of Lamb, Quo Vadis
Serves 3–4

2-pound rack of lamb
2 small carrots, peeled and minced
1 medium onion, minced
1 tablespoon butter, cut into bits
1 cup stock (lamb or chicken)
¼ cup bread crumbs
¼ cup minced parsley
Salt and pepper

Preheat oven to 500 F. In a shallow roasting pan, put lamb, fat-side-down, on spread-out carrots, onions and butter. Place in oven and roast for 20 minutes. Reduce heat to 400 F., turn the lamb over, add ½ cup of the stock to the pan, and roast for 10 minutes more.

Mix bread crumbs and parsley together; sprinkle over lamb and put under the broiler for 4 or 5 minutes, until crisp and brown. Remove to a hot platter and keep warm.

Add the rest of the stock to the pan; mix, and put entire contents of pan into blender at high speed for 1 minute. Correct seasoning, with salt and pepper, and serve as a sauce for the lamb. Serve the lamb with paper frills on the bone ends, and garnish the platter with watercress.

Lamb Shoulder

Serves 6 or more

Lamb shoulder, usually about 4–5 pounds, is, in the opinion of many gastronomes, the most flavorful and juiciest part of the animal. It is spectacular when boned and butterflied, with excess fat removed, then grilled over charcoal or broiled. Do not marinate it, but make a basting mixture of equal parts—about ½ cup each—of olive oil and wine (red or white), with a couple of lightly crushed cloves of garlic. Brush the meat frequently with this mixture during the cooking, which won't take very long—about 15 or 20 minutes—over a hot fire, or close to the heat under the broiler. Carve in thin slices across the grain; spoon over the glorious juices which will accumulate in the platter.

Simplicity is the keynote when cooking lamb shoulder, as in the famous Irish stew:

Irish Stew

Serves 6

2 good-size potatoes
2 medium onions
6 lamb shoulder chops
Salt and pepper
½ teaspoon thyme
Cold water or lamb broth if available

Peel potatoes and slice thin (about ⅛ inch); peel onions and slice equally thin. In a deep baking dish (having a cover) arrange a layer of half of the potatoes, top with a layer of half of the onions, sprinkle with salt and pepper. Arrange lamb chops on top of the onions, season with salt, pepper, and thyme; then top with a layer of the remaining onions, and finally with the rest of the potatoes. Heat oven to 350 F. Add water (or lamb broth, or a mixture of both) to come just to the top of the potatoes. Bring to a boil on top of the stove; then, put into oven, covered, and cook until lamb is tender—about 1 hour. Or cook only on the top of the stove over medium heat if you prefer. Serve in bowls, as the sauce will be rather thin.

About Pork

In recent years, pork has become one of the best meat buys available. Not only is it lower in price than other meats; but, through careful breeding, it has lost a great deal of the fat content which many people found disagreeable. Today's pork has less than 50 per cent of the fat content which was present thirty years ago. While this is a blessing to those of us who are on low-fat diets or who fear cholesterol, it does pose a problem, because the meat has a tendency to become dry in cooking; so it is a good idea to use some sort of liquid addition. It has also been found that pork need not be cooked to 185 F. internal temperature, as most instructions of yesterday specified; instead, 160 F. is ample, and provides a juicier and more tender roast.

Why the Commodities Exchange trades only in "pork bellies" is one of life's great mysteries, as is the fact that the entire back structure of the porker, from shoulder to ham, is called the loin, a cut of meat about 3 feet long. However, the loin is customarily cut into the center, the rib end, and the loin end, which contains the tenderloin. When loin chops are cut, the tenderloin is often removed. Old cookbooks call for "a pork tenderloin, about 3 or 4 pounds," but don't try to find one that size today, for they just do not exist. A pork tenderloin now weighs 1½ pounds, and is wondrously good.

PORK CUTS

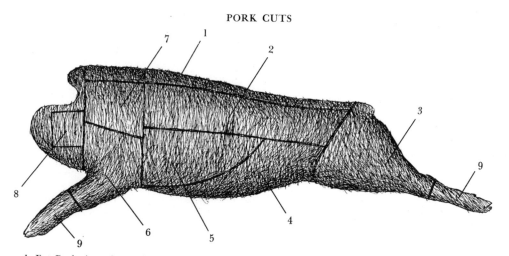

1. Fat Back: in strips to bard meat and pates, as lard for baking and frying; 2. Loin: rib chops, loin chops, country style ribs, loin roast (boned or whole), tenderloin; 3. Leg: fresh or smoked ham; 4. Bacon; 5. Spareribs and Salt Pork; 6. Picnic Shoulder: ground pork, sausage, smoked or fresh roast and hocks; 7. Blade: stew meat, smoked shoulder roll, braising roasts; 8. Jowl; 9. Pig's Feet

Pork Tenderloin

The easiest way with pork tenderloins, and one of the best, is to make scallops of them—a tenderloin, weighing about 1½ pounds, serves three. Trim off all fat and the fibrous sheath, then cut crosswise about 1½ inches thick. Lay these little rounds on a sheet of wax paper; cover with another sheet; and pound them out very thin with a mallet or the flat side of a cleaver or heavy knife, until 4 inches or so in diameter.

Dredge the pieces with flour seasoned with salt, pepper and thyme, and sauté quickly in plenty of butter. Keep the cooked ones warm in a 120 F. oven until all are done. These lovely little morsels will cook in a few minutes on a side. Add another lump of butter to the pan, let it foam up, and pour over the meat. Garnish with minced parsley.

Pork Tenderloin en Croûte

Serves 6

MEAT
2 pork tenderloins
1 tablespoon butter
1 tablespoon peanut oil
Salt and pepper
½ teaspoon thyme

PASTRY
2 cups flour
1 teaspoon salt
⅓ cup butter
⅓ cup lard
⅓ cup cold water
1 egg, lightly beaten

Trim tenderloins carefully, and remove tail ends, or tuck them under and tie. Heat butter and oil in a sauté pan; brown tenderloins on all sides, turning often. Remove from pan, season with salt, pepper and thyme, and let cool while you make the pastry.

Heat oven to 350 F. Mix flour and salt, and work in shortenings with fingertips. Add water, a little at a time, and mix well, working quickly until dough will form a soft ball.

Roll dough out on a floured surface in an oblong about ⅛ inch thick and just big enough to enclose tenderloins placed side by side in the center, thick end to thin end. Brush the tenderloins with the butter and oil from the sauté pan, and wrap in the pastry, sealing edges and ends well.

Place seam-side-down on a lightly greased cookie sheet. Make 3 or 4 slits in the top with the tip of a sharp knife; brush with beaten egg, and bake in oven for about 30 minutes, or until brown and beautiful.

Marinated Pork Loin Roast with Prunes

Serves 8–10

This Scandinavian specialty is not only a delight to eat, it has great eye appeal as well, for each slice has a center bull's-eye of dark, delicious prunes. It must be started 2 days before your dinner. While easiest to prepare and slice boned, this dish may be made with the meat on the bone.

---

1 12-ounce box pitted prunes
Cognac
5–6-pound pork-loin roast, center or rib end
    (boned: loin in one piece, and bones
    in one piece. Reserve bones)
3 tablespoons butter
2 tablespoons oil
1 clove garlic, crushed
1 teaspoon dried thyme
Salt and pepper

MARINADE MIXTURE
2 large onions, peeled and sliced
2 carrots, peeled and sliced
2 stalks celery, sliced
4 bay leaves
6–8 peppercorns
Dry red wine (enough to cover meat)

Put prunes into a jar, cover with Cognac, and let stand for 24 hours.
Have your butcher bone the loin so that the meat is in one piece and the bones in one piece (the bones to be used as a rack on which to roast the loin). With a long, sharp-pointed knife make an incision in thickest part of meat and ex-

tending its entire length. If necessary, enlarge opening a bit to hold soaked prunes and stuff them in with a long-handled spoon or other long, blunt instrument. Roll meat and tie in several places with white cotton string. Put meat into 4-quart mixing bowl with marinade mixture and refrigerate for 24 hours.

Preheat oven to 450 F. Remove meat from marinade, drain and dry it; strain marinade to use as basting liquid. Heat butter and oil in a skillet and brown roast on all sides. Put reserved bones in roasting pan; place meat on them as if they were a rack; baste well with strained marinade, and roast for 15 minutes. Reduce heat to 350 F. and, basting from time to time with the strained marinade, roast until done— about 1 hour or until a thermometer inserted in meat reads 160 F.

Remove meat to a warm platter and keep warm while you make gravy with the pan juices, first skimmed, then seasoned with a little pounded garlic and finely minced fresh thyme (or crumbled, if dried). Cook it on top of the range over high heat, scraping up and stirring in the brown bits adhering to the pan. If it seems too thick, add more marinade. Serve roast sliced thin, garnished with sautéed apple slices, and with a little gravy poured over, the rest in a separate dish.

NOTE: This recipe may be prepared as above, using a pork loin that has not been boned. Stuff roast, but do not tie with string. Marinate as above, but roast 1½ hours or until thermometer inserted in meat reads 160 F.

Roasted Pork Loin with Green Pepper Butter

Serves 8–10

This is a miraculous way with pork. I make a deep bow to Elizabeth David for introducing me to the wonders of green peppercorns, and to this butter, which goes well with any number of dishes. Green peppercorns can be bought bottled or canned. Sometimes difficult to find, they are well worth searching for.

FOR MEAT

5–6-pound pork loin roast, center or rib end
3 tablespoons butter
2 tablespoons oil
1 cup Madeira (or more)

GREEN PEPPER BUTTER

2 teaspoons, bottled or canned, green peppercorns, drained
1 small clove garlic
½ teaspoon ground cinnamon
2 ounces (½ bar) butter
½ teaspoon salt

Have your butcher bone the pork loin so that the meat is in one piece and the bones in one piece.

Reserve the bones.

In a mortar, crush the drained green peppercorns along with the garlic and cinnamon until smooth; then, work in the butter. When thoroughly amalgamated, add the salt and work in well. Larger quantities of green pepper butter can be made and kept in the freezer. Other spices, such as coriander, cumin and ginger may be combined with the cinnamon, or used instead, and the proportion of the spices may be altered to your taste.

Preheat oven to 375 F. Spread out the boned pork loin and make a slit the entire length of the meat. Fill it with the green pepper butter; roll up and tie. Brown on all sides in the heated butter and oil, and, using the bones as a rack, put in a roasting pan. Pour Madeira into pan; cover with foil if pan has no cover. Roast in oven, basting with more Madeira now and then, until done—1½ hours, or until thermometer inserted in meat reads 160 F. Thicken the sauce, if necessary, with *beurre manié.** Serve it with pride.

* Flour and butter kneaded together in a one-to-one proportion.

About Pork Legs and Shoulders

While fresh pork legs and shoulders are sometimes available in markets, most of them are made into ham, a great favorite on American tables. Alas, most of today's hams have little flavor, and need a good deal of enhancement. Here is a good recipe:

Ham Chablisienne

Serves 6

---

4 shallots (or green onions), peeled and chopped
1 cup good Chablis
1 teaspoon dried tarragon
1 cup stock (chicken, beef or pork)
½ cup tomato sauce
Heavy cream, approximately 1 cup
2 tablespoons butter, cut into bits
6 hot slices cooked ham, ¼-inch thick

Over high heat, boil the shallots, Chablis and tarragon together until reduced to about ⅓ cup. Add stock and tomato sauce. (Homemade tomato sauce is infinitely preferable to the canned variety; it may be made in large batches and kept in the freezer.) Mix well, and simmer over very low heat for 30 minutes or more. Add an amount of heavy cream equal to the entire contents of the pan. (In many parts of our country, heavy, or "whipping," cream is the only sort available.) Mix well and simmer for another 10 minutes.

Put the sauce through a sieve, reheat, and just before serving add butter, beating in well. Serve this sauce over hot slices of cooked ham. If ham has cooled, heat briefly in sauce before serving.

About Veal

Unfortunately, really good white veal is difficult to find in most places: and when you do find it, the price seems exorbitant. Most veal goes into the restaurant market. Little is left for the household consumer.

The one cut which is most often seen is the shank, and from this piece comes one of the greatest of all entrées, a specialty of northern Italy, especially Milan.

Ossi Bucchi

Serves 4

2 veal shanks
Seasoned flour (½ cup flour, 1 tablespoon salt, freshly ground black pepper)
2 tablespoons butter
2 tablespoons olive oil
1 cup dry white wine (Soave or Frascati)
1 tin (28-ounce) Italian-style tomatoes with basil
1 cup stock (or more)
Salt and black pepper

Have veal shanks cut into slices 1½ inches thick. (Make stock from the end portions, seasoning water with onion, bay leaf, and basil; cook as long as time allows—not less than 1 hour, not more than 4.) Dust the meat (there should be about 8 pieces) with the seasoned flour. In a large skillet, heat the butter with the oil and brown the meat on all sides. If it seems too dry, add a bit more oil to the pan. Arrange the browned slices in a baking pan, marrow-side-up; pour the wine over, and let cook slowly, on top of the stove, for about 10 minutes. Set aside.

Heat oven to 325 F. Drain the tomatoes (save the juice for basting later, if necessary), chop them and add to the pan along with the stock. Season with salt and pepper, cover, and put into oven for about 1½ hours, or until tender. Watch to see if it is dry; if so, baste with reserved tomato juice. Before serving, sprinkle with:

GREMOLATA
2 cloves garlic, peeled and chopped (not pressed; the bits of garlic should be tangible in the finished product)
Grated peel of 1 lemon
A handful of fresh parsley, finely chopped

Toss lightly together and strew over the veal just before serving.

NOTE: This dish is invariably served with Risotto Milanese.

Variety Meats

The most popular of these parts of the various animals is liver. Consequently, the price rises regularly. However, such cuts (called offal in England, and sometimes called innards here) are pretty economical as they contain little waste, no bone, little or no fat. There are those who object to eating such meats, without having tried them. In my experience, many people, once exposed to these good things, become instant exponents of their glories.

Most of what is called calves' liver, at least in my part of the country, is really from young beef. (As mentioned before, there is little veal to be had.) For a splendid party dish try it this way:

Roast Liver

Serves 8–10

Have a 3- to 5-pound calf or beef liver skinned and tied into a compact shape. Heat oven to 350 F. Cover liver completely with slices of bacon, fastening the ends with toothpicks. Put it on a rack in a baking dish and cook in oven until a meat thermometer inserted in the center reads 150 F. By this time the bacon should be crisp and ruffled along the edges. Serve the liver in thin slices, with Béarnaise * sauce, accompanied by chopped spinach and a gratin of potatoes.

* Use recipe for CLASSIC HOLLANDAISE (see page 34). Before beginning, in small pan reduce ½ teaspoon dried tarragon, 3 chopped shallots and 1 cup dry white wine over high heat to ⅓ cup. Add to sauce when adding lemon juice.

Beef Tongue

Beef tongues vary in weight from about 2½ to 4 pounds, the difference being largely due to the way the tongue was trimmed to begin with. Larger ones will have the bones and gristle lurking in the back (large) end. Whatever their weight (a 2½- to 4-pound tongue will serve 4 or more), they must be cooked until tender in water to cover, along with a bay leaf, an onion, a carrot, salt, peppercorns, celery tops, parsley—the same things you'd add for making any kind of stock. Bring to a boil; skim, and simmer until tender—2–3 hours. Remove, let cool just until cool enough for skin to be removed and the whole trimmed neatly, getting rid of the bones (if any) and the fat portion around the root. At this point it may be sliced and served with mustard, or may be made into something special.

Cooking water may be used as stock; but only for strongly flavored peasant dishes such as cabbage soup or lentil purée.

Baked Tongue

Cook tongue (page 179), trim and let cool. Heat oven to 375 F. About 30 minutes before serving, spread the tongue all over with Dijon-style prepared mustard; then coat completely with fine, dry bread crumbs. Put into roasting pan, root side down, and roast in oven until the crumbs are nicely browned, about 20–25 minutes.

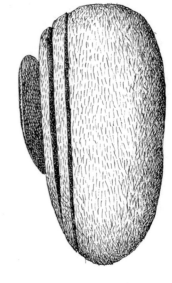

To serve, use a very sharp slicing knife and cut slices lengthwise; this way each slice contains some of each part of the tongue, from tip to root. Pass a mustard-flavored Béchamel * sauce, made with the stock. Serves 4 or more, depending on what accompanies it.

* See page 115. Add 1 tablespoon Dijon-style mustard for each 2 cups of sauce.

Braised Tongue, Raisin Sauce

Serves 4 or more

Cook a beef tongue as above until just tender; cool and remove skin. Soak ½ cup raisins in 1 cup white wine 1–2 hours. In a skillet, melt 4 tablespoons of butter and brown the tongue all over, then remove tongue to an ovenproof glass casserole.

Heat oven to 350 F. To the skillet, add 3 tablespoons of flour; stir and cook for a couple of minutes, then add ½ cup each of diced carrots and minced onion. Cook for a few minutes, until onions are just soft; then add raisins and wine, ½ cup of the tongue stock, salt and pepper to taste. Cook until slightly thickened (you may need to add a little more stock), and pour over the tongue. Cook in oven until the tongue is glazed and very tender when pierced with a fork or the tip of a sharp knife.

Sweetbreads

Because of the scarcity of veal, really good sweetbreads are difficult to come by. The ones ordinarily available come from older animals and need more cooking, but one must take care that they are not over-cooked lest they become rubbery. They do have great flavor, however, and this is a good way to use them:

Sweetbreads in Sherry, Rice Ring
Serves 4–6

RICE MOLD
3 cups water
1 teaspoon salt
1½ cups rice
3 tablespoons butter
1 cup stemmed and chopped watercress

SWEETBREADS
2 pairs sweetbreads
½ lemon
1 tablespoon grated onion
¼ cup butter
¼ cup flour
2 cups cream
Salt
¼ cup medium-dry sherry
1 tablespoon lemon juice
2 egg yolks

Bring water to a boil with salt; cook rice, covered, until tender and water is absorbed. Heat oven to 180 F. Mix rice with butter and chopped watercress, and pack into a well-buttered 1-quart ring mold. Turn out on a platter and keep warm in the oven.

Cover the sweetbreads with cold water, add the half lemon, squeezed and the shell dropped in; bring to a boil; reduce heat to moderate and cook for 15 minutes. Drain and plunge into ice water; then remove membranes and separate sweetbreads into their natural divisions.

In a saucepan big enough to hold the sweetbreads, eventually, cook the onion in the butter. When soft, add flour and cook, stirring, for a couple of minutes. Separately —it's easier this way—heat the cream, salt and sherry together; then add the lemon juice. Gradually, over low heat add heated liquid to the onion mixture, whisking constantly, until you have a slightly thickened sauce. Beat the egg yolks lightly; add a little of the hot sauce, beating all the time, then combine with sauce in saucepan and cook, over low heat, stirring until thickened. Add sweetbreads, correct seasoning—salt, pepper, perhaps a touch of cayenne—and pour into the rice ring.

Kidneys

Kidneys, favorites of European gastronomes, have never been too popular in this country, perhaps because they are misunderstood. When properly prepared they are flavorful and tender and altogether delightful. While those from veal are in short supply, lamb kidneys are nearly as good.

Lamb Kidney Sauté

Serves 3–4

4 tablespoons butter
8 lamb kidneys, with fat and membrane removed
1 tablespoon Dijon-style mustard
1 jigger Cognac
Salt and pepper

Melt butter in a skillet, add lamb kidneys, and sauté quickly until browned on all sides, tossing them around to cook evenly. Lift kidneys from the pan to a dish deep enough to catch the juices that will run from them. Split them and remove white cores, cut in half crosswise, making 4 pieces from each kidney.

Add the mustard to the pan and heat, stirring, until it is thoroughly incorporated with the butter. Return kidneys and juices to the pan. Over high heat, pour on Cognac, and flame. Season with salt and pepper and toss kidneys until blood is no longer running, or is just set, and the sauce slightly thickened—2 or 3 minutes should be plenty. Serve at once.

Brains Vinaigrette

Serves 4–6

Among the best of all dishes for a first course, or for inclusion in a cold buffet, this is also one of the easiest of delicacies to prepare.

Wash 2 sets of brains under cold water, rinsing off any blood and pulling off membranes; trim soft parts, if desired.

Cover brains with cold water; add ½ lemon, squeezed, and the shell dropped in. Bring to a boil, and simmer for 10 minutes. Remove from the heat; drain well; plunge brains into a bowl of ice water and, when thoroughly cooled, refrigerate.

Make a vinaigrette sauce with 2 tablespoons white wine vinegar, ½ cup olive oil, salt and pepper beaten well together.

Slice the brains evenly, arrange in a shallow dish, and pour the sauce over. Before serving, sprinkle with capers and minced chives.

THE GREAT COOKS COOKBOOK

Wines for Meats

ALEXIS BESPALOFF

Most people think of red wine with meat, and red wine of one kind or another can certainly be served with the dishes in this chapter. Pork could be accompanied by white wine, and a rich, semisweet white wine such as a Rhine wine or California Sauterne might be used to partner those sweet dishes that contain raisins, prunes, or oranges. This section will focus on red wines, however, and the easiest way to discuss them is to group them loosely into three basic categories: light, fruity, delicate; dry, brisk, slightly tart; and big, robust, generous wines.

Light red wines are among the easiest to drink, and are perfect for casual occasions and simple foods. Beaujolais, or wines from villages within the Beaujolais region such as Brouilly, Fleurie or Morgon; wines from Italy such as Valpolicella and Bardolino, Barbera and Grignolino; and Gamay, Gamay Beaujolais and Zinfandel from California—these are all uncomplicated and appealing wines. Many people enjoy light wines at cellar temperature, and cool them for 20 minutes on a window sill in winter, in the refrigerator in summer. Served cool, these wines also have the advantage of cutting through the richness of certain sauces and of dishes cooked with fruit.

The prototype of dry, brisk wines with a touch of astringency is red Bordeaux, which can range in quality and price from regional wines labeled Bordeaux Rouge, Médoc, St. Emilion, Margaux and St. Estèphe to famous château-bottled wines produced in limited quantities and correspondingly expensive. Bordeaux is made principally from the Cabernet Sauvignon grape; and similar wines, labeled with the grape name rather than the place of origin, are produced in California, Chile, Yugoslavia and other countries. These examples are generally less intense than the wines of Bordeaux, but they are less expensive as well. The Rioja district, in Spain, produces wines in the style of Bordeaux, although some of the *reservas,* which are aged longer than other Riojas before being bottled, are softer and more in the style of Rhône wines. Perhaps the most popular wine in this category is Chianti, although the wines can vary greatly in style from one producer to another. Dão, from central Portugal, is a less familiar but well-made dry wine.

The classic full-bodied wines are those of Burgundy, such as Pommard, Nuits-Saint-Georges, and Gevrey-Chambertin. These are now expensive wines, and although there is nothing that exactly resembles them in taste, there are a number of wines that have the same generous, mouth-filling quality that so many people enjoy. Moulin-à-Vent from the Beaujolais region, Châteauneuf-du-Pape and Côtes-du-Rhône from the Rhône Valley, and the wines labeled Corbières and Minervois from southern France—each has its own personality, and all of them have the fullness of body that makes them good accompaniments to hearty dishes. Other choices include Barolo and Gattinara from northern Italy, Pinot Noir, Barbera, and Petite Sirah from California. Remember also that inexpensive California Burgundies, especially those sold in jugs, are generally round and full-bodied in style.

Whether you serve an inexpensive wine from a carafe, or a fine Bordeaux or Burgundy, or anything in between, the choice among red wines is enormous and varied in every price range.

Years ago, when I worked at the Plaza Athenée Hotel in Paris, we were five chefs at the vegetable section. When I came to this country and joined the famed Le Pavillon in New York, there was, to my surprise, only one chef assigned to the vegetables—and he was in charge of the soups as well. I soon discovered that most restaurants did not have a professional at the vegetable station. The vegetable man is usually a kitchen helper, and his lack of professionalism is reflected in the quality of vegetable dishes served to diners. Humble vegetables are treated only as such—and unjustly so—as if relegated to the role of satellites of glorious meat and fish dishes. Yet they can be glorious on their own, or equally as important as accompaniments and garnishes. In all fairness, diners should not be subjected to the inescapable breaded and broiled tomato halves, for example, whenever a steak or a piece of chicken is ordered.

All in all, vegetables are made too little of on American tables. And more often than not, they are tasteless, badly presented, over- or undercooked, and rarely made from fresh products. Vegetables make healthy, attractive and inexpensive dishes. And the variety from which to choose is far greater than that of meat, poultry or fish; so much so, in fact, that I had great difficulty limiting this chapter to only twenty-three recipes. I have tried to confine my recipes to vegetables that are interesting in their own right, rather than simply being bland accompaniments. They are often important enough to be served on their own as a vegetable course or as an *hors d'oeuvre*. While my selection is very arbitrary, I do not mean to minimize the importance of other vegetables that are not listed. Because of lack of space, I did not give recipes for familiar vegetables such as green beans, broccoli, asparagus, celery and the like. I also bypassed some of those less frequently served, such as white turnips, rutabaga, sorrel, cardoons, salsify, Jerusalem artichokes, fennel, and collard greens—to name some, but hardly all. Except for navy beans, I have not given recipes for other legumes—such as red kidney beans, lentils, black-eyed or chick peas, limas or favas—all of which make excellent casserole dishes.

The quality of green vegetables—green beans, artichokes, peas, spinach, asparagus and others—varies considerably, depending upon the seasons and, therefore, the freshness of the product. Some vegetables are good even though frozen, but canned vegetables are dreadful. You do not know the true taste of vegetables unless you have eaten them fresh.

As a general rule, all green vegetables should be cooked in lots of salted boiling water, and you must be careful not to overcook them. They must be cooled immediately under cold running water to stop their cooking and so retain their taste, color and crispness. When cold, they should be drained, covered and kept cool, but not too cold, until they are ready to be reheated and served.

I have featured twenty different vegetables, giving one recipe for each, except for the potato. Among some of the 200 different ways of preparing the potato, I chose three which I believe reflect its versatility. On the whole, it is a good policy to decide which vegetable you will serve when you have seen the best that your market has to offer, even if it means a slight change in your menu.

Artichauts Ménagère

[STUFFED ARTICHOKES]
Serves 6

Artichokes, cultivated in France since the sixteenth century, are not often seen on the American table although increasing in popularity. Very small, pointed, young—still faintly purple—artichokes are eaten raw with salt and pepper. Mature globe artichokes are usually boiled and served cold with a vinaigrette, or warm with melted butter or HOLLANDAISE.*

Like most vegetables, artichokes are better if they have not been refrigerated. To prepare them for cooking, first the stems are cut off, then about 1½ inches of their top leaves trimmed. For aesthetic purposes, the top of each remaining leaf is snipped with scissors. The artichokes are then cooked in a lot of salted boiling water —about 45 minutes—and checked for doneness by pulling out a leaf; if it comes out easily, the artichoke is done.

Artichoke bottoms or hearts are the center of the vegetable left after all the leaves and choke have been removed. When prepared separately, they are usually cooked in lemony water, kept in the cooking liquid until needed and used in countless recipes as a garnish.

---

6 artichokes (8 to 10 ounces each), medium globe, prepared as above but *not cooked*

* See page 34.

4–5 slices fresh white bread, diced (2 cups)
¾ cup lukewarm milk
1 tablespoon olive oil
1 large onion, peeled and chopped (about 1 cup)
1 large tomato, peeled, seeded and coarsely chopped, about 1 cup (see NOTE, p. 188)
2–3 garlic cloves, peeled, crushed and chopped fine
½ teaspoon salt
½ teaspoon freshly ground black pepper
3 tablespoons fresh chopped parsley
2 eggs
6 large slices of bacon
1½ cups dry white wine
1 tablespoon sweet butter
1 tablespoon flour

Drop the artichokes into a large pot of salted boiling water. Bring to a boil again and cook for 15 minutes. Place immediately under cold running water until the artichokes have cooled. Lift each one by hand from the water and, holding upside down, gently squeeze out excess water. Pull out the delicate center leaves all at once to expose the choke. Set aside the center leaves and reserve for use later. With a teaspoon, scoop out the whole choke and discard, leaving a central cavity in each artichoke.

Mix the bread cubes and milk together. Heat the oil in a saucepan and add the onion; cook 2 minutes, stirring to prevent the onion from burning. Add the tomatoes and garlic and, over medium heat, cook 2 minutes more. Remove from heat and combine with the bread mixture. Add the salt, pepper and parsley, and then the eggs. Mix well.

Stuff the cavity of each artichoke with part of the mixture. Set the reserved central leaves on top of the mixture to close the opening. Wrap each artichoke with one slice of the bacon so it will keep these top leaves in place. In a saucepan just large enough to hold all the artichokes, arrange them top-side-up and touching each other. This will keep the bacon in place. Pour the wine around them and bring to a boil. Cover, and simmer over low heat for 1 hour.

In a small pan, mix the butter and flour to a smooth paste. Pour the liquid (a good cupful) from the artichokes into the butter mixture. Combine well with a whisk. Bring to a boil, stirring constantly to prevent scorching. Reduce heat and simmer very slowly for 6–8 minutes. Taste for seasoning; it may need salt and pepper. Arrange the artichokes on a serving platter and pour the sauce over. Serve immediately, either as a first course or as the main course of a light lunch, accompanied by salad and cheese.

NOTE: To peel tomatoes, drop them into boiling water for 30–40 seconds. Lift out with slotted spoon and peel under cold water. Slice in half, between stem and bottom, and squeeze out seeds.

Aubergines Sautées Monégasque

[FRESH EGGPLANT WITH ONIONS AND OLIVES]

Serves 6

For this recipe, use the small, round type of eggplant, about 5 inches long by 2 inches wide. Do not peel the eggplant, but remove stem and cut it lengthwise into ½″ slices. Discard the first and last slices of each eggplant; they will be mainly skin. You should have 12 nice slices, 2 per person. With the point of a knife, slash the slices about ⅛ inch deep and sprinkle on both sides with 1 teaspoon of salt. Place the slices flat on a cookie sheet and put another sheet on top of them, weighted with heavy objects. Let stand for 30 minutes. Pressing the slices with salt draws out the bitter liquid and the eggplant does not absorb as much oil while cooking.

---

3 small eggplants (about 2¼ pounds), cut into 12 half-inch slices
5 medium onions, peeled and sliced thin (about 3 cups)
½ cup water
½ teaspoon salt
¼ teaspoon freshly ground white pepper
1 tablespoon sweet butter
½ cup flour
½ cup vegetable oil
1 cup small black fresh olives
2 tablespoons fresh chopped parsley

Slash, salt and press eggplant slices as described (left). Meanwhile, place the sliced onions, water, salt, pepper and butter in a saucepan and bring to a boil. Cover, and cook over medium heat for about 10 minutes, until all the liquid has evaporated. Remove the lid and continue cooking over low heat, stirring once or twice, for another 8–10 minutes, until the onions are translucent and slightly gold in color. Set aside.

Heat oven to 200 F. With a paper towel, pat dry the wet, pressed eggplant slices. Dip each slice in flour and shake lightly to rid of excess flour. Divide the oil between 2 large, heavy skillets. When the oil is hot, place the slices flat in it (do not overlap) and cook over medium to low heat for about 4 minutes on each side, or until golden brown. When done, place slices on a cookie sheet and keep warm in oven.

When ready to serve, remove eggplant from oven and bring oven to 450 F. Arrange all the cooked slices on a warm platter, slightly overlapping, in a nice pattern, and top each slice with a good tablespoon of the cooked onion. Embed 3 olives in each onion mound and place in hot oven for 3–4 minutes. Sprinkle with parsley and serve immediately. These are good by themselves as a first course or luncheon dish or as an accompaniment to braised brains *provençales* or any roast.

Carottes Vichy

[STEAMED CARROTS]

Serves 6

This dish is especially good when made with fresh, sweet carrots. However, lacking a nearby garden or farm, the conventional supermarket carrots will do, with an addition of a small amount of sugar. If fresh carrots are used, cut the amount of sugar by half. Remember that the carrots must be sliced as thin as possible. If you are not professional enough with a knife, use an automatic slicer.

2½ pounds fresh carrots (15–22 carrots, depending on size) ; peeled, then sliced very thin (about 8 cups)
½ stick sweet butter (4 tablespoons)
4 teaspoons sugar
2 teaspoons salt

4 cups water, approximately
½ tablespoon fresh, finely chopped parsley (if you have no fresh parsley, omit it)

Place all the ingredients, except the parsley, in a heavy glass-ceramic casserole. The carrots should be covered, just barely, with water. Bring to a boil. Boil, uncovered, over high heat until all the liquid has evaporated and the carrots shine and start to glaze; this should take about 40 minutes. Place in a serving bowl and sprinkle with the chopped parsley. Serve immediately, customarily with lean broiled beef—a steak—or veal or braised ham.

Champignons Farcis

[STUFFED MUSHROOMS]

Serves 6

25 firm white mushrooms (about 2 inches in diameter) , approximately 1½ pounds
1 teaspoon salt
⅔ stick sweet butter (5½ tablespoons)
1 large onion, peeled and chopped very fine (¾ cup)
1 rib celery, washed, peeled and chopped fine (⅓ cup)
⅛ teaspoon freshly ground white pepper
1 clove garlic, peeled, crushed and chopped very fine (¼ teaspoon)

3 slices fresh white bread; trimmed, cubed, and crumbed in the blender at medium speed (about 1 cup)

Preheat oven to 400 F. Wash the mushrooms. Select 20 of the nicest; break off the stem inside the cap so that each cap becomes a receptacle; reserve the stems. Place the 20 caps, hollow-side-up, on a baking pan; sprinkle with ½ teaspoon of the salt and place in oven for 5

THE GREAT COOKS COOKBOOK

minutes. Remove from oven, turn caps over to drain and cool for 5 minutes. Drain off any liquid in pan. Raise oven heat to 450 F.

To make the stuffing, chop the 5 remaining mushrooms and all of the stems very fine (about 2¾ cups). Melt ⅓ of the stick of butter in a heavy saucepan over medium heat; add the onions and cook 2 minutes. Add the celery and cook another 2 minutes, stirring with a spoon to prevent scorching. Add the chopped mushrooms, the remaining ½ teaspoon salt, and the pepper; cook for about 5 minutes. The mushrooms will throw off liquid; continue cooking until it has evaporated. Add the garlic, cook for about 1 minute, and then set this stuffing mixture aside to cool to lukewarm.

Melt the remaining butter in a skillet. Add the bread crumbs and, stirring constantly, cook until the bread is loose again and begins to brown.

Transfer crumbs to a plate; they will continue to brown for a few seconds. Fill each mushroom cap with stuffing; you will have enough of the mixture to shape it into a nice rounded dome in each cap. Dip the mushrooms stuffed-side-down into the bread crumbs, or press the bread crumbs evenly on each dome, heavily enough so that the whole top is coated. Arrange in a baking dish and place in oven for 8–10 minutes. Serve immediately. These make a lovely first course or an *hors d'oeuvre* with drinks. They are equally excellent with fillet of beef or a leg of veal.

Choufleur Polonaise

[SAUTÉED CAULIFLOWER]
Serves 6

1 large, or 2 small cauliflowers (about 3½ pounds)
1 stick sweet butter (¼ pound)
1 tablespoon vegetable oil
1 teaspoon salt
¼ teaspoon freshly ground white pepper
1 hard-cooked egg, peeled and pushed through a metal sieve, or chopped very fine
1 tablespoon fresh chopped parsley
1–2 slices fresh white bread, cubed, and crumbed in the blender at medium speed (¾ cup)

Bring a large pot of salted water to a boil. Choose white, firm heads of cauliflower with small flowerets, compact and tight together. Cut the leaves from the stem, and separate the flowerets from the core by cutting around each one with a knife. If the cauliflower is older and tough, pull off the hard skin around the stem of each floweret.

Place the flowerets in the boiling water. Bring the water to a boil again; reduce the heat and boil slowly for 10–12 minutes—until the stems are tender when pierced with the point of a knife. To stop the cooking, put the pot under cold running water, placing at once a long-handled spoon across top of the pot so water will bounce off it gently onto the cauliflower. This procedure prevents the tender flowerets from breaking under the force of the running water. When flowerets are cold, lift each by hand from the water; drain on paper towels. Set aside.

Melt half of the butter in a very large, heavy skillet. If you do not have an extra-large skillet, use two. Add the oil. When the mixture is hot, carefully place each floweret head-down into it. Sprinkle with salt and pepper and cook over medium to low heat for 5–7 minutes until the floweret heads are golden brown.

To present the flowerets as a reconstituted head of cauliflower, arrange in the following way. (Depending on the number of flowerets you have, reconstitute either one or two heads of cauliflower.) On a dinner plate (or 2, for 2 heads), make a circle of flowerets—this outermost circle should be about 5 or 6 inches in diameter —with the stems pointing toward the center of the plate. Continue building up by placing flowerets, stems always pointed down toward the center of the plate, in smaller and smaller circles until the construction resembles a head of cauliflower.

Mix the chopped egg and chopped parsley together, and sprinkle on the cauliflower. Melt the remaining butter in a skillet and add the bread crumbs. Cook, shaking the skillet constantly, until the crumbs are golden brown. Pour immediately on the cauliflower and serve right away, in elegant solitary splendor as a vegetable course or as a pleasant contrast to a stew such as *coq au vin* or veal goulash.

Concombres Persillés

[PARSLEY CUCUMBERS]
Serves 6

Cucumbers are not usually served as a hot vegetable. However, they are one of the best accompaniments for poached fish in sauce. A variation may be made on the recipe below. When the cucumbers are heating in the butter, add half a cup of cream and some chopped tarragon, instead of parsley, and cook a few minutes until the cream coats each piece of cucumber.

4 good-size cucumbers (about 14 ounces each)
3 tablespoons sweet butter
½ teaspoon salt
¼ teaspoon freshly ground white pepper
1 tablespoon freshly chopped parsley

Bring a large pot of salted water to a boil. Trim each cucumber at both ends. Cut each one across widthwise into 4 pieces. You now have 4 cylinders for each cucumber. Place each cylinder flat-side-down on a board and quarter it. With a small paring knife, remove the seeds and cut the skin off each piece, shaping it as you go along. All the pieces should be about the same shape and size; this ensures proper cooking. Place the cucumbers in the boiling water and bring to a boil again. Reduce heat and boil slowly for 6–8 minutes until the pieces are tender when pierced with the point of a knife. To stop the cooking, put the pot under cold running water, placing at once a long-handled spoon across the top of pot so water will bounce off it gently onto the cucumbers. This procedure prevents the tender pieces from breaking under the force of the running water. When the cucumbers are cold, drain in a colander and cover with paper towel.

Melt the butter in a saucepan until it foams. Add the cucumber, salt, pepper, and cook over medium heat for 5–6 minutes—just enough so that the pieces are very hot. Add the chopped parsley; mix, then pour into a serving dish. Serve immediately with poached fish or a well-sauced veal dish.

Côtes de Blêtes au Gratin
[SWISS CHARD AU GRATIN]
Serves 6

Although readily available here in most Italian markets, Swiss chard is relatively unknown in the United States. It is commonly served in France, especially around the Lyonnais region. In France, it is called *Blêtes, Bettes* or *Carde Poirée*. The green leaves may be used in soup or prepared like spinach.

In the following recipe, only the central rib, or stalk, is used. The green part is cut off from both sides of the rib. The fibrous membrane of the leaf on both sides of the rib is removed by cutting each rib across halfway through, breaking the rib at the cut and pulling off the membrane. If the rib is curled, cut into halves lengthwise; you will have 2 narrow, flat pieces. Cut the clean stems into 2–2½-inch pieces. Save the removed part of the leaf for soup or a purée.

3 pounds (approximately) Swiss chard (2 large bunches) ; peeled and cut into pieces (about 3½ cups)
½ stick sweet butter
3 tablespoons flour
2 cups milk
½ cup cream
½ teaspoon salt
¼ teaspoon freshly ground pepper
1 tablespoon grated Parmesan cheese

Drop the Swiss chard pieces into enough salted boiling water to cover. Bring back to a boil and cook, uncovered, for 6–8 minutes, or until tender. Drain in a colander.

Butter a gratin dish (I use an oval dish 1½″ x 12″ x 5″) . Set aside.

In a heavy saucepan, over medium heat, melt the butter, add the flour and mix well. Add the milk and, stirring constantly with a whisk to prevent scorching and lumps, bring to a boil. When the mixture begins to boil, reduce heat and simmer for 4–5 minutes. Add the cream, salt and pepper; mix well.

Heat oven to 400 F. Place the cooled and drained Swiss chard in the buttered gratin dish; pour the cream sauce over. Be sure that all the pieces are sauced. Sprinkle with cheese and place on a cookie sheet in oven for 30–35 minutes until golden brown. Serve at once as an unusual side dish for any roast.

Courgettes Farcies
[STUFFED ZUCCHINI]
Serves 6

This recipe will make 6 large portions (or 12 garnishes if you serve only ½ zucchini per person).

---

6 medium-size zucchini (about 3 pounds)
3 teaspoons salt (this recipe needs a lot of salt)
½ cup rice (nonconverted rice; or use Carolina rice)
1½ cups water
3 tablespoons olive oil
1 medium onion, peeled and chopped fine (about ¾ cup)
3 medium-large tomatoes, split into halves horizontally, and squeezed to remove the seeds; coarsely chopped (2 cups pulp)
3 large cloves garlic, peeled, crushed and chopped (2 teaspoons)
½ teaspoon freshly ground black pepper
1 piece hot chili pepper without seeds; chopped fine (1½ teaspoons)
1 cup grated Swiss Gruyère or Emmenthaler cheese
3 small slices fresh white bread, cubed and crumbed in blender at medium speed (1 cup)
⅓ cup vegetable oil

Trim both ends of zucchini slightly; wash under cold running water. Cut into halves lengthwise. With a teaspoon, remove the seeds and scoop some of the pulp out of each half so as to obtain a shell about ¼ inch thick; be careful not to break through the zucchini shells. Keep the seeds and pulp and chop them coarsely; you should have about 4 cups. Arrange the shells next to each other in a large oven-proof glass baking dish, scooped-out-side-up. Sprinkle with 1 teaspoon of the salt. Combine the rice and water in a small, heavy saucepan and bring to a boil over medium heat. Cover and simmer very slowly for 20 minutes until all the water is absorbed.

To make the stuffing, first heat the olive oil in a saucepan. Add the onion; sauté, stirring, for 2–3 minutes. Add the zucchini pulp, tomatoes, garlic, pepper, remaining salt, and hot chili pepper. Cook over medium heat for 10 minutes to reduce most of the liquid, stirring once in a while to prevent scorching. Combine with rice and cool slightly, about 15 minutes.

Heat oven to 400 F. Empty each zucchini shell of any accumulated liquid. Fill with the stuffing so that it slightly overlaps the rim of the shell. Combine the grated cheese and bread crumbs well, and top stuffing heavily with the mixture. With a teaspoon, sprinkle the vegetable oil on top of the bread crumb mixture. Place in oven for a good hour until golden brown. Allow to rest for at least 10 minutes before serving 2 pieces per person as a first course (serving 6) or 1 piece per person as a garnish for stuffed flank steak or a sautéed veal chop.

Crêpes de Maïs

⟦CORN CRÊPES⟧
Serves 6

This is an original recipe I developed; it was suggested by my wife, who is a corn lover. It is easy to make, quite elegant, and delicate in texture and taste.

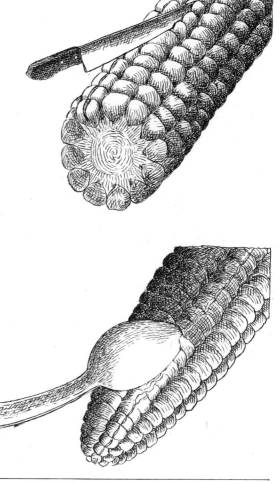

5 medium-size ears of corn, husked, and silk removed
4 tablespoons flour
4 eggs
1 teaspoon salt
¼ teaspoon freshly ground pepper
½ cup heavy cream
½ stick (¼ cup) of sweet butter, melted

Bring a pot of salted water to a rolling boil. Drop the husked, cleaned corn into the water and let come to a boil again. Remove corn from water immediately, and let cool until it can be handled. With a sharp knife, cut straight down the middle of each kernel row, slitting each kernel open. Then hold the ear in one hand, the top of the ear resting on the table, and, with a spoon, scrape the pulp out of the opened kernels, extracting all of it as you scrape down the full length of the ear, and all around the ear, row by row. The skin of the kernel that held the pulp will remain attached to the ear; the pulp will be removed. You will have about 1¼ cups of pulp.

Put the pulp in a large bowl and sprinkle with the flour. Mix well with a whisk. Add the eggs, salt and pepper, mixing to blend all ingredients well. Add the cream and combine well. Finally, add the melted butter and mix together once more.

Heat oven to 180 F. Place a crêpe pan or a seasoned heavy iron pan over low to medium heat. When hot, pour 2 tablespoons of the mixture into the pan. This amount is enough for 1 crêpe. If the skillet is large enough to hold 2 crêpes, make 2 at a time, otherwise use several pans. Each crêpe should be about 4″ in diameter. Cook 40 seconds on one side; flip over or turn with a large spatula, and cook 30 seconds on the other side. Keep the finished crêpes hot in oven while you are making the others. Makes about 20 crêpes to serve as a first course or with beef, veal or rabbit stews.

Endives Meunière

[SAUTÉED ENDIVES]
Serves 6

The best endives come from Belgium. Even in France, where great quantities of endives are grown every year, the best restaurants still get their supply from Belgium. The Belgians, however, call endive *chicon,* and the curly chicory salad *endive,* which makes menu-reading a little confusing.

In the following recipe, the first step is to braise the endives, the second, to finish the endives just before they are served.

10 medium-size, white, firm, Belgian endives
1½ teaspoons salt
1½ teaspoons sugar
Juice of 1 lemon
⅓ cup water
1 stick sweet butter
¼ cup brown gravy (optional)
1 tablespoon fresh, chopped parsley

Heat oven to 375 F. Remove any bruised leaves from the endives. Wash carefully under cold water and arrange the endives in a glass-ceramic casserole which has a cover. Sprinkle with 1 teaspoonful of the salt, then the sugar, lemon juice, water and 2 tablespoons of the butter cut in little bits.

Cover and bring to a boil. Remove from heat; cover the endives with a piece of wax paper and place a small saucer on top to keep the paper in place. The endives, also, will be slightly pressed down. Replace pan lid. Place in oven for 35 to 40 minutes. (If you prefer, you may braise them on top of the stove over very low heat and for the same length of time.) When braised, the endives should be tender but not mushy. Let cool to room temperature. Place endives in an earthenware or glass tureen; pour the cooking juices over

THE GREAT COOKS COOKBOOK

and cover with wax paper. At this point, they may be refrigerated for one week and used as needed. Endives may also be served plain, directly from the hot broth.

Just before finishing the endives, remove them from the broth and gently squeeze out the excess liquid. Place them on an even surface and flatten them lightly with the broad side of a knife. If the endives are large, cut them lengthwise in half.

You will probably need 2 large, heavy saucepans. Put 2 tablespoons of butter in

each one; heat, place the endives, flattened or cut-side-up, into the butter, allowing enough room so they do not overlap. Sauté over medium to low heat for about 4½ minutes on each side until they are golden brown. Arrange the endives side by side on a large serving platter. Warm the gravy and pour it around them in a thin ribbon-like stream. Melt the remaining butter in a skillet until it turns a nice hazelnut color, then pour over the endives. Sprinkle with the parsley and serve immediately, with roast fish or beef.

Gratin Dauphinois
[SCALLOPED POTATOES IN GARLIC AND CREAM]
Serves 6

One of the simplest ways to prepare potatoes—that is, GRATIN DAUPHINOIS, or scalloped potatoes in garlic and cream—might very well be the most sublime way to treat the vegetable. Although the dish is a specialty of Grenoble, a town on the edge of the Alps, it is well known in eastern France—particularly around the Rhône Valley, where it is made with varying success in many restaurants. Around Grenoble it is considered heretical to sprinkle it with cheese, but around Lyon it is an accepted practice. Actually, the cheese is necessary only if you use a good deal of milk in the recipe, since it helps the gratin achieve a beautiful golden color. Expensive restaurants, however, often use only cream. When prepared that way, the potatoes turn beautifully golden without the addition of cheese.

2 pounds boiling potatoes (will be 5–6 cups, sliced)
1 large clove garlic (or 2 small cloves)
2 cups milk
1½ cups heavy cream
¾ teaspoon salt (approximately)
½ teaspoon freshly ground white pepper
1 tablespoon butter
½ cup grated Swiss cheese (about 2 ounces)

Peel the potatoes, wash, and dry thoroughly. Slice fairly thin—⅛-inch thick—with a sharp knife or slicer. Do not soak the sliced potatoes in water or they will lose the starch needed for the dish to be smooth.

Peel the garlic; crush it with the broad side of a knife and chop it very fine. It should have the consistency of a purée. In a large, heavy saucepan, combine the potato slices with the garlic, milk, cream, salt and pepper. Bring to a boil over medium heat, stirring with a wooden spoon to prevent scorching (and the mixture can scorch very easily). As the liquid gets hotter, the mixture will thicken slightly; remove from heat.

Preheat oven to 400 F. Butter a shallow glass baking dish, about 1½-inches deep, and pour in the potato mixture. Sprinkle cheese all over the top; place dish on a cookie sheet (to catch any spills and to allow more even transfer of heat), and bake about 1 hour, until potatoes are golden brown and tender when pierced with the point of a knife. Let rest for 15–20 minutes before serving with saddle or leg of lamb.

NOTE: There should be enough for 6 good supper servings. If you have any leftovers, follow this Grenoble tradition. Serve the cold potatoes for lunch the next day with a green salad, seasoned with oil and vinegar and a lot of chopped garlic.

Gratin de Courge Bressane
[PUMPKIN AU GRATIN]
Serves 6

It is unusual in the United States to utilize pumpkin in ways other than in pumpkin pie. In the part of France from which I come, Bourg-en-Bresse, pumpkin is never served sweet as dessert but cooked, *au gratin,* and served as a vegetable.

---

1 small to medium-size pumpkin; peeled, seeded, and cut into 3″ chunks (approximately 3 pounds raw pulp)
2 teaspoons salt
1 teaspoon sweet butter, softened
3 large eggs
1 cup heavy cream
½ teaspoon freshly ground white pepper

Place the pumpkin chunks in a large saucepan with 1 teaspoon of the salt. Cover with cold water and bring to a boil. Cover, and simmer slowly for 20–25 minutes, until the pumpkin is tender when pierced with a fork or tip of a knife. Drain thoroughly in a colander. Put through a food mill to give it the consistency of a nice purée.

Heat oven to 450 F. Butter a shallow gratin dish, approximately 1½ inches deep and large enough to hold 6 cupfuls. With a fork, beat the eggs until well combined and mix with the cream until blended. Combine the pumpkin purée, egg mixture, remaining salt and the pepper, and pour into the gratin dish. Place dish on a cookie sheet (to catch any spills, and to conduct and distribute the heat more evenly), and transfer to oven. Cook for about 1 hour, until golden brown. Remove from oven; let rest 10 minutes before serving. This is very good with broiled steak, lamb chops or chicken.

Gratin de Poireaux Savoyarde

⟦LEEKS AU GRATIN⟧
Serves 6

Leeks, although widely used throughout France as a vegetable, *hors d'oeuvre,* or in sauces and garnishes, are little known in the United States. In France, often served cold with a VINAIGRETTE,* leeks are called the asparagus of the poor because they are so inexpensive. In America, however, they are more expensive than real asparagus.

8–10 large leeks
10 slices bacon
1 cup water
⅛ teaspoon dried thyme
¼ teaspoon freshly ground white pepper
2½ tablespoons sweet butter
2½ tablespoons flour
1 cup milk
1 cup heavy cream
Dash salt (depending on saltiness of bacon)
1 tablespoon grated Parmesan cheese

---

*T*rim the roots, and, using only the white and light-green parts, cut each leek into 2″ pieces, then into quarters (about 6 cups), and wash thoroughly in a good amount of water. Lift them from the water by hand; if you just

* See page 41.

drain them, they may retain some of the sand.

Cut each bacon slice into quarters, and sauté in a saucepan until golden brown. Add the leeks, water, thyme, and pepper. Cover tightly, and cook over medium heat for 20 minutes; the leeks should be tender and the water cooked away. Melt 2 tablespoons of the butter in a saucepan; add flour, mixing well with a whisk. Add milk and bring to a boil, stirring constantly with a whisk to prevent scorching. Add the cream, dash of salt (about ¼ teaspoon) and bring to a boil, stirring again to prevent scorching. Remove from heat.

Heat oven to 375 F. Butter a shallow ovenproof glass baking dish (about 1½ inches deep and large enough to hold 6 cupfuls) with the remaining butter. Place the leeks in the dish and pour the sauce over, making sure all the leeks are coated. Sprinkle with the cheese; place dish on a cookie sheet (to catch spillage and to conduct and distribute heat more evenly); place in oven for 30 minutes, or until golden brown. Remove from oven. Let dish rest for at least 10 minutes before serving beside a roast beef or pot roast.

Haricots Bretonne

[BRAISED PEA BEANS]
Serves 6

Most dried beans sold in supermarkets are not more than a year old and do not require long soaking before they are cooked. They may even be cooked without any soaking if they are started in *cold* water. However, if you wish to soak, 1½–2 hours in cold water is sufficient. With long soaking, 12 or more hours, the beans begin to ferment and may even become slightly toxic. In any case, with long soaking the chances for successful cooking are lessened, rather than increased. If the cooking of the beans is started in hot or boiling water, they will toughen; eventually, they will soften but be mushy.

---

1 pound Boston navy (pea) beans, presoaked for 2 hours in cold water
6 cups cold water
2 teaspoons salt
1 very large onion (8–10 ounces), peeled
4 cloves
¼ teaspoon dried thyme
2 bay leaves
3 medium carrots, peeled
5 tablespoons sweet butter
3 medium tomatoes, peeled and seeded (see NOTE page 188 for procedure), chopped coarsely (about 2 cups)
2–3 cloves garlic; peeled, crushed and chopped fine (1 teaspoon)
½ teaspoon freshly ground black pepper
¼ cup fresh parsley, chopped

Lift the beans by the handful from the soaking liquid. (Do not drain in a colander; grains of sand may be mixed with the beans.) Put them in a heavy saucepan and add the water. Add 1½ teaspoons of the salt, the onion stuck with 4 cloves, thyme, bay leaves and the carrots. Bring to a boil and skim off the foam. Cover, and simmer slowly for 1 hour and 45 minutes, until most of the liquid has cooked away.

While the beans cook, melt 3 tablespoons of the butter in a saucepan and add the chopped tomatoes. Cook for 5 minutes over medium heat; add the garlic, remaining salt, and the ½ teaspoon pepper. Mix well and set aside.

Remove the onion and carrots from the cooked beans; discard the cloves. Chop the onion and carrots coarsely and put back with the beans. Combine the parsley with the tomato mixture and add to the beans. Add the remaining 2 tablespoons butter; simmer over moderate heat for 5 minutes. Serve immediately as a classic friend to roast lamb or pork.

If you would like to reheat the beans (they develop flavor and are quite good reheated), start heating them with ¼ cup of water and cook, covered, over low heat; make sure they don't scorch.

Laitues Braisées

[BRAISED LETTUCE]
Serves 6

Braised heads of lettuce are usually cooked with pork rind, carrots, onions, parsley and herbs. However, if you have a good brown sauce, it is simpler to just blanch the lettuce in boiling water and finish the dish with the sauce. The result is just as good.

6 small to medium heads of Boston lettuce
½ teaspoon salt
½ teaspoon freshly ground white pepper
5 tablespoons sweet butter
1 cup good brown gravy (homemade, or good quality canned)
1 tablespoon freshly chopped parsley

Remove and discard any bruised leaves, then wash heads of lettuce in cold water, spreading gently to rid them of sand. Drop the heads of lettuce into a large pot of salted boiling water; cover; let come to a boil again. Remove cover (or lettuce will turn yellow) and continue to boil for 15 to 20 minutes until the cores become tender but not mushy. Remove from heat; drain off all hot water by holding cover partially over pot. Place a long-handled spoon or spatula across top of pot and run cold water over it so that it falls lightly onto the lettuce to cool it. This procedure prevents the tender leaves from breaking under the force of the water. When cool, lift each one by hand from the water and squeeze to remove as much water as possible, but be careful to keep the shape of the lettuce intact.

Split each head of lettuce into halves lengthwise and lay cut-side-up on a board. With not too much pressure, flatten each one with the broad side of a knife. One by one, fold the tips of the leaves over on themselves 1″; press; turn over, and trim the core. You now have 12 neat little packages. Sprinkle on both sides with salt and pepper.

Heat oven to 180 F. Melt 3 tablespoons of the butter in a large skillet or saucepan (with an ovenproof handle, if possible) and place lettuce packages in it side by side, folded-side-up; do not let them overlap. Cook over medium heat 5–6 minutes until they are slightly browned. Turn over and cook for another 5–6 minutes. Cover with aluminum foil and keep warm in oven.

When ready to serve, arrange packages attractively on a warm platter and coat with heated gravy. In a small saucepan, over medium heat, melt the remaining butter until it turns hazelnut color and pour directly over the lettuce. Sprinkle with parsley and serve immediately.

Petits Choux Braisés

[[SMALL BRAISED CABBAGES]]
Serves 6

---

1 large green cabbage
10 slices of bacon (½ pound), coarsely
    chopped
1 medium-size well-ripened tomato, cubed
    (1 cup)
2 medium onions, peeled and thinly sliced
    (1¾ cups)
5 cloves garlic; peeled, crushed and coarsely
    chopped (1 good tablespoon)
5 carrots, peeled and thinly sliced (1½
    cups)
¼ teaspoon freshly ground black pepper
½ teaspoon dried thyme
2 bay leaves, broken into pieces
1 teaspoon salt
2 cups chicken stock
1 tablespoon good wine vinegar
2 tablespoons water
1 tablespoon arrowroot or cornstarch

Clean cabbage and remove any bruised leaves. Cut out the central core to separate the leaves. Try not to damage the large leaves; you will need them later to use as wrappers for the inside of the cabbage. Drop all the leaves into a large pot of salted boiling water. Push the leaves into the water and bring to a boil again. It will take at least 5 minutes for it to start boiling once more; when it does, cover, and continue to boil for 12 minutes more. Place the whole pot of cabbage under cold running water until the leaves are thoroughly cold. Drain in a colander. Select 10 of the largest leaves and set aside to use as wrappers. You will make about 10 little cabbages of these leaves. Cut away the triangular rib sections, which are tough.

Have a 6-ounce round ladle handy. Place a large leaf in the cup of the ladle so that it hangs over the sides. Fill the center of it with more cabbage, pushing to make it compact. Fold the overhanging leaf onto the center, and unmold. You will have a nice round little cabbage. Press it gently to draw out some of the excess water. Repeat until you have used all of the cabbage to make about 10 miniature cabbages.

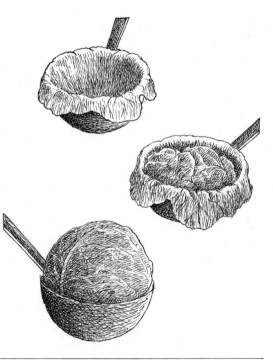

Heat oven to 400 F. Put the chopped bacon in a large, flat, overproof glass baking dish. Top with the tomato, half of the onion, the garlic, half of the carrots, and the pepper; arrange the little cabbages on it. Sprinkle over them the remaining carrots, onion, thyme, bay leaves, and salt; pour the chicken stock over. Bring to a boil on top of the stove. Cover tightly with a large piece of aluminum foil, place on a cookie sheet in oven for 1 hour. Reduce oven to 350 F. and cook 1 hour longer.

Remove from the oven. Take off the aluminum foil; place little cabbages on a platter, and garnish by sprinkling all of the cooked vegetables on top of them. You should have about 1½ cups of juice left in the gratin dish; mix the vinegar and water with the arrowroot until smooth and add it to the juices. Stirring constantly, bring to a boil. Let boil for a few seconds, then pour over the cabbages. Serve hot as a whole meal with a salad. (Very good reheated.)

Petits Pois à la Française

[STEWED PEAS, FRENCH STYLE]
Serves 6

This recipe is especially good in the summertime when fresh peas, fresh tiny white onions and fresh Boston lettuce are available. If you are adamantly averse to shelling peas, use frozen peas—the smallest you can find, but never canned peas. If tiny white onions are not available, split large onions into chunks.

½ pound (30–35) tiny white onions about the size of large olives
1 large Boston lettuce, sliced across into ½-inch wide slices, then washed and drained
1 teaspoon salt
2 teaspoons sugar
1 cup water
2 tablespoons sweet butter
1 pound (about 2½ pounds in the pod) shelled peas (fresh, if possible)
1 tablespoon flour

Peel the onions, and place them with the sliced lettuce, salt, sugar, water and 1 tablespoon of the butter in a heavy saucepan (not aluminum, if possible). Bring to a boil. Cover, and simmer for 15 minutes. Add the peas, and simmer slowly for 10 minutes more.

In a bowl, mix the remaining butter and flour to a smooth paste. Strain the liquid from the simmered vegetables over it, mixing fast with a whisk to blend well. Pour the mixture back into the saucepan of vegetables and bring to a boil. Cover, and simmer slowly for 6–8 minutes. Taste for seasoning before serving; it may need more salt or sugar. An almost invariable twosome with pigeon, this is equally good with chicken.

Pommes Dauphine

[CREAM PUFF POTATOES]
Serves 6

3–4 medium potatoes (¾ pound, depending on size)
1½ teaspoons salt
1 cup water
⅓ stick sweet butter, cut into bits
¼ teaspoon freshly ground white pepper
1 cup all-purpose flour
4 large eggs
Vegetable oil for frying

Wash the potatoes; cover with cold water; add 1 teaspoon of the salt and bring to a boil over high heat. Reduce heat and boil slowly for 25–30 minutes until they are tender when pierced with the point of a knife. Make sure the potatoes are covered with water through-out the cooking time. When done, remove potatoes from water with a slotted spoon and let cool for 15–20 minutes. Peel the potatoes, cut into large pieces and, with your fingers or a spoon, push through a metal sieve or food mill; there should be about 1½ cups of pulp.

Put the cup of water into a saucepan, add the butter bits, salt, pepper, and bring to a boil. As soon as the water boils, add the flour all at once. Remove from heat and stir the mixture vigorously with a wooden spatula for 1 minute so that all the ingredients form a smooth, homogeneous mass of dough. Put back over low heat and continue working with the spatula for 3–4 minutes to dry; a crust should form in the bottom of the saucepan. Transfer the dough to a clean bowl (discard the dry crust that sticks to the bottom of the pan). Let dough cool for at least 10 min-utes. One at a time, add the eggs, beating well after each addition. (If you do not cool the mixture, it may scramble your eggs and ruin the whole dish.) Mix in the potato pulp.

Heat the oven to 180–200 F. Heat the oil in a saucepan at least 2″ deep. The oil must be at least 1½ inches deep. Using a thermometer, bring the oil to 350 F. One tablespoonful at a time, place the mixture into the hot oil, pushing the dough out of the spoon with your fingers. Depending on the size of your pan, you can make as many as 15 to 20 puffs at the same time. Cook for 8–10 minutes, turning the potatoes in the oil so they brown evenly all over. As soon as they are done, remove with a skimmer to a tray lined with paper towels. Keep warm in a 180–200 F. oven while you are cooking another batch. There is enough to make about 60 potato puffs. Sprinkle lightly with salt and serve as soon as possible or the potatoes will lose their crispness. Roast chicken, steak or veal chops are good with these.

Pommes Persillées

[PARSLEY POTATOES]
Serves 6

This is one of the easiest potato dishes to make, and it is excellent when done properly. In restaurants, for example, simple boiled potatoes are rarely good because, once boiled, potatoes cannot be kept in water for any length of time without becoming soggy and tasting reheated.

It is important that the potatoes be the same size to ensure proper cooking. If you cannot find tiny boiling potatoes, cut large ones into chunks, trimmed so you have pieces the same size and shape (about 1½″ in diameter).

3 pounds small potatoes, peeled; or 30
    potato pieces made of large potatoes
1 teaspoon salt
½ stick sweet butter
3 tablespoons fresh, finely chopped parsley

Cover the potatoes with cold water, add the salt and bring to a boil. Boil slowly for 18–20 minutes, until the potatoes are soft when pierced with the tip of a knife. Drain in a colander and put potatoes back in the saucepan over medium heat for a few seconds so that any residual water will evaporate. This method ensures very moist and rich-textured potatoes. Add the butter and parsley; cook just long enough for the butter to melt and coat the potatoes. Serve immediately. These are very good as an accompaniment for poached fish, pot roast, steaks—to name just a few dishes that they so appropriately complement.

Purée de Marrons

[CHESTNUT PURÉE]
Serves 6

When buying chestnuts, watch out for the little holes which indicate that they are wormy.

2 pounds chestnuts (about 1 pound 5
    ounces left after peeling)
⅓ rib of celery
2½ cups good chicken stock
½ stick sweet butter

1 cup heavy cream
1 teaspoon freshly ground white pepper
¼ teaspoon salt (depending on the
    saltiness of your stock)

Heat oven to 400 F. With the point of a paring knife, score each chestnut on both sides. The incisions help the skin to break open during roasting. Place on a flat cookie sheet (chestnuts should not overlap) and put into preheated oven for 20–30 minutes. (Do not brown to the point where part of the flesh is roasted black; they will become too dehydrated and be difficult to cook.) Remove from the oven. Peel the chestnuts, but hold them with a towel to avoid burning your hands. Both inner and outer skin must come off. Discard any bad chestnuts.

Put the peeled chestnuts in a heavy saucepan, add the celery and chicken stock; bring to a boil. Cover, and simmer slowly for 2 hours. There will be very little stock left in the pot. Put the entire mixture through a food mill. Place this purée in a clean saucepan and add the butter. Stir vigorously with a wooden spatula until it is well blended. Add the cream, pepper and salt as necessary, and stir again until mixture comes to a boil. Cover with plastic wrap and keep warm in a double boiler until serving time. In France, this usually goes with venison, roast goose or turkey.

Ratatouille

[PROVENCE'S VEGETABLE STEW]
Serves 6

This is the epitome of vegetable stews! Yet it is common fare in the south of France. In the following recipe, the vegetables are sautéed in oil, individually, before being stewed, and this is the usual practice, by the way, in good restaurants. However, if you prefer, you can put all the cubed vegetables into a casserole, top with the seasonings and water; cooked this way, the result is quite satisfactory and much less time-consuming. RATATOUILLE is excellent reheated, and superb cold as an *hors d'oeuvre*, top with small black olives and olive oil.

¼ cup olive oil
¼ cup vegetable oil
1 eggplant (1¼ pounds); ends cut off, washed and cut, with skin on, into 1-inch cubes (about 4 cups)
3 medium zucchini (about 1¼ pounds, washed, ends removed, cut in 1-inch cubes (about 3 cups)
¾ pound onions (2–3 depending on size) washed, peeled and cut into 1-inch cubes
1 pound sweet green peppers (2–3, depending on size); washed, seeded, and cut into 1″ squares (about 3 cups)
4–5 well-ripened tomatoes; peeled, seeded and coarsely cubed (about 4 cups) (see NOTE page 188)
5–6 cloves garlic; peeled, crushed, chopped very fine (about 1 tablespoon)
½ cup water
3½ teaspoons salt (that is a lot of salt, but this recipe requires it)
½ teaspoon freshly ground black pepper

Heat some of each oil in one or, better, two large skillets, and first sauté all of the eggplant cubes; remove with slotted spoon. Then sauté all of the zucchini cubes. (Allow 8 minutes for each.) (The eggplant will absorb more oil while cooking than the other vegetables.) When browned, place them in a large, heavy casserole that has a cover. In more oil, sauté the onions and peppers together for about 6 minutes. Add them to the casserole.

Add the remaining ingredients to the casserole and bring to a boil over medium heat. Reduce heat, cover, and cook over slow heat for 1½ hours. Remove the cover, increase the heat to medium, and cook another 30 minutes, uncovered, to reduce some of the liquid. Stir once in a while during the cooking to prevent scorching. Let the RATATOUILLE rest for at least 30 minutes before serving.

Timbales d' Épinards

[[SPINACH MOLDS]]
Serves 6

TIMBALES:

3 tablespoons vegetable oil
4½ tablespoons sweet butter
6 slices firm white bread, cut into rounds about 2½ inches in diameter
1 pound fresh spinach
Salt
½ teaspoon freshly ground white pepper
⅛ teaspoon nutmeg, preferably freshly grated
2 tablespoons flour
¾ cup milk
½ cup heavy cream
3 eggs

SAUCE:

1 tablespoon butter
1 tablespoon flour
¼ cup milk
¼ cup heavy cream
1 hard-cooked egg, shelled

Heat the oil and 1 tablespoon of the butter in a skillet, and sauté the rounds of bread on both sides until golden brown. Put on kitchen towel to drain. Set aside. Using ½ tablespoon of the butter, grease 6 small dariole or baba molds measuring 2¼ inches in diameter and 2″ high. Set aside.

If you have large leaves of spinach with thick stems, it is preferable to remove the stems. Fold each leaf underside-up with one hand. Grasp the stem with other, and rip it off. Wash the spinach and drop into a large pot of salted boiling water. Boil, uncovered, over high heat for 5–6 minutes. Cool under cold running water. Press the spinach to rid it of excess water. Chop the spinach coarsely; it will come to about 1 loose cupful. Sprinkle with the salt, pepper and nutmeg.

Melt the remaining 3 tablespoons butter in a heavy saucepan and cook until it is literally black and smoking. (Black or burned butter gives a nutty taste to the spinach.) Still over high heat, add the spinach and mix well with a fork. Sprinkle with the flour and mix well. Add the milk and cream and mix well. Reduce heat to medium, and, stirring constantly, bring to a boil. Remove from heat and cool to luke-warm.

Heat oven to 375 F. Beat the eggs with a fork to combine well and stir them into the spinach mixture. With this, fill the buttered molds and place them in a pan. Fill the pan with cold water to reach about ⅔ of the way up the molds. Bake in oven for 25–30 minutes, or until set. Tip of knife inserted should come out clean.

Meanwhile, prepare the sauce. Melt the 1 tablespoon of butter in a saucepan, add the flour and mix well with a whisk. Add the milk and cream and, stirring constantly, bring to a boil. Let simmer for 5 minutes over very low heat. Chop the

hard-cooked egg coarsely and set aside.

To serve, run a knife around the inside of the molds to loosen the *timbales.* Unmold each *timbale* on a sautéed round of bread, and arrange around a roast, or serve separately as a vegetable course. Pour 1 tablespoon of the white sauce on each *timbale.* Sprinkle with the chopped egg. Serve as a first course, a main course for lunch, or with the simplest broiled fish or chicken.

NOTE: Instead of using 6 individual molds, this recipe can be made in a large charlotte or soufflé mold. It will take 5–10 minutes longer in the oven.

Tomates Provençales

[TOMATOES WITH GARLIC]
Serves 6

An easy-to-prepare, unsophisticated dish, TOMATOES WITH GARLIC is very often featured in country restaurants.

6 medium tomatoes, very ripe (about 2 pounds)
1½ tablespoons olive oil
1½ tablespoons vegetable oil
1½ teaspoons salt (this recipe needs lots of salt)
½ teaspoon freshly ground white pepper
½ stick sweet butter
2 tablespoons freshly chopped parsley
5–6 cloves garlic; peeled, crushed, chopped very fine (about 1 tablespoon)

Heat oven to 300 F. Remove tomato stems, and cut each tomato horizontally into halves. Mix oils to-gether and heat in a very large skillet (or two if necessary). When hot, add the tomatoes, cut-side-down, and cook over high heat for about 3 minutes. Sprinkle with half of the salt and pepper. Turn the tomatoes over; sprinkle with the remaining salt and pepper and, over high heat, cook another 3 minutes. They should be slightly browned on both sides. Be careful: the oil splatters while cooking. Transfer the tomatoes to a serving gratin dish, cut-side-up and one touching the other, and put in oven for 10 minutes.

Meanwhile, melt the butter. When it sizzles, add the parsley and garlic and, shaking the pan constantly, cook about 45 seconds. Do not allow the garlic to burn or the dish will be completely ruined. Pour evenly over the tomatoes and serve immediately with any broiled meat.

Baking, Sweet and Savory

With the exception of making bread—an art that was rediscovered a few years ago —most people think of baking as preparing cakes, pastries, buttercreams or anything sweet. But what would a chicken pie be without its shawl of pastry? Or *empanadas* without their flaky crust? *Pâté en croute* without its casing? Impossible. Of course, all this is baking also: savory style. Don't most people immediately associate baking with an oven? What about crêpes; are they not baked on top of the stove, just as pancakes in a skillet over direct heat? The point is made. Baking is many things.

As distinguished from cooking, baking is more scientific and infinitely more precise. If a sauce is simmering too fast, you can adjust the heat. If a cake is baking too fast, it is too late. Lowering the heat at that point usually won't solve the problem. When a soup needs more seasoning, you add it. When a loaf of bread tastes flat, chances are it does not have enough salt; but you cannot do anything about it. This matter of precision is one of the reasons that so many people shy away from baking. They think it is too difficult. How often do you hear: "I like it, but it takes too much time." A little bit of patience and practice go a long way and pay off. Even the most proficient among us had to start learning at some point. What a pleasure it is when you can marvel at your own achievement and proudly compare what you have produced with the commercial product—if it is available at all. It is a feeling hard to come by in our world of hectic living where money and time seem to mean everything. I would not trade the hours in which baking afforded me an opportunity to leave this frantic world behind for a while to indulge in the pleasure of kneading my own dough, or to drink in the rich aroma of a yeast bread in the oven. What relaxation! What rewards! Above all, then, *baking is fun.*

Proper equipment is the cornerstone of good baking. Always read the entire recipe ahead of time to make sure you have all the right utensils. Let me share with you some thoughts on a few essentials. If you have to use your oven, make sure it is properly calibrated. An oven that does not produce the degree of heat for which it is set is a very common problem; it plays havoc with your cake. If you have had consistently bad luck in baking, even though you have followed the recipes exactly, ask your local appliance dealer to check the oven.

A ruler always comes in handy. You may not believe it, but there are recipes that call for measuring dough as you work with it. It is always a good idea to check the measurements of the equipment the recipe specifies. The difference between an eight-inch pie dish and one that measures ten inches usually means the difference between success and failure. If the instructions call for an 11 x 16-inch jelly-roll pan, don't stretch the dough to make it fit a pan that is larger. It won't work.

Baking time usually varies, depending on the type of vessel you use. Breads and pastries bake faster in glass than they do in metal. When a recipe calls for one cup of flour, don't measure it in a coffee cup. Use U. S.-standard measuring cups and spoons. They are inexpensive and should be in every baker's kitchen (a cook's too, for that matter). Beware of imported equipment because it is not always exact, or it may be designated in different or unfamiliar units. Don't trust your eyes measuring off ¼ to ½ cup in a one-cup measure. Incorrect quantities will throw off the ratio of ingredients.

Wooden spoons of varying sizes are always useful for baking. And rubber spatulas are indispensable in any kitchen. Try to find one with a wooden handle. Not only will it give you a better grip than the one with a smooth, plastic handle, but also it tends to be made of a better grade of rubber. When buying cookie sheets or jelly-roll pans, get the heaviest-gauge metal you can find. They bake more evenly, will last a lifetime and are therefore worth the extra money.

And now for the ingredients. Precision and quality are as important as the equipment. Here are a few basic hints.

The size of eggs varies considerably. The wrong size takes its toll on your recipe. The PÂTE À CHOUX recipe, for instance, calls for four U. S.-graded large eggs. If you use extra-large eggs, the paste becomes too fluid to shape with a pastry bag. In making the CHICKEN LIVER GOUGÈRE, it would be impossible to line the dish with the paste. For the DACQUOISE you would have too much egg white to make the meringue. If you tried to correct the problem by using larger layer-cake pans, thereby increasing the size of the meringue layers, the ratio of the sugar and almonds would be off. When you buy eggs, open the carton to see whether they are clean, and jiggle each one to make sure it is not stuck. You know what that means. Not only is a cracked or broken egg a nuisance and waste, but is also constitutes a health hazard because it can harbor bacteria.

I always make an issue about the use of "unsalted" butter. There is often a distinct difference between what is labeled "sweet" and "unsalted" butter. Unfortunately, some dairy producers label a package of butter as "sweet" in large print, and you don't discover until you come home— or not at all—that the fine print underneath specifies "lightly salted." To remind you of the difference, I always call for unsalted butter in my recipes. Make it a practice to smell butter before you buy it. If it has an aroma of cheese, it is not fresh.

A wide variety of flour is available in most markets, and it is easy to become confused. All-purpose flour is the most versatile. It can be used for cakes, breads and pastries. That is why I specify this type of flour in my recipes. Besides, it is less expensive than cake flours, which usually do not make much difference in the quality of the finished product, particularly if the cake is leavened with eggs. In preparing the recipes in this chapter, you must avoid using self-rising flour because it contains salt and baking powder.

Like film for your camera, yeast is marked with an expiration date. Check it to make sure that you get active yeast. If you plan to make a pastry which calls for heavy cream, buy it two days before you intend to use it. As heavy cream stands in the refrigerator, it thickens and therefore whips to a richer consistency than does fresh cream.

Now a final word on yeast dough, because it is used in so many baking recipes and abounds in myths. Don't be concerned over where you let your dough rise. It does *not* require a warm place to grow in bulk. You can even place it in the refrigerator! The only difference that temperatures make is the time it will take for the dough to rise. Avoid bringing the dry yeast in close contact with butter because it will

coat the yeast and make it difficult to activate. Proofing the yeast is as simple as anything. Don't be alarmed if the process described in the recipes that follow differs from the more involved one your mother used to use.

Go to it; find out that you, too, can bake. Join in the fun.

Almond Butter Cakes
Makes about 12

¾ pound (1½ cups) unsalted butter, softened, plus 1 tablespoon
1¾ cups granulated sugar
3 eggs, U. S.-graded large
1½ cups flour
1 teaspoon vanilla
¾ cup blanched almonds, coarsely chopped

Preheat oven to 350 F. Grease a 7 x 12 x 2-inch heat-resistant glass baking dish with the one tablespoon of butter. Place the sugar and softened butter in a large mixing bowl. Beat with a wooden spoon or electric mixer until light and fluffy. Beat in the eggs, one at a time, and then the flour and vanilla. Spoon the batter into the prepared baking dish and spread evenly. Sprinkle the top with the chopped almonds and bake 15 to 20 minutes, or until the cake is golden. Remove from oven and place the cake, still in the dish, on a wire rack to cool before cutting into small squares.

Baba au Rhum

Serves 8–10

BATTER:
¼ cup warm water (110 to 115 F.)
1 package active dry yeast
¼ cup granulated sugar
2 cups all-purpose flour
4 eggs, U. S.-graded large
¼ cup milk
½ cup unsalted butter, softened, plus
    1 tablespoon

To make the batter: Place the water, yeast and ½ teaspoon of the sugar in a small bowl. Stir once or twice and let stand until the mixture bubbles (4 to 6 minutes). In a large bowl, combine the flour, eggs, milk and the remaining sugar. Add the yeast mixture. With a wooden spoon, beat the batter until all the ingredients are well blended. Cover the bowl and let the batter rise until doubled in bulk (about 45 minutes).

Stir the batter down and beat in the softened butter. With the remaining tablespoon of butter, lightly grease a 1½-quart oblong heat-resistant glass baking dish and pour in the batter. Let rise for the second time. After it has been rising for 15 minutes, preheat the oven to 400 F. When the dough has doubled, place it in the oven and bake for 10 minutes. Reduce the oven temperature to 350 F. and continue to bake the *Baba* for an additional 20 minutes or until golden brown. Remove from oven and cool on cake rack.

SYRUP:
1 cup sugar
2 cups water
½ cup dark rum

To make the syrup: Combine the sugar and water in a 1-quart saucepan. Place the pan on high heat until the sugar dissolves. Remove from the heat and allow to cool to room temperature. Stir in the rum.

TO FINISH:
½ cup apricot preserve, heated and put
    through a sieve.
2½ cups rum syrup

To finish the Baba au Rhum: Invert the cooled cake onto a serving plate. Slowly spoon about 1 cup of the rum syrup over it, allowing the cake to absorb the syrup. Continue in this fashion until you have used all the syrup. If an excessive amount collects on the serving dish, spoon it back over the cake. This should take 20 minutes to ½ hour overall. Brush the surface with the warm apricot preserve. Cut as ALMOND BUTTER CAKES (page 212). Serve at room temperature.

Cheese Bread

Makes 1 Loaf

1 cup lukewarm water (110–115 F.)
1 envelope active dry yeast
½ teaspoon sugar
3½ to 4 cups sifted all-purpose flour
2 teaspoons salt
1½ cups grated sharp Cheddar cheese
3 eggs
2 teaspoons unsalted butter
2 tablespoons milk

Place the water, yeast and sugar in a small bowl. Stir once or twice and let stand until mixture bubbles (4 to 6 minutes). Combine 3½ cups flour, salt, cheese and two of the eggs in a large mixing bowl. Add the bubbled yeast mixture and stir with a wooden spoon until all the liquid has been absorbed. With your hands, gather the dough into a ball. Place it on a lightly floured surface and knead for about 10 minutes. If the dough sticks to your hands or to the kneading surface, knead in a few tablespoons of flour at a time. Continue to knead until the dough is smooth.

With 1 teaspoon of the butter, lightly grease a bowl. Put in the dough and sprinkle it with a little flour. Cover with a towel and let the dough rise until double in bulk (about 1 hour). When the dough has risen, punch it down. Cover again with the towel and let it rise for the second time (30 to 40 minutes). With the remaining butter, grease a 9 x 5 x 3-inch ovenproof glass bread pan.

When the dough has risen, punch it down again. Preheat oven to 375 F. Shape the dough into a loaf and place it in the prepared pan. Brush top with mixture made by lightly beating together the milk and the remaining egg. Bake bread until golden brown (about 45 minutes). Remove from pan and cool on cake rack.

THE GREAT COOKS COOKBOOK

Chicken Liver Gougère

Serves 4

PÂTE À CHOUX
Choux Pastry
1 cup water
½ teaspoon salt
6 tablespoons unsalted butter
1 cup all-purpose flour, sifted
4 eggs, U. S.-graded large
1 egg beaten with 2 tablespoons milk, for
    topping

FILLING
4 tablespoons unsalted butter
1 cup chicken livers (about 8 ounces)
2 tablespoons finely chopped shallots
1 cup sliced fresh mushrooms
1 tablespoon flour
½ cup chicken broth
1 medium tomato, peeled, cut into wedges,
    and seeded
Salt and freshly ground pepper
1 tablespoon finely chopped fresh parsley

To make the pastry: Place the water, salt and butter in a small saucepan. Bring to a boil. When butter melts, remove pan from heat and add the flour all at once. Beat the mixture with a wooden spoon until the dough leaves the sides of the pan. Return to medium heat and cook, beating vigorously for 1 minute.

Remove from heat and beat in the 4 eggs, one at a time, beating well after each addition. Continue to beat the mixture until smooth and shiny.

To make the filling: Heat the butter in a small skillet until very hot. Add the chicken livers and sauté them on all sides until nicely browned (about 3 minutes). With slotted spoon, remove livers from skillet. To the butter remaining in the skillet, add the chopped shallots and cook over medium heat until transparent. Stir in the mushrooms and cook for 2 minutes. Stir in the flour, broth and tomato. Simmer for 4 to 5 minutes, then add the chicken livers. Taste for salt and pepper. Remove from heat.

Preheat the oven to 400 F. Divide choux pastry into 4 equal portions. Line 4 lightly buttered individual ovenproof glass dishes, about 3½ inches in diameter and about 2 inches deep, with the pastry, by gently pressing it against the dish with your fingers. Brush pastry with the egg-milk mixture. Divide the filling evenly into the 4 dishes. Place in oven and bake the GOUGÈRE for about 20 minutes or until pastry is well puffed and nicely browned. Sprinkle with chopped parsley before serving.

Chocolate Prune Roll

Serves 8–10

THE FILLING:

8 ounces pitted prunes
1 stick (½ cup) unsalted butter
½ cup granulated sugar
½ teaspoon vanilla
1½ ounces semisweet chocolate, melted

To make the filling: Place the prunes in a medium-size saucepan and cover with cold water. Bring to a boil, reduce heat and let simmer for 12 to 14 minutes or until the prunes are soft. Pour off the water and dry the prunes with paper towels. Using a food mill, purée the prunes; discard the skins. With a large wooden spoon, beat the butter, sugar and vanilla in a medium-size bowl until fluffy and light in color. Beat in the puréed prunes and melted chocolate. Refrigerate for about 1 hour.

THE CAKE:

4 teaspoons butter, softened, plus 2 tablespoons flour
5 eggs, U. S.-graded large
1 cup superfine sugar
1 cup all-purpose flour, sifted
4 tablespoons butter, melted and cooled
2 teaspoons lemon rind, grated
½ cup confectioners' sugar, sifted

To make the cake: Preheat the oven to 350 F. Spread an 11 x 16-inch jelly-roll pan with 2 teaspoons of the softened butter and line the pan with wax paper. Spread the remaining 2 teaspoons of softened butter on the wax paper, then sprinkle it with the 2 tablespoons of flour. Tip the pan from side to side to cover the butter evenly with flour. Turn the pan upside down and knock out any excess flour.

Place the eggs and sugar in a large mixing bowl. Beat with an electric mixer until triple in bulk. With a rubber spatula fold in the flour, a few tablespoons at a time. Add the butter and lemon rind in the same fashion. Pour the mixture into the prepared jelly-roll pan. Bake for 12 to 16 minutes or until the cake is golden brown and shrinks slightly away from the sides of the pan. Remove the cake from the oven and allow to cool in the pan on a wire cake rack. Turn out onto a fresh sheet of wax paper. Carefully peel off buttered wax paper.

Using an icing spatula, spread the prune filling evenly over the cake. Starting at a long edge, roll it into a cylinder. Wrap in foil and refrigerate. To serve, unwrap the cake; place on a long platter and dust with the confectioners' sugar.

Crab Turnovers

Serves 8

THE FILLING:

3 tablespoons unsalted butter
3 tablespoons flour
1 cup milk
1 pound crabmeat, with all cartilage picked
 out
¼ teaspoon cayenne pepper
1 teaspoon salt
2 tablespoons chopped chives
2 tablespoons chopped fresh parsley

THE PASTRY

8 sheets filo pastry (see NOTE)
¼ pound unsalted butter, melted

To make the filling: In a heavy, 1-quart saucepan, melt the butter over medium heat. Add the flour and mix well. Stirring with a wire whisk, pour in the milk and cook over high heat until mixture comes to a boil and thickens. Reduce heat to low and let simmer for 2 or 3 minutes. Remove from heat, and stir in the crabmeat, pepper, salt, chives and parsley. Taste for seasoning and cool to room temperature.

To make the turnovers: Preheat the oven to 400 F. Spread one sheet of 12 x 16-inch filo flat, and brush the entire surface with about 1 tablespoon of the melted butter. Fold the pastry over once from a 12-inch side and once from a 16-inch side. The pastry now has four layers and measures 6 x 8 inches. Brush 2 inches of the edge of one 8-inch side with butter and fold over to make a 6-inch square. Spread ⅛ of the crabmeat filling onto the center of the square.

Brush the edges of the square with additional melted butter. Fold the squares in half, diagonally, to form a triangular turnover. Press the edges down to seal. In the same fashion, make 7 more turnovers. Place them on a lightly buttered cookie sheet and bake in the middle of the oven for 15 to 25 minutes or until the pastry is crisp and lightly browned.

NOTE: Filo is a Greek sheet pastry that can be bought, fresh or frozen, in most specialty food stores.

Croissants

Makes 18

1 cup warm water (110 to 115 F.)
1 package active dry yeast
½ teaspoon sugar
3 cups all-purpose flour
2 teaspoons salt
1 tablespoon (plus, separately, 1 teaspoon)
   unsalted butter
1 cup unsalted butter (chilled)

Place the water, yeast and sugar in a small bowl. Stir once or twice and let stand until the mixture bubbles (4 to 6 minutes). In a large bowl, combine the flour, salt and 1 tablespoon butter. Add the yeast mixture. Stir with a wooden spoon until all the liquid is absorbed. With your hands, gather the dough into a ball. Place it on a lightly floured surface and knead for about 10 minutes. If the dough sticks to your hands or to the kneading surface, knead in a few tablespoons of flour at a time. Continue to knead until the dough is smooth.

Lightly grease a large bowl with 1 teaspoon of butter. Place the dough in the bowl; sprinkle it with a little flour. Cover with a towel and let the dough rise until double in bulk (about 1 hour). When the dough has risen, punch it down; sprinkle with a little flour and wrap in foil. Place in the refrigerator until well chilled (about 2 hours).

Remove from refrigerator and, on a lightly floured surface, roll the dough into an oblong shape ¼-inch thick. Place the oblong so that its long side faces you horizontally. Visualize it as being folded into thirds, which will finally make 3 layers.

Begin at the right: dot only two-thirds of the surface with ¼ of the chilled butter (scooped out of cup about 1 teaspoonful at a time). Leave last third *un-buttered*.

Begin now on the left with the un-buttered end: lift, and fold it over the center buttered third. Fold remaining buttered third over center, thus forming 3 layers.

Roll the dough again into a ¼-inch oblong shape and proceed as just described until all the chilled butter has been used. Wrap dough in foil and chill for 2 hours.

Preheat oven to 350 F. On a lightly floured surface, roll the chilled dough into a square measuring approximately 15½–16 x ¼ inch. Using a ruler, measure off a 15" x 15" square and, with a pastry wheel or sharp knife, cut the dough to this measurement. In the same fashion, measure and cut this dough into nine 5-inch squares. Place 8 of the squares on a large cookie sheet and refrigerate (to prevent the dough from softening) while you make the first two CROISSANTS.

Cut the 5-inch square diagonally, creating 2 triangles. Elongate each triangle by rolling with a rolling pin to ⅛-inch thickness. Hold the point opposite the wide base with one hand and, with the palm of the other, roll up the dough from the base. Stretch it slightly as you roll.

Remove a 5-inch square from cookie sheet in refrigerator and replace with the two rolled triangles, turning the ends in slightly to form a crescent, or croissant. One at a time, remove, cut and shape the remaining squares, returning each to refrigerator after rolling, until all are formed.

Transfer all croissants to a lightly greased baking sheet. Bake on middle shelf of oven until golden brown (about 20 minutes).

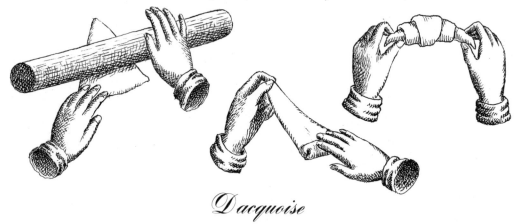

Dacquoise

Serves 8–10

MERINGUE INGREDIENTS
10 tablespoons granulated sugar
1 cup blanched almonds, toasted and
    ground
2 tablespoons cornstarch
¼ cup unsweetened cocoa
6 egg whites, from U. S.-graded large eggs
1 teaspoon unsalted butter

BUTTERCREAM INGREDIENTS
1 cup confectioners' sugar, plus 2
    tablespoons
2 egg yolks, from U. S.-graded large eggs
½ cup milk
2 sticks (½ pound) unsalted butter
½ cup unsweetened cocoa

To make the meringue: Preheat oven to 250 F. In a small bowl, mix 2 tablespoons of the granulated sugar, ground almonds, cornstarch and ¼ cup cocoa. Set aside. In a large bowl, beat egg whites with an electric mixer until they begin to form soft peaks. Add the remaining 8 tablespoons granulated sugar; continue to beat until egg whites are very firm. With a rubber spatula, fold the almond mixture thoroughly into the meringue. Bottom-side turned up, butter with 1 teaspoon butter, and lightly flour two 9-inch layer cake pans. Spread half the mixture on the bottom of each upside-down pan. Bake the meringue 60 to 90 minutes or until it feels dry and crisp to the touch. Remove from the oven and allow to cool on the pans.

To make the buttercream: In a heavy saucepan, mix the confectioners' sugar and egg yolks with a wooden spoon until well blended. In a second saucepan, heat the milk until small bubbles appear around the edge. Gradually, pour the hot milk into the combined sugar and egg yolks, constantly beating with a wire whisk. Place the mixture on medium to low heat and cook, stirring constantly, until it coats a spoon heavily. Do not allow mixture (custard) to boil. Pour the custard into a large bowl and cool it by beating with an electric mixer at high speed until it reaches room temperature. Soften the sticks of butter with your hands quickly, preventing lumps and an oily texture. Set aside. Beat

the cocoa into the custard. Add the butter, about 2 tablespoons at a time. Continue to beat the buttercream until it is smooth and fluffy.

To assemble the DACQUOISE: Loosen meringue layers with a metal spatula. Place one layer on serving dish. Spoon the chocolate buttercream into a pastry bag fitted with a #5 star tube. Pipe rosettes all around the top edge of one layer. Continue in this pattern toward the center until the entire layer is covered with rosettes. Gently place the second layer of meringue on top of the buttercream. For decoration, form one large rosette in the center of the top layer. Chill the DACQUOISE for one hour. Before serving, sprinkle with the 2 tablespoons confectioners' sugar and place on cake dish.

Empanadas
Makes 20–24

PASTRY:
3 cups all-purpose flour
4 tablespoons vegetable shortening, chilled
½ teaspoon salt
1½ sticks (12 tablespoons) unsalted butter, chilled, plus 2 tablespoons softened (for greasing cookie sheets)
4 to 6 tablespoons ice water

To make the pastry: Place the flour in a medium-size bowl. Add the vegetable shortening and salt. Cut the chilled butter into small pieces and place them on top of the flour. With your

fingertips, work the ingredients together quickly (to prevent softening of the butter and shortening) until they look like coarse meal. Pour 3 tablespoons of the ice water over the mixture, stir with fingers and gather into a ball. If the dough crumbles, add additional ice water a tablespoon at a time. Wrap in plastic wrap and refrigerate for one hour.

THE FILLING:
3 tablespoons oil
½ cup chopped onions
½ teaspoon finely chopped garlic
½ pound lean ground beef

THE GREAT COOKS COOKBOOK

½ pound lean ground pork
¼ teaspoon ground cumin
½ teaspoon salt
¼ teaspoon cayenne pepper
8 pitted black olives, coarsely chopped
3 hard-cooked eggs, coarsely chopped

To make the filling: Heat the oil in a medium-size skillet until very hot. Add the chopped onions and garlic and cook until the onions are transparent. Add the ground meats and stir with a wooden spoon, breaking up any lumps. Continue to cook until the meat loses its pink color. Scrape the meat mixture into a bowl and add the cumin, salt, cayenne pepper, chopped olives and eggs. Mix well and taste for seasoning. Allow to cool to room temperature.

TO SHAPE AND BAKE THE EMPANADAS:
2 tablespoons unsalted butter, softened
Flour

Lightly grease two large cookie sheets with the softened butter. On a lightly floured surface, roll out the chilled pastry to ⅛-inch thickness. Using a 3-inch cookie cutter, stencil out pastry rounds. Gather the scraps, reroll and continue to cut rounds until all the pastry is used. Place a teaspoon of filling on each round of pastry. Moisten the edges of the pastry with a little water. Fold the dough over, making a turnover shape, and press the edges together with your fingers to seal in the filling. Preheat the oven to 350 F. Place the EMPANADAS on the prepared cookie sheets and chill for 15 minutes. Bake the EMPANADAS on the middle shelf of the oven for 10 minutes, or until they are lightly brown.

NOTE: This Latin-American dish is particularly nice with cocktails or a before-dinner drink.

Frangipan Gâteau
[[ALMOND CAKE]]
Serves 8–10

THE PASTRY:
1¼ cups all-purpose flour
2 egg yolks, U. S.-graded large
2 tablespoons granulated sugar
1 stick (8 tablespoons) unsalted butter

To make the pastry: Place the flour in a medium-size bowl. Add the egg yolks and sugar. Cut the butter into small pieces and place them on top of the flour. With your fingers, mix the ingredients together until well blended into a medium-firm paste. Wrap in wax paper and refrigerate for 1 hour.

THE FILLING:
1 stick (8 tablespoons) unsalted butter
1 cup almond paste *
¼ cup all-purpose flour, sifted
3 eggs U. S.-graded large
½ teaspoon vanilla
1 teaspoon grated lemon rind

* Available frozen and in cans.

To make the filling: In a medium-size bowl, cream the butter by beating it with a wooden spoon. Gradually add the almond paste and continue to beat until smooth. Beat in the flour, the eggs—one at a time—and then the vanilla and the lemon rind.

TO MAKE THE GÂTEAU:
2 teaspoons unsalted butter, softened
¾ cup apricot jam
1 cup sliced almonds, toasted

Preheat oven to 350 F. Grease a 9-inch heat-resistant glass layer-cake pan with 2 teaspoons softened butter. Roll out the pastry between two pieces of wax paper until about ¼ inch thick and slightly more than 9 inches in diameter. Remove top piece of wax paper. Invert the cake pan onto the rolled-out dough and press firmly (as with a cookie cutter) to cut dough to fit the pan. Insert palm of hand under the wax paper and turn pan and pastry right-side-up so that the 9-inch circle of pastry falls into the pan. Gently peel off the paper and remove excess pastry.

Prick the pastry 6 to 8 times with the tines of a fork. Place in the preheated oven and bake until light golden (about 15 minutes). Remove from oven and allow to cool to room temperature on cake rack. Coat the pastry with ¼ cup of the apricot jam. Spread the almond filling evenly over the top of the coated pastry and smooth with a spatula. Bake 25 to 30 minutes, or until cake tester comes out clean and the cake is dark golden brown. Cool on a cake rack for about 30 minutes. Invert cake onto a plate and, holding cake and plate together, turn right-side-up onto a serving plate. Coat the top of the cake with the remaining apricot jam and sprinkle with the toasted almonds.

Frozen Walnut Cream Torte
Serves 8

CAKE:
4 teaspoons unsalted butter, softened
2 tablespoons flour
5 egg yolks, U. S.-graded large
¾ cup sugar
1 teaspoon vanilla
¼ cup fresh bread crumbs, toasted in oven
1 cup ground walnuts
5 egg whites

Prepare the cake pans: Spread the inside of each of two 9-inch heat-resistant glass layer-cake pans with 1 teaspoon of the softened butter. Line the bottom of the pans with wax paper and coat the paper with the remaining butter. Sprinkle each pan with 1 tablespoon of flour. Tip the pans side to side several times, allowing flour to coat the butter evenly. Turn the pans upside down and shake out any excess flour.

To make the cake: Preheat the oven to 350 F. Place the egg yolks, sugar and the 1 teaspoon of vanilla in a large mixing bowl and beat with an electric mixer until triple in bulk. Stir in the bread crumbs and ground walnuts. Clean the beaters.

In another large bowl, beat the egg whites with an electric mixer until they are stiff enough to stand in firm peaks. With a rubber spatula, stir ¼ of the whites into the yolk mixture. Pour it over the remaining egg whites and gently fold them together. Pour the batter into the prepared layer-cake pans. Bake on the middle shelf of the oven for 12 to 15 minutes, or until the cake shrinks away slightly from the sides of the pans. Remove the cakes from the oven and allow them to cool in the pans on cake racks. Unmold and peel off wax paper if it adheres to the cake.

TO PUT THE CAKE TOGETHER:
2 cups heavy cream, chilled
¼ cup confectioners' sugar, sifted
2 teaspoons vanilla

Putting the cake together: When the layers have cooled, whip the heavy cream until firm enough to stand in soft peaks. Beat in the confectioners' sugar and the 2 teaspoons vanilla. Place one layer on a serving plate and spread the top with whipped cream. Place the second layer on top of the first and spread it with whipped cream. Finally, spread the remaining whipped cream on the sides. Place the cake in the freezer. When the cream is firm— about 1 hour—gently wrap cake in foil and return to freezer. One hour before serving, remove foil and place the cake in refrigerator.

German Crumb Cake
Serves 4–6

THE DOUGH:
¼ cup warm water (110 to 115 F.)
1 package active dry yeast
⅓ cup granulated sugar
1½ cups flour
2 eggs
¼ cup milk
4 tablespoons unsalted butter, softened— plus 1 teaspoon

THE TOPPING:
12 tablespoons unsalted butter, chilled, plus 4 tablespoons, melted
1½ cups flour
12 tablespoons granulated sugar
1 teaspoon cinnamon

To make the dough: Place water, yeast and ½ teaspoon of the sugar in a small bowl. Stir once or twice and let stand until the mixture bubbles (4 to 6 minutes).

In a large bowl, combine the flour, eggs, milk, 4 tablespoons butter and remaining sugar. Add the yeast mixture. With a wooden spoon, mix until all the liquid has been absorbed.

With your hands gather the dough into a ball. Place it on a lightly floured surface and knead for about 10 minutes. If the dough sticks to your hands or to the kneading surface, knead in a few tablespoons of flour at a time. Continue to knead until the dough is smooth. With 1 teaspoon butter, lightly grease a bowl. Put in the dough and sprinkle it with a little flour. Cover with a towel and let the dough rise until double in bulk (about 1 hour).

To make the topping: With your fingertips, rub the butter and the dry ingredients together quickly (to prevent softening of the butter) until they form large crumbs.

To make the cake: Preheat the oven to 350 F. After the dough has risen, punch it down and roll it to fit a 7 x 12 x 1½-inch heat-resistant glass baking dish. Place the dough in the dish. If necessary, stretch it until it covers the bottom of the dish smoothly. Sprinkle the crumbs evenly over the dough. Spoon the melted butter on top. Bake for 30 minutes or until the top is crusty. Serve at room temperature.

Honey Cake
Serves 8–10

12 tablespoons vegetable oil, plus 2 tablespoons for preparing baking dish
1 cup granulated sugar
1 tablespoon baking powder
2 cups all-purpose flour
8 ounces ground walnuts or pecans
1 cup raisins
3 eggs
1 (16-ounce) jar of honey
1 tablespoon grated lemon rind
4 tablespoons lemon juice
¾ cup strong coffee, cooled

Preheat oven to 350 F. Grease 2 8½ x 4½ x 2½-inch heat-resistant glass baking dishes, using 1 tablespoon oil. Line with wax paper and grease again with the second tablespoon of oil.

Sift the sugar, baking powder and flour together into a large bowl. Blend in the nuts and raisins.

In another large bowl, mix eggs, honey, grated lemon rind, lemon juice, remaining oil and cooled coffee. With a large wooden spoon, stir the flour mixture into the honey mixture until all ingredients are well blended. Divide the batter evenly into the two prepared baking dishes. Bake for 30 to 40 minutes or until the cakes are dark brown.

Islander Lime Pie

Serves 6–8

PASTRY:

1½ cups all-purpose flour
2 tablespoons vegetable shortening, chilled
1 tablespoon granulated sugar
¼ teaspoon salt
6 tablespoons unsalted butter, chilled, plus 2 teaspoons softened
3 to 4 tablespoons ice water

To make the pastry: Place the flour in a medium-size bowl. Add the vegetable shortening, sugar and salt. Cut the butter into small pieces and place them on top of the flour. With your fingertips, work the ingredients together quickly (to prevent softening of the butter and shortening) until they look like coarse meal. Pour 3 tablespoons ice water over the mixture, mix with a fork and gather the mixture into a ball. If the dough crumbles, add the additional tablespoon of ice water. Wrap in plastic wrap and refrigerate for 1 hour.

Lightly grease a 9-inch glass pie dish with the softened butter. On a lightly floured surface, roll the pastry into a 14-inch circle. To prevent the pastry from sticking, turn it clockwise several times as you roll it. With the help of a metal spatula, roll the pastry onto a rolling pin and unroll it over the rim of the pie dish. Press gently into place until the dish is evenly lined. With a small knife, trim the excess pastry from the rim. Chill for 30 minutes.

To bake the pie shell: Preheat the oven to 400 F. Place a circle of wax paper on top of the chilled pastry. (It should extend about 2 inches beyond the edge of the pie plate to facilitate lifting it out after the shell is set.) Fill the pastry shell with rice and bake on the middle shelf of the oven for 10 minutes. Remove the rice and wax paper. Prick the pastry with a fork in several places, and return it to the oven for 8 to 10 minutes or until it is golden brown. Remove from oven and, leaving the shell in the dish, place on a wire rack to cool.

FILLING:

1¼ cups granulated sugar
1 envelope unflavored gelatin
3 egg yolks
¾ cup evaporated milk
¾ cup fresh lime juice, strained
4 tablespoons grated lime rind
3 egg whites
1 cup heavy cream
2 tablespoons confectioners' sugar

To make the filling: In a 1-quart heavy saucepan mix the granulated sugar and gelatin. Beat the egg yolks into the sugar mixture. Slowly stir in the evaporated milk. Place the mixture on medium heat and cook, stirring constantly, until it coats a spoon. Do not allow mixture (custard) to boil.

Pour the custard into a large bowl and beat in the lime juice and 3 tablespoons of the grated lime rind. Let the custard cool to room temperature.

When the custard has cooled, beat the egg whites until they are very firm. With a rubber spatula, stir ¼ of the egg whites into the custard, then pour the custard over the remaining egg whites and gently fold together.

Pour the filling into the prepared pastry shell and refrigerate for at least 2 hours. Just before serving, whip the heavy cream until firm enough to stand in soft peaks. Beat in the confectioners' sugar and spread cream over the top of the pie with an icing spatula. Sprinkle top with remaining 1 tablespoon lime rind.

The Matured Pound Cake

Serves 8–10

2 sticks unsalted butter, plus 2 teaspoons softened
1¼ cups granulated sugar
5 eggs, U. S.-graded large
1 teaspoon grated lemon rind
1 teaspoon vanilla
2 cups all-purpose flour, sifted
½ cup coarsely chopped walnuts or pecans

To make the cake: Preheat the oven to 350 F. Grease a 5 x 3 x 9-inch heat-resistant glass loaf pan with the softened butter. Place the remaining butter and sugar in a large mixing bowl and beat with an electric mixer until light in color. One at a time, beat in the eggs; add lemon rind and vanilla. With a rubber spatula, fold in the flour very gently but thoroughly.

Place mixture in loaf pan and sprinkle the top with the chopped nuts. Bake for 1 to 1¼ hours, or until cake tester stuck in middle comes out clean. Remove from oven and allow to cool in pan on cake rack. The cake should be allowed to mature for at least 4 to 6 hours. Unmold and serve.

A Most Untraditional Chicken Pie

Serves 6

THE DOUGH:

¼ cup warm water (110 to 115 F.)
1 package active dry yeast
½ teaspoon sugar
3½ cups all-purpose flour
1½ teaspoons salt
8 tablespoons unsalted butter, softened
¾ cup milk
1 egg yolk and 2 tablespoons milk beaten
  together

To make the dough: Place the water, yeast and sugar in a small bowl. Stir once or twice and let stand until mixture bubbles (4 to 6 minutes).

Combine flour, salt, 6 tablespoons of the softened butter, and milk in a large bowl. Add the yeast mixture. With a wooden spoon, stir until all the liquid has been absorbed.

With your hands, gather the dough into a ball. Place it on a lightly floured surface and knead for about 10 minutes. If the dough sticks to your hands or to the kneading surface, add a few tablespoons of flour at a time. Continue to knead until the dough is smooth.

Grease a large bowl with 1 tablespoon butter, place the dough in it and sprinkle lightly with flour. Cover with a towel and let the dough rise until it is double in bulk (about 1 hour). When the dough has doubled, punch it down. Cover with the towel and let rise until it is doubled in bulk again (this time 30 to 40 minutes).

THE FILLING:

4 tablespoons unsalted butter
½ cup chopped onion
¼ cup chopped green pepper
½ teaspoon finely chopped garlic
1 cup canned tomatoes, drained and
  chopped
2½ cups cooked chicken meat, diced into
  ½-inch pieces
½ teaspoon salt
¼ teaspoon freshly ground black pepper
2 tablespoons chopped fresh parsley

To make the filling: While the dough is rising, heat the butter in a large skillet until very hot. Add the onions, green pepper, garlic and, stirring, cook at medium heat for about 8 minutes or until the vegetables are soft. Stir in the tomatoes, raise the heat to high and cook until the liquid has evaporated. Add the chicken, salt, pepper, and parsley. Taste for seasoning and cool to room temperature.

To roll the dough: Preheat the oven

to 350 F. With the remaining tablespoon of butter, grease a 9-inch heat-resistant glass pie dish. After the dough has risen the second time, punch it down again, roll on a lightly floured surface and shape it into a 22-inch round. With the help of a metal spatula, roll the dough onto a rolling pin. Unroll it loosely over the rim of the dish. Press gently into place until the dish is evenly lined. Let excess dough hang over the rim. Spoon in the filling. Gather the excess dough and overlap it evenly at the center of the dish to cover the filling completely. Brush with the egg yolk and milk mixture. Bake for 40 to 50 minutes, or until the crust is golden brown.

One-Crust Apple Pie

Serves 8

PASTRY:
1½ cups all-purpose flour
2 tablespoons vegetable shortening, chilled
1 tablespoon granulated sugar
¼ teaspoon salt
6 tablespoons unsalted butter, chilled, plus 3 tablespoons, softened
3 to 4 tablespoons ice water

THE FILLING:
4 tablespoons unsalted butter
3 pounds Greening apples, cored, peeled and cut into ¼-inch slices
½ to ¾ cup granulated sugar, depending on the tartness of the apples
2 teaspoons vanilla

To make the pastry: Place the flour in a medium-size bowl. Add the vegetable shortening, sugar and salt. Cut the 6 tablespoons chilled butter into small pieces and place them on top of the flour. With your fingertips, work the ingredients together quickly (to prevent softening of the butter and shortening) until they look like coarse meal. Pour 3 tablespoons ice water over the mixture and gather it into a small ball. If the dough crumbles, add the additional tablespoon ice water. Wrap in plastic wrap and refrigerate for 1 hour. Grease a 9-inch heat-resistant glass pie dish with the softened butter.

To make the filling: Heat the butter in a large skillet. Add the sliced apples and sugar. Sauté them 4 to 6 minutes, shaking the pan so the butter coats the apples on all sides. Remove from heat and stir in the vanilla. Place the apple mixture in the buttered pie dish, and allow to cool to room temperature.

To make the pie: On a lightly floured surface, roll the pastry into an 11-inch circle. To prevent the pastry from sticking, turn it clockwise several times as you roll it. With the help of a metal spatula, roll the pastry onto a rolling pin and unroll it over the pie dish with the apple filling. With a small knife, trim off the excess pastry around the edge of the pie dish.

Press the edge of the pastry against the top edge of the pie plate with the tines of a fork. With a small knife make 2 slits toward the center of the pastry to allow the steam to escape. Place the pie in the refrigerator for 30 minutes. Bake in a preheated 350 F. oven until the crust is golden brown (40 to 50 minutes).

Pizza Siciliana

Serves 6–8

THE DOUGH:
1 cup warm water (110 to 115 F.)
1 package active dry yeast
½ teaspoon granulated sugar
3½ cups all-purpose flour
2 teaspoons salt
2 tablespoons oil

To make the dough: Place the water, yeast and sugar in a small bowl. Stir once or twice and let stand until mixture bubbles (4 to 6 minutes). Combine flour and salt in a large mixing bowl. Add the yeast mixture. With a wooden spoon, stir until all the liquid has been absorbed.

With your hands, gather the dough into a ball. Place it on a lightly floured surface and knead for about 10 minutes. If the dough sticks to your hands or to the kneading surface, knead in a few tablespoons of flour at a time. Continue to knead until the dough is smooth.

Grease a large bowl lightly with 1 teaspoon of the oil. Place the dough in it and sprinkle it lightly with flour. Cover with a towel and let the dough rise until it is doubled in bulk (about 1 hour). When the dough has doubled, punch it down.

Cover again with the towel and let it rise for a second time (30 to 40 minutes). With the remaining oil, grease two 7 x 12-inch heat-resistant glass baking dishes, about 1½–2-inches high.

TOMATO SAUCE:
4 tablespoons olive oil
½ cup finely chopped onions
1 teaspoon finely chopped garlic
2 1-pound cans whole tomatoes
1 tablespoon dried basil
1 teaspoon salt
½ teaspoon freshly ground black pepper
½ teaspoon sugar
¼ cup tomato paste

To make the sauce: Heat the oil in a large skillet until very hot. Add the onions and the garlic and, stirring, cook for about 8 minutes, or until the onions are soft. Stir in the tomatoes and their liquid, the basil, salt, pepper, sugar and tomato paste. Bring to a boil, lower the heat and let simmer, uncovered, for 30 minutes.

THE TOPPING:
1 pound mozzarella cheese, grated
¼ cup Parmesan cheese, grated

1 large green pepper, halved, seeded, and
    cut into 1/4-inch strips
1/2 cup finely chopped onions
6 anchovies, chopped
12 pitted black olives
1/2 teaspoon dried orégano
2 tablespoons olive oil

To bake the PIZZA: Preheat the oven to 450 F. When the dough has risen for the second time, punch it down and cut it in half. Roll each half to fit the prepared baking dishes. Place the dough in the dishes and, if necessary, stretch and smooth it out with your hands until it covers the bottom of the dish. Spread the sauce evenly over the top of the dough. Bake in the middle of the oven for 15 minutes, then sprinkle the pizzas with the mozzarella and Parmesan cheese, green peppers, chopped onions, chopped anchovies, black olives and orégano. Spoon the olive oil over the top and bake for an additional 10 minutes. Remove from oven and allow the pizzas to rest for 5 minutes before slicing them into squares.

Very Sticky Buns
Makes 10–12

THE DOUGH:
1/4 cup warm water (110 to 115 F.)
1 package active dry yeast
1/2 cup granulated sugar
3 1/2 cups all-purpose flour
1/2 teaspoon salt
1 1/4 cups milk
2 teaspoons grated lemon rind
1 egg
9 tablespoons unsalted butter

FILLING:
1/2 cup raisins
1 1/2 teaspoons cinnamon
3 tablespoons sugar
1 cup pecans, coarsely chopped
5 tablespoons butter, melted
1 cup maple syrup

To make the dough: Place the water, yeast and 1/2 teaspoon of the sugar in a small bowl. Stir once or twice and let stand until mixture bubbles (4 to 6 minutes). Combine flour, salt, remaining sugar, milk, lemon rind, egg, and 8 tablespoons of the butter. Add the yeast mixture with a wooden spoon; stir until all the liquid has been absorbed.

With your hands, gather the dough into a ball. Place it on a lightly floured surface and knead for about 10 minutes. If the dough sticks to your hands or to the kneading surface, knead in additional flour a few tablespoons at a time. Continue to knead until the dough is smooth. Grease a large bowl with the remaining 1 tablespoon of butter, place the dough in it and sprinkle lightly with flour. Cover with a towel and let the dough rise until it doubles in bulk (about 1 hour).

To make the filling: Combine the raisins, cinnamon, sugar and 1/2 cup of the pecans. Set aside.

To make the buns: On a lightly

THE GREAT COOKS COOKBOOK

floured surface roll the dough into a rectangle about 10 x 12 inches. Brush the dough with 4 tablespoons of the melted butter. Sprinkle the filling evenly over the dough. Cover with a piece of wax paper and gently press the nut mixture into the dough. Remove wax paper and, starting from a long edge, roll the dough into a cylinder.

Grease a 9½-inch heat-resistant glass round baking dish with the remaining 1 tablespoon butter. Pour half of the maple syrup into the prepared dish and sprinkle with remaining ½ cup of pecans. Slice the cylinder into 1-inch rounds and arrange them in the dish. Pour the other half of the syrup on the rounds. Preheat the oven to 350 F. Let the buns rise for 20 minutes. Bake for 30 minutes. Serve at room temperature from the baking dish.

Viennese Crescents

Makes about 2 dozen

2 cups all-purpose flour
4 tablespoons confectioners' sugar, plus ½ cup for dusting baked cookies
⅛ teaspoon salt
1½ sticks unsalted butter, melted and cooled
½ cup ground walnuts

Sift the flour, the 4 tablespoons confectioners' sugar and the salt together. Pour the melted butter into a medium-size bowl. Gradually, add the flour mixture a few tablespoons at a time, beating with a wooden spoon after each addition. After all the flour mixture has been incorporated, beat in the ground walnuts. Place the mixture in the refrigerator until well chilled (about 2 hours).

Preheat the oven to 350 F. Roll 2 tablespoons of the dough at a time between the palms of hands until it becomes a cylinder about ½ inch thick and 2½ inches long. Place on a cookie sheet and curve the ends to form a crescent. Bake on the middle shelf of the oven until lightly browned (about 12 minutes).

Remove to a wire rack, dust with the remaining ½ cup of confectioners' sugar and allow to cool.

About Desserts

Desserts may be said to be the exclamation point to the meal! Their style varies with the country in which one is eating and with the meal at which it is served. A rich, heavy meal, for example, should be followed by a reasonably light dessert, whereas a more simple meal could be finished with something rich.

In Britain, at many tables dessert is followed by a savoury, which is what it says, and is in many respects what we in America serve with cocktails. In any case, it is highly seasoned and highly unlikely—such as deviled cheese, scrambled eggs on toast, anchovies or sardines with mustard sauce —the principle being that this morsel clears the palate for the port that follows.

In French, dessert is derived from the word *desservir,* meaning to clear the table and, in a manner of speaking, set the stage for the finale, or dessert, as we know it. Many food experts feel that the dessert course is the *pièce de résistance* of the meal and is more likely to be remembered than any other part of it. One reason is that such a variety is available to suit the taste and circumstances of almost any dinner party. Within this chapter you will find desserts rich and desserts plain. I have not included fresh fruit except in a compote, but very often a bowl of fruit is the perfect choice after a rich course. For summer meals it is difficult to equal if served alongside good cheese and crisp bread. Many desserts can be prepared ahead of time and some may be frozen. In Europe and on many French menus in this country, you will find the term *entremets.* This is a sweet we in America call dessert. The sweet in this case should be a very small portion (obviously without fruit), but fruit and cheese may follow. Originally, it was a course served between meat courses at a time when meals were Gargantuan and the *entremets* created a pause or change of pace from the next meat course.

One of the most impressive desserts is the soufflé, hot or cold. For the hot ones, almost all preparation can be done ahead of time. In the baking, timing is important. I know one cook who makes two, one to be served when the meal is finished and another for dawdlers. Hot dessert soufflés demand punctuality, and the waiting should be on the part of the diner rather than the other way around. Cold soufflés are a delight. They are airy and can be sparkling when made with fresh citrus juices. Most can be made early in the day, and many the day before.

Now a word for the weight-conscious. A small helping of dessert, even one as waistline-destroying as PARIS-BREST, that mouth-watering dream of buttercream and other temptations, will not make that much difference in your over-all calorie intake and may be very good for your personality. You can always cut down on one meal or another during the next few days and be happy with your memory.

Pear and Strawberry Compote

Serves 6–8

POACHING SYRUP
2 quarts water
3 cups sugar
4 sticks cinnamon
8 whole cloves
1 lemon, cut in quarters

FRUITS
8 Anjou or Comice pears
2 pints strawberries

*T*o make the poaching syrup, dissolve the sugar in the water in a large pan with a lid. Add the cin-namon sticks, cloves and lemon quarters. Simmer for half an hour with the lid on.

Peel the pears. Cut in half and carefully remove the core. Simmer gently in the poaching syrup until they are soft when pierced with a toothpick. Time will vary with the degree of ripeness of the pears. Allow to cool in the syrup.

Wash and hull the strawberries.

Mix cooled pears and 2 cups of the poaching syrup with the strawberries.

(Pears may be poached days ahead of time, refrigerated in the syrup. Add strawberries just before serving.)

Serve in a glass dish.

Cold Apricot Soufflé

Serves 6–8

SOUFFLÉ
16 dried apricots
½ cup apricot liqueur
Vegetable oil
1 package unflavored gelatin
¼ cup cold water
1 cup milk
4 egg yolks
½ cup sugar
4 tablespoons lemon juice
1 cup heavy cream
7 egg whites
½ cup crushed macaroon crumbs for garnish

APRICOT CREAM

*I*n a small bowl, pour enough water over the apricots to cover. Soak for 12 hours; drain and pour on apricot liqueur.

Fold over lengthwise a long strip of aluminum foil and oil it on one side. Tie it neatly around a 1-quart glass soufflé dish, oiled side in, to make a collar standing 3 inches above the top.

Sprinkle the gelatin over the ¼ cup water to soften.

Heat the milk in the top of a double boiler. In a bowl, beat the egg yolks with the sugar until they are light and lemon-colored, and pour the hot milk over them. Beat. Return the mixture to the top of the double boiler and add the gelatin.

Cook the mixture over hot water, stirring or whisking constantly until it is thick and creamy, being careful that it does not boil. Remove the pan from the heat and let the mixture cool.

Rub the apricots in the liqueur through a fine sieve and stir into the cooled custard. Stir in the lemon juice. Refrigerate the mixture until it begins to thicken.

Whip the cream until it is thick but not stiff and fold into the apricot-custard mixture. Refrigerate the mixture until it is just beginning to set.

Beat the egg whites until they are stiff but not dry and fold them gently into the mixture with a large metal spoon. Spoon the soufflé into the prepared soufflé dish and chill it for at least 3 hours.

Remove the collar before serving and pat the crushed macaroon crumbs over the sides.

Decorate the top with rosettes of APRICOT CREAM.

APRICOT CREAM
½ cup apricot jam or purée, the tarter the better
1 cup (½ pint) heavy cream, well chilled

If using jam, put through a fine strainer. Add the strained jam or the purée to the cream. Beat together until the right consistency for piping through a forcing bag, using a #7 star tube.

Deep Dish Apple Pie

Serves 6–8

FILLING

6 Greening or other cooking apples
½ cup sugar
8 whole cloves
2 sticks cinnamon broken in half
Grated rind of 1 lemon

GLAZE

¼ cup cream
1 egg yolk
superfine sugar for dusting

PASTRY

2 cups all-purpose flour
½ teaspoon salt
3 tablespoons cold shortening
1 stick cold butter
Cold water

Prepare Filling: Peel and core apples. Slice thin. In a bowl, toss apples, sugar, cloves, cinnamon sticks and grated lemon rind.

Prepare Pastry: Sift the flour and salt into a mixing bowl. Add the shortening and chip the cold butter into the bowl. Break up with a pastry blender until the mixture is coarse and mealy. Add just enough cold water to form a nonsticky ball (about 3 tablespoons), handling as little as possible.

Transfer the dough to a floured board. Spread out with the heel of your hand once, gather into a ball and seal in plastic bag or wrap. Place in refrigerator for at least 2 hours.

To assemble: Preheat oven to 350 F. Fill glass casserole (1-quart capacity, 2½ inches deep) with sliced apple mixture, mounding to form a dome. Add water to half fill dish.

Roll out pastry—about ¼ inch thick.

Moisten edge of dish. Lay pastry over apples, pressing to rim of dish. Trim excess dough. Reroll trimmings and cut strip of pastry the same width as dish rim; reserve extra pastry. Moisten edge of pastry and lay the strip neatly around the rim, pressing so that it makes a firm contact. Crimp, making deep indents with finger and thumb of left hand and first finger of right.

To glaze: Mix the cream with the egg yolk and brush the entire surface with the mixture. Make cut-outs with remaining pastry and arrange on top. Brush with egg-cream mixture.

Bake in preheated oven for 1 hour. A steam vent is unnecessary. If pastry is taking on too much color, cover with a sheet of foil.

Dust with fine sugar while still hot.

Strawberry Sorbet

Serves 6–8

2 pints strawberries
3 cups sugar
1 cup hot water
4 tablespoons lemon juice
2-quart electric ice-cream freezer
freezing salt
2 egg whites
SAUCE DIJONNAISE

Wash and hull strawberries in that order. Purée in a food mill or force through a wire sieve or strainer. Do not use a blender.

In a heavy pan, dissolve the sugar in hot water. When completely dissolved, bring to a boil over high heat. As it reaches a rolling boil, the temperature will be 216 F. If you have a candy thermometer, use it to test. Take pan off heat immediately and chill syrup over iced water. When cold, mix with strawberry purée and lemon juice and pour into ice-cream freezer.

Pack the space around the container with alternating layers of crushed ice and freezing salt in proportions of three parts ice to one part salt, using 2-cup measures as the unit. Put dasher and lid in place, start the motor and freeze for 20 minutes.

Beat egg whites with a pinch of salt until they hold soft peaks.

Remove cover from freezer and remove dasher. Stir in beaten egg whites and reassemble the ice-cream maker. Freeze for another 20 minutes.

SAUCE DIJONNAISE
1 10-ounce package frozen raspberries, thawed and drained
½ cup black currant jam

Rub both the raspberries and the black currant jam through a fine sieve. Mix thoroughly and serve with the SORBET.

Serve in glass dish. Pour a little of the sauce over the SORBET and pass the remainder in a sauceboat.

Uncooked Almond Pudding

Serves 6–8

1 package (3 ounces) sponge fingers
    (ladyfingers)
½ cup (1 stick) unsalted butter, slightly
    softened
3 large eggs
8 ounces (approximately) granulated
    sugar
8 ounces (approximately) ground almonds
1 cup heavy cream

*L*ine a plain 1-quart mold or mixing bowl with strips of waxed paper. (This makes it easier to unmold the pudding.) Line bottom and sides with sponge fingers.

Beat butter until light and creamy.

Weigh 3 large eggs in shell (approximately 8 ounces).

Beat the same weight of granulated sugar and the same weight of ground almonds into the butter.

Add eggs, one at a time, beating well before adding another.

Pour mixture into mold lined with sponge fingers. Cover with remaining sponge fingers.

Place a saucer or plate with heavy weight on the top.

Refrigerate for 24 hours.

Lift out of mold; remove paper strips; slice thin. Serve with whipped cream.

Iced Coffee Mousse

Serves 6–8

Vegetable oil
1 package unflavored gelatin
¼ cup cool water
3 eggs
½ cup sugar
1½ cups milk
¼ cup brandy
6 tablespoons freeze-dried coffee
½ pint (1 cup) heavy cream
2 egg whites
½ cup macaroon crumbs or lightly buttered cake crumbs

*F*old over lengthwise a long strip of aluminum foil and oil it on one side. Tie it neatly around a 1-quart glass soufflé dish, oiled side in, to make a collar standing 3 inches above the top.

Dissolve gelatin by sprinkling it over cool water.

Separate the eggs. In top of glass double boiler—no heat—beat together the egg yolks and sugar until creamy. In another pan, heat the milk until almost boiling. Spoon a little of the milk into the egg-yolk mixture; then pour the egg-yolk mixture into the remaining hot milk, whisking it vigorously. Return to the top of double boiler.

Add brandy and coffee, and cook over simmering water until the mixture reaches the thickness of heavy cream, whisking all the time. Stir in gelatin and allow to cool. When it begins to set, whip cream until thick and fold in. Whip egg whites until stiff and fold them in.

Pour the mixture into the soufflé dish and chill for at least 2 hours.

Remove collar before serving and pat cake or macaroon crumbs onto the side.

Bread Pudding, French Style, with Sabayon Sauce

Serves 6–8

PUDDING
Butter
½ cup white raisins
¼ cup rum, heated
6 thin slices white bread, crusts removed
3 cups milk
⅔ cups sugar
4 whole eggs
2 egg yolks
1 teaspoon vanilla

SABAYON SAUCE
4 egg yolks
1 cup sugar
1 cup dry white wine, or dry Sherry, or
     dry Vermouth

Preheat oven to 350 F. Butter well an 8 x 11 x 1½-inch ovenproof glass baking dish.

Plump the raisins in the heated rum for about 10 to 15 minutes and drain thoroughly.

Butter the bread. Cut each slice into four squares. Scatter the raisins over the bottom of the dish, then cover with the buttered squares of bread.

Heat the milk until a film shines on the top. Stir in the sugar until dissolved. Beat the eggs and yolks together well. Add the hot milk slowly to the eggs, beating constantly. Stir in the vanilla, and pour the mixture over the bread.

Place the baking dish in a roasting pan with enough hot water to reach to two-thirds the depth of the dish. Bake for 40 to 50 minutes or until a knife inserted about an inch from the edge comes out dry. Cool at room temperature.

To prepare SABAYON SAUCE: Combine the yolks and sugar in the top of a glass double boiler. Beat with an electric beater for 2 minutes.

Beat in the wine slowly, then place over hot (not boiling) water and cook, whipping constantly with a wire whisk for 8 to 10 minutes. At this point you should have a creamy, fluffy mixture with enough body to leave a clear path when you pull the whisk through it. At the end of the cooking time, pour the SABAYON into a serving bowl.

Serve tepid with the BREAD PUDDING.

Crystallized Strawberries

Serves 6–8

Strictly speaking, this is not a dessert at all. It is a little something sweet to eat with coffee after a meal so rich that it requires no dessert, or to add an extra, after-dessert touch to an elegant dinner.

Don't attempt this at all unless you can get perfect, unblemished strawberries with stems long enough so you won't burn your fingers on the sugar syrup.

¼ cup hot water
1 cup sugar
Vegetable oil
1 pint large, perfect strawberries with
    long stems

Pour the hot water over the sugar in a small pan and stir until it has dissolved. Lightly oil baking sheet.

Put the pan over the highest heat possible and boil for 8–10 minutes or until the temperature on a candy thermometer reaches 280 F. If a candy thermometer is not available, heat until the liquid forms a thin, hard thread when a metal spoon is dipped into it and then lifted. Remove syrup from heat.

Hold a strawberry by its stem, dip it into the syrup and swirl to coat thoroughly. Hold it up to allow the excess to drip off. Retain in your hand for a few seconds to dry before placing it on the lightly oiled baking sheet.

(The strawberries may be prepared 2 hours ahead of time, but they will not retain their crystallized state much longer; they will get soggy.)

Walnut and Raspberry Cream Torte

Serves 6–8

CAKE
Butter
Flour
4 egg whites
1 cup superfine sugar
¼ teaspoon red wine vinegar
1 teaspoon almond extract

1 cup chopped walnuts

FILLING
1 cup heavy cream
1 cup raspberries
Confectioners' sugar
2 8-inch round cake pans

reheat oven to 325 F. Prepare the cake pans by buttering them and dusting thoroughly with flour. Shake off any excess flour.

Beat egg whites until stiff. Continue beating until very stiff, adding the sugar gradually. Continue beating for at least 5 minutes more.

Add vinegar and almond extract. Fold in chopped walnuts.

Spoon into prepared pans and smooth the tops gently.

Bake for 35 minutes; keep oven door ever so slightly ajar. Cool thoroughly.

For the filling, whip the cream thoroughly. Fold in the raspberries. Remove the meringues from their pans. Place one meringue on a glass serving dish. Spread with filling. Place other meringue on top and chill.

Dust with confectioners' sugar before serving.

Gâteau Basque

[BASQUE CAKE]
Serves 6–8

ALMOND PASTRY
6 tablespoons butter
2 tablespoons shortening
1-½ cups all-purpose flour
Pinch of salt
3 tablespoons ground, blanched almonds
¼ cup sugar
1 egg yolk
½ teaspoon almond extract
2–3 tablespoons ice water

FILLING
¾ cup plum jam, preferably damson

GLAZE
1 egg white, lightly beaten
Granulated sugar for dusting

n a bowl, rub butter and shortening into flour and salt. Add ground almonds and sugar.

Mix egg yolk with almond extract and water and add to flour mixture. Work lightly with a spoon to a smooth dough and chill, covered, for about 1 hour.

Preheat oven to 400 F. Roll out two-thirds of the dough on a floured surface and line an 8-inch flan ring or 7½-inch oven-proof glass pie plate. Fill with jam. Roll out the remaining dough to a 9-inch circle and cover the cake. Seal the edges and mark the top in cartwheel fashion with the point of a knife, cutting through to the layer of jam.

Bake for 15 minutes or until the top is golden brown.

Just before the end of cooking, brush the top of the GÂTEAU with the beaten egg white, sprinkle with granulated sugar and return to the oven for about 2 minutes. (Sugar must be dusted onto egg white quickly so that the heat of the pastry has a chance to make a meringuelike topping of frost.)

Serve hot or cold.

Lemon Ice Cream

Makes 3 Cups

3 tablespoons lemon juice
2 teaspoons grated lemon rind
1 cup sugar
2 cups (1 pint) light cream
⅛ teaspoon salt

Combine the juice, rind and sugar and blend well. Slowly stir in the cream and salt. Mix well.

Pour into a freezing tray and freeze until solid around the outside and mushy in the middle. Stir well with a wooden spoon and refreeze until solid.

Dolce Maddalena

Serves 5–6

1 package (3 ounces) ladyfingers or sponge
   fingers
¼ cup Marsala (sweet)
2 eggs, separated
½ cup sugar
¾ cup ricotta or cream cheese
4 ounces candied fruit
4 ounces grated chocolate
16 double Amaretti (macaroons), crushed

Sprinkle ladyfingers with Marsala. Beat the egg yolks thoroughly with the sugar and cheese until smooth and thick.

Beat the egg whites until stiff peaks are formed. Fold the candied fruit, grated chocolate and crushed macaroons into the beaten egg whites.

Line a 1-quart charlotte mold or glass bowl with the well-sprinkled ladyfingers.

Fold egg yolk and egg white mixtures carefully together and place in the lined mold.

Freeze overnight or for 8 hours. (The dessert keeps well if frozen.)

Unmold; slice thin because it is so rich, and serve.

Orange Moss

Serves 8–10

1 envelope unflavored gelatin
¼ cup water
10 ounces (1¼ cups) fresh orange juice
1 can (6 ounces) frozen orange juice
    concentrate, undiluted
Sugar to taste, if any

*S*often gelatin by sprinkling over water and allow to stand for 3–4 minutes. Dissolve over very gentle heat.

In a 3-quart bowl, whisk dissolved gelatin into fresh orange juice mixed with concentrate—and sugar, if desired. An electric beater is almost essential for this recipe, but it can be accomplished by hand if you have the endurance.

Stand orange-juice bowl in a larger one of ice and beat until the volume is increased sixfold and the mixture stands in peaks.

Spoon into glass dish and store in the refrigerator. May be made a day in advance. This is the perfect dessert for the diet-conscious.

Simple Syllabub

Serves 10–12

¼ cup granulated sugar
4 tablespoons lemon juice
Grated rind of 1 lemon
6 tablespoons dry white wine
4 tablespoons fine brandy
2 tablespoons medium dry sherry
2 cups (1 pint) heavy cream
½ teaspoon grated nutmeg

*C*ombine all ingredients except cream and nutmeg in ceramic or glass mixing bowl. Allow to stand for at least 2 hours.

Strain into a clean 2-quart bowl. With electric hand beater or in mixer, beat at the same speed as would be used with a large balloon whisk, adding the cream slowly. If you have the endurance, use the balloon whisk.

When all the cream is in and the mixture is holding soft peaks, add the grated nutmeg. Spoon into individual small glasses or 1-quart glass bowl.

NOTE: A little goes a long way. It is superb with fresh berries—strawberries, blueberries or raspberries—and is better if made a day ahead.

Rhubarb Fool

Serves 8–10

1 pound young, tender, pink rhubarb
1 cup granulated sugar
1 ounce (2 tablespoons) preserved ginger
2 cups heavy cream

Remove leaves and root end of rhubarb stalks. Wash and cut in 2-inch chunks.

In a heavy pan, with close-fitting lid, combine sugar, ginger and rhubarb. Cook over gentle heat until tender, about 10 minutes. Water is not needed.

Drain, and purée the rhubarb in blender or food mill. Cool thoroughly.

Chill the cream and whip until just thickened. I find a balloon whisk and chilled bowl produce the best results.

Combine the cream with the rhubarb and spoon into parfait glasses or glass bowl. Chill thoroughly.

German Apple Pie

Serves 6–8

5–6 tart apples—Greenings are best, but
  McIntosh will do
4 tablespoons lemon juice
1 cup sugar
½ teaspoon powdered cinnamon
4 tablespoons (½ stick) butter
1 egg, lightly beaten
½ cup all-purpose flour
1 teaspoon baking powder

Heat oven to 350 F. Peel and core apples. Slice thin. Sprinkle with lemon juice and toss with ½ cup of the sugar and the cinnamon.

Melt half the butter in a heavy skillet large enough to hold the apples comfortably. Add apples. Over medium heat, toss and shake till apples are heated through.

In a bowl, cream remaining butter and sugar and mix in beaten egg.

Sift flour and baking powder together and stir into egg and butter mixture to make a batter.

Spoon apples into an 8 x 8-inch glass baking dish; level the surface and drop the batter by spoonfuls over apples.

Bake for 45 minutes. Serve hot or at room temperature.

Soufflé à l'Orange

Serves 6–8

Vegetable oil
Granulated sugar
1 large navel orange
1/3 cup plus 2 tablespoons sugar
3 tablespoons sifted flour
3/4 cup milk
4 egg yolks
2 tablespoons softened butter
5 egg whites
Pinch cream of tartar
4 tablespoons Cointreau
Powdered sugar

Heat oven to 400 F. Oil lightly a 6-cup heat-resistant glass soufflé dish and roll granulated sugar around in it to coat lightly. Shake out the excess.

Peel the orange with a vegetable peeler, taking care not to include any of the white pith. Chop the peel and crush it with 1 tablespoon sugar in a bowl or with pestle and mortar.

In a glass-ceramic saucepan, mix the flour and 1/3 cup sugar. Add a little of the milk to blend. Beat in the remaining milk and the mashed orange peel and sugar. Stir over gentle heat until the mixture thickens and reaches the boiling point. Boil for 30 seconds only. Remove the pan from the heat and allow to cool slightly.

Beat the egg yolks into the sauce one at a time. Beat in 1 tablespoon softened butter and dot top of sauce with the remaining tablespoon of butter.

In a bowl beat the egg whites and cream of tartar until soft peaks are formed. Sprinkle on 1 tablespoon sugar and beat until stiff peaks are held.

Stir the Cointreau into the sauce; then stir in 1/4 of the egg whites. Fold in the remaining whites and turn mixture into the prepared soufflé dish, leaving a space of 1 1/4 inches below the rim.

Put a baking sheet in the center of the oven and put the soufflé on it. Reduce the heat to 375 F. and bake for 20 minutes.

Quickly sprinkle the soufflé top with powdered sugar and bake for 10 to 15 minutes longer. The top should be pleasantly browned.

Paris-Brest

Serves 6–8

This is one of the most delicious and rich pastries in French cuisine.

PRALINE POWDER
¾ cup sugar
¼ cup water
¼ teaspoon cream of tartar
½ cup blanched almonds

---

*P*lace all ingredients in heavy pan, not tin-lined—preferably glass-ceramic. Heat and stir until sugar dissolves. Continue to heat, without stirring, until the color is dark amber. Pour onto lightly greased cookie sheet, with edges, and cool. Break into rough pieces and pulverize in a blender. Store in a screw-top jar in the refrigerator.

CHOUX PASTE RING
1 teaspoon softened butter
Flour
1 cup water
6 tablespoons unsalted butter
Pinch of salt
1 cup all-purpose flour
4 large eggs
1 egg for glazing, beaten
1 tablespoon water
Slivered almonds

CRÈME PRALINÉE
¾ cup less 1 tablespoon sugar
¼ cup water
3 egg yolks

6 ounces (1½ sticks) butter, softened
½ cup PRALINE POWDER

TO ASSEMBLE
1 cup heavy cream

To Make Choux Ring: Grease a baking sheet lightly with softened butter and coat with flour. Shake off excess. Draw an 8-inch circle in the middle.

Place water, butter and salt in heavy pan and heat until butter has melted. Bring to a rolling boil and throw in all the flour at once. Stir, off the heat, until mixture leaves sides and bottom of pan. Transfer to a clean mixing bowl; cool slightly, and stir in eggs one at a time. Beat well after each addition. If you have a mixer, use it with the dough-mixing attachment.

Heat oven to 450 F. Fill a pastry bag, fitted with a large, plain #8 tube, with the CHOUX PASTE. Squeeze out a ring of the paste about 1 inch high and 2 inches thick inside the circle marked on the baking sheet. Brush with beaten egg mixed with 1 tablespoon water, and scatter some almonds on top.

Bake for 15 minutes at 450 F., then reduce heat to 350 F. Bake for 40 minutes longer and allow to cool in oven after heat has been turned off.

To make Crème Pralinée: In a heavy pan—preferably glass-ceramic—melt the sugar in water without stirring. Boil until a long thread is spun or temperature of

240 F. is reached on candy thermometer. Remember: do not stir.

Beat egg yolks. From a height, pour the syrup in a thin stream into the egg yolks and continue to beat. Continue to beat until the mixture is thick and heavy and cool. Beat in the softened butter and stir in PRALINE POWDER.

To Assemble Paris-Brest: Split the CHOUX PASTE RING halfway between top and bottom. Fill the bottom half with CRÈME PRALINÉE. With remaining crème fill the dents in the inside of the upper half.

Whip cream until stiff. Pile on bottom half of pastry ring and cover with top half, almond-side-up.

This dessert may be made ahead of time and assembled the afternoon of your dinner party.

Meringue aux Pommes

Serves 8

6–7 large apples, Greenings or, failing that, firm McIntosh
½ cup dry white wine
2 tablespoons butter, approximately
Grated rind of 1 lemon
½ cup red currant jelly

MERINGUE
6 egg whites
2 cups granulated sugar
1 teaspoon vinegar
1 teaspoon vanilla extract

Peel and core apples. Slice—not too thin—into 2-quart pan with lid. Add white wine and cook slowly over low heat. Shake the pan every now and again, holding the lid firmly in place so that apple slices will be rotated in pan. Cooking time over low heat is about 10–15 minutes. Do not cook to a pulp.

Butter 2¾-quart ovenproof dish and spread the cooked apples evenly over the bottom. Dish should be about ⅔ full. Sprinkle with grated lemon rind. Dot with red currant jelly. Preheat oven to 275 F.

Beat egg whites with an electric mixer or with hand beater until soft peaks are formed. Add sugar gradually while continuing to beat. Add vinegar and vanilla extract and continue to beat for at least 8 minutes.

With a #7 star tube and pastry bag, pipe meringue over apples. Shell shapes look good.

Bake in preheated oven for 50 minutes to 1 hour. After 20 minutes look at MERINGUE and if it is becoming dark in color, lower heat to 250 F. and cover with a sheet of brown paper or foil.

Do not refrigerate unless the atmosphere is very humid. It *may* be made with success in the morning for that evening.

Parfait d'Or

Serves 6–8

---

2 cups (1 pint) heavy cream
¾ cup sugar
⅓ cup hot water
3 egg yolks
Pinch of salt
2 teaspoons vanilla extract

---

*C*hill cream and beater. In a heavy pan pour hot water over sugar and stir until dissolved. Boil over high heat until it reaches 230 F. on candy thermometer, or until a teaspoon of the syrup, dropped into cold water and molded with finger and thumb, forms a soft ball.

While syrup is cooking, beat egg yolks with salt in a bowl until light and creamy. Add syrup in a thin stream while continuing to beat. Beat until mixture cools. This can be accelerated by standing mixing bowl in a larger one of crushed ice.

Separately, beat cream with vanilla until a soft peak is formed. Fold egg mixture into cream and spoon into a glass bowl, or individual ramekins, or 6-ounce custard cups. Freeze till firm.

The parfait keeps well if frozen and covered.

Wines for Desserts

ALEXIS BESPALOFF

Nowadays, even those who enjoy serving their guests a variety of red and white wines during a meal will usually serve coffee with dessert. There are many simple occasions when an additional wine may be inappropriate, and there are desserts with which it is difficult to serve any wine—citrus fruits, ice cream, and chocolate dishes, for example. A special dessert, however, will be shown off to even greater advantage if it is accompanied by a wine of its own, and serving an interesting and unusual wine at the end of a meal when it is unexpected provides your guests with a delightful surprise.

Champagne will provide a happy ending to any meal, but you may prefer an Extra Dry, which is really semidry, rather than the drier Brut. California and New York State Champagnes are widely available, and some of the least expensive are also among the least dry, because sweetness is used to mask the taste of an inexpensive wine. This makes some inexpensive champagnes a poor choice as an apéritif, but good value with dessert. The most distinctive of all sparkling wines is Asti Spumanti, made in Italy from the Muscat grape. Its sweetness and intense flavor enable it to stand up to even the sweetest and richest desserts.

Among the sweet white wines traditionally served with dessert, Sauternes—from the Bordeaux region of France—is the most famous. It is made from overripe and shriveled grapes which produce a sweet, luscious wine with a special undertaste of its own. Many firms market a regional Sauternes or Barsac (which is an inner district within Sauternes), and there are a number of well-known château-bottled wines to be found as well. The best of the château-bottled wines are more expensive, but they also have a more concentrated and complex flavor.

The basic grape varieties used to make Sauternes are the Sauvignon Blanc and Semillon, and many California wineries market a Sweet Sauvignon Blanc and Sweet Semillon, as well as wines labeled Sauterne or Haut Sauterne. These wines are most appealing, but they are generally less sweet than a Sauternes from France, and less intense in flavor. As a result, they are overwhelmed by a particularly rich dessert.

The greatest rivals to Sauternes as a dessert wine are the sweeter German wines from the Rhine and Moselle. The very sweetest of them, labeled Beerenauslese and Trockenbeerenauslese, are remarkable wines that cost as much as $100 a bottle. They are best appreciated by themselves, without food. Those labeled Spätlese or Auslese, however, can be most enjoyable with lighter desserts, fruit, or cake. Rhine wines, in brown bottles, are generally richer and sweeter than Moselles, in green bottles. Whether you prefer the richness of a Sauternes or the spiciness, flowery bouquet and balancing acidity of a German wine can only be discovered by trying good examples of these wines for yourself.

Somewhat different in style is Tokay, the most famous wine of Hungary. It is made in the same general way as is Sauternes, but is aged longer in the barrel before being bottled. The wine is honeyed in taste, and has a drier finish than a Sauternes. The sweetest Tokay—some are dry—is called Aszu, and the sweetest of the Aszu wines is labeled "5 *puttonos.*"

Cream sherry and port are traditionally served after dinner, but they can also be used to accompany dessert. These wines have enough richness and sweetness to stand up to most desserts, and a glass is as much as most people will want. This holds true of most dessert wines, by the way, and you will find that a half-bottle goes further with dessert than with any other course.

Although you may feel that serving a dessert wine is an unnecessary embellishment, the variety of choices may tempt you, at least occasionally, to treat yourself and your guests to wines that are not often seen on the dinner table any more.

THE GREAT COOKS COOKBOOK

Index